Next Generation Databases

NoSQL, NewSQL, and Big Data

Guy Harrison

Apress®

Next Generation Databases

ISBN-13 (pbk): 978-1-4842-1330-8

ISBN-13 (electronic): 978-1-4842-1329-2

Managing Director: Welmoed Spahr
Lead Editor: Jonathan Gennick
Development Editor: Douglas Pundick
Technical Reviewer: Stephane Faroult
Editorial Board: Steve Anglin, Pramila Balen, Louise Corrigan, Jim DeWolf, Jonathan Gennick, Robert Hutchinson, Celestin Suresh John, Michelle Lowman, James Markham, Susan McDermott, Matthew Moodie, Jeffrey Pepper, Douglas Pundick, Ben Renow-Clarke, Gwenan Spearing
Coordinating Editor: Jill Balzano
Copy Editor: Carole Berglie
Compositor: SPi Global
Indexer: SPi Global
Artist: SPi Global
Cover Designer: Anna Ishchenko

Distributed to the book trade worldwide by Springer Science+Business Media New York, 233 Spring Street, 6th Floor, New York, NY 10013. Phone 1-800-SPRINGER, fax (201) 348-4505, e-mail orders-ny@springer-sbm.com, or visit www.springer.com. Apress Media, LLC is a California LLC and the sole member (owner) is Springer Science + Business Media Finance Inc (SSBM Finance Inc). SSBM Finance Inc is a Delaware corporation.

For information on translations, please e-mail rights@apress.com, or visit www.apress.com.

Apress and friends of ED books may be purchased in bulk for academic, corporate, or promotional use. eBook versions and licenses are also available for most titles. For more information, reference our Special Bulk Sales–eBook Licensing web page at www.apress.com/bulk-sales.

Any source code or other supplementary material referenced by the author in this text is available to readers at www.apress.com. For detailed information about how to locate your book's source code, go to www.apress.com/source-code/.

To Catherine Maree Arnold (1981-2010)

Contents at a Glance

Contents

About the Author

Guy Harrison started working as a database developer in the mid-1980s. He has written numerous books on database development and performance optimization. He joined Quest Software (now part of Dell) in 2000, and currently leads the team that develops the Toad, Spotlight, and Shareplex product families.

Guy lives in Melbourne Australia, with his wife, a variable number of adult children, a cat, three dogs, and a giant killer rabbit.

Guy can be reached at guy.a.harrison@gmail.com at http://guyharrison.net and is @guyharrison on Twitter.

About the Technical Reviewer

Stéphane Faroult is a French consultant who first discovered relational databases and the SQL language 30 years ago. Stéphane joined Oracle France in its early days (after a brief spell with IBM and a period of time teaching at the University of Ottawa), and developed an interest in performance and tuning topics, on which he soon started writing training courses. After leaving Oracle in 1988, Stéphane briefly tried going straight and did a bit of operational research, but after only a year he succumbed again to the allure of relational databases. He is currently visiting faculty in the Computing and Information Science Department at Kansas State University. For his sins, Stéphane has been performing database consultancy continuously ever since; he founded RoughSea, Ltd. in 1998. In recent years, Stéphane has had a growing interest in education, which has taken various forms, including books (*The Art of SQL*, soon followed *by Refactoring SQL Applications*, both published by O'Reilly) and more recently a textbook (*SQL Success*, published by RoughSea), a series of seminars in Asia, and video tutorials (`www.youtube.com/user/roughsealtd`).

Acknowledgements

I'd like to thank everyone at Apress who helped in the production of this book, in particular lead editor Jonathan Gennick, coordinating editor Jill Balzano, and development editor Douglas Pundick. I'd like to especially thank Stéphane Faroult, who provided outstanding technical review feedback. Rarely have I worked with a reviewer of the caliber of Stéphane, and his comments were invaluable.

As always, thanks to my family—Jenni, Chris, Kate, Mike, and Willie—for providing the emotional support and understanding necessary to take on this project.

This book is dedicated to the memory of Catherine Maree Arnold, our beloved niece who passed away in 2010. I met Catherine when she was five years old; the first time I met her, she introduced me to the magic of Roald Dahl's *The Twits*. The last time I saw her, she explained modern DNA sequencing techniques and told me about her ambition to save species from extinction. She was one of the smartest, funniest, and kindest human beings you could hope to meet. When my first book was published in 1987, she jokingly insisted that I should dedicate it to her, so it's fitting that I dedicate this book to her memory.

—Guy Harrison
Melbourne, Australia
December 2015

PART I

■ ■ ■

Next Generation Databases

CHAPTER 1

■ ■ ■

Three Database Revolutions

Fantasy. Lunacy.

All revolutions are, until they happen, then they are historical inevitabilities.

— David Mitchell, Cloud Atlas

We're still in the first minutes of the first day of the Internet revolution.

—Scott Cook

This book is about a third revolution in database technology. The first revolution was driven by the emergence of the electronic computer, and the second revolution by the emergence of the relational database. The third revolution has resulted in an explosion of nonrelational database alternatives driven by the demands of modern applications that require global scope and continuous availability. In this chapter we'll provide an overview of these three waves of database technologies and discuss the market and technology forces leading to today's next generation databases.

Figure 1-1 shows a simple timeline of major database releases.

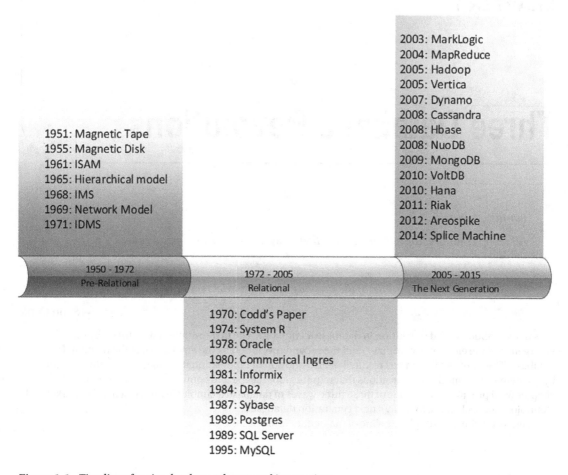

Figure 1-1. *Timeline of major database releases and innovations*

Figure 1-1 illustrates three major eras in database technology. In the 20 years following the widespread adoption of electronic computers, a range of increasingly sophisticated database systems emerged. Shortly after the definition of the relational model in 1970, almost every significant database system shared a common architecture. The three pillars of this architecture were the relational model, ACID transactions, and the SQL language.

However, starting around 2008, an explosion of new database systems occurred, and none of these adhered to the traditional relational implementations. These new database systems are the subject of this book, and this chapter will show how the preceding waves of database technologies led to this next generation of database systems.

Early Database Systems

Wikipedia defines a *database* as an "organized collection of data." Although the term *database* entered our vocabulary only in the late 1960s, collecting and organizing data has been an integral factor in the development of human civilization and technology. Books—especially those with a strongly enforced structure such as dictionaries and encyclopedias—represent datasets in physical form. Libraries and other indexed archives of information represent preindustrial equivalents of modern database systems.

We can also see the genesis of the digital database in the adoption of punched cards and other physical media that could store information in a form that could be processed mechanically. In the 19th century, loom cards were used to "program" fabric looms to generate complex fabric patterns, while tabulating machines used punched cards to produce census statistics, and player pianos used perforated paper strips that represented melodies. Figure 1-2 shows a Hollerith tabulating machine being used to process the U.S. census in 1890.

Figure 1-2. *Tabulating machines and punched cards used to process 1890 U.S. census*

The emergence of electronic computers following the Second World War represented the first revolution in databases. Some early digital computers were created to perform purely mathematical functions—calculating ballistic tables, for instance. But equally as often they were intended to operate on and manipulate data, such as processing encrypted Axis military communications.

Early "databases" used paper tape initially and eventually magnetic tape to store data sequentially. While it was possible to "fast forward" and "rewind" through these datasets, it was not until the emergence of the spinning magnetic disk in the mid-1950s that direct high-speed access to individual records became possible. Direct access allowed fast access to any item within a file of any size. The development of indexing methods such as ISAM (Index Sequential Access Method) made fast record-oriented access feasible and consequently allowed for the birth of the first OLTP (On-line Transaction Processing) computer systems.

ISAM and similar indexing structures powered the first electronic databases. However, these were completely under the control of the application—there were databases but no *Database Management Systems* (*DBMS*).

The First Database Revolution

Requiring every application to write its own data handling code was clearly a productivity issue: every application had to reinvent the database wheel. Furthermore, errors in application data handling code led inevitably to corrupted data. Allowing multiple users to concurrently access or change data without logically or physically corrupting the data requires sophisticated coding. Finally, optimization of data access through caching, pre-fetch, and other techniques required complicated and specialized algorithms that could not easily be duplicated in each application.

Therefore, it became desirable to externalize database handling logic from the application in a separate code base. This layer—the Database Management System, or DBMS—would minimize programmer overhead and ensure the performance and integrity of data access routines.

Early database systems enforced both a schema (a definition of the structure of the data within the database) and an access path (a fixed means of navigating from one record to another). For instance, the DBMS might have a definition of a CUSTOMER and an ORDER together with a defined access path that allowed you to retrieve the orders associated with a particular customer or the customer associated with a specific order.

These first-generation databases ran exclusively on the mainframe computer systems of the day — largely IBM mainframes. By the early 1970s, two major models of DBMS were competing for dominance. The *network model* was formalized by the CODASYL standard and implemented in databases such as IDMS, while the *hierarchical model* provided a somewhat simpler approach as was most notably found in IBM's IMS (Information Management System). Figure 1-3 provides a comparison of these databases' structural representation of data.

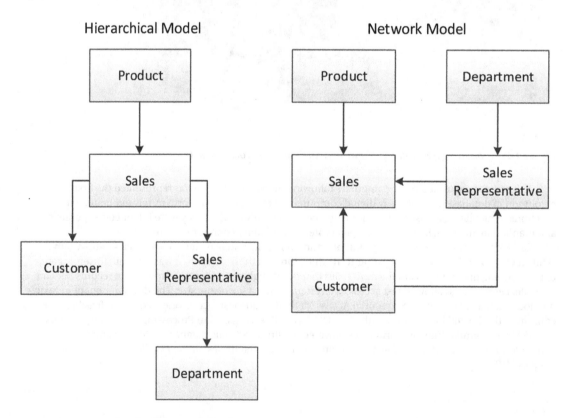

Figure 1-3. *Hierarchical and network database models*

■ **Note** These early systems are often described as "navigational" in nature because you must navigate from one object to another using pointers or links. For instance, to find an order in a hierarchical database, it may be necessary to first locate the customer, then follow the link to the customer's orders.

Hierarchical and network database systems dominated during the era of mainframe computing and powered the vast majority of computer applications up until the late 1970s. However, these systems had several notable drawbacks.

First, the navigational databases were extremely inflexible in terms of data structure and query capabilities. Generally only queries that could be anticipated during the initial design phase were possible, and it was extremely difficult to add new data elements to an existing system.

Second, the database systems were centered on record at a time transaction processing—what we today refer to as CRUD (Create, Read, Update, Delete). Query operations, especially the sort of complex analytic queries that we today associate with business intelligence, required complex coding. The business demands for analytic-style reports grew rapidly as computer systems became increasingly integrated with business processes. As a result, most IT departments found themselves with huge backlogs of report requests and a whole generation of computer programmers writing repetitive COBOL report code.

The Second Database Revolution

Arguably, no single person has had more influence over database technology than Edgar Codd. Codd received a mathematics degree from Oxford shortly after the Second World War and subsequently immigrated to the United States, where he worked for IBM on and off from 1949 onwards. Codd worked as a "programming mathematician" (ah, those were the days) and worked on some of IBM's very first commercial electronic computers.

In the late 1960s, Codd was working at an IBM laboratory in San Jose, California. Codd was very familiar with the databases of the day, and he harbored significant reservations about their design. In particular, he felt that:

- **Existing databases were too hard to use**. Databases of the day could only be accessed by people with specialized programming skills.

- **Existing databases lacked a theoretical foundation**. Codd's mathematical background encouraged him to think about data in terms of formal structures and logical operations; he regarded existing databases as using arbitrary representations that did not ensure logical consistency or provide the ability to deal with missing information.

- **Existing databases mixed logical and physical implementations**. The representation of data in existing databases matched the format of the physical storage in the database, rather than a logical representation of the data that could be comprehended by a nontechnical user.

Codd published an internal IBM paper outlining his ideas for a more formalized model for database systems, which then led to his 1970 paper "A Relational Model of Data for Large Shared Data Banks."[1] This classic paper contained the core ideas that defined the *relational database model* that became the most significant—almost universal—model for database systems for a generation.

Relational theory

The intricacies of relational database theory can be complex and are beyond the scope of this introduction. However, at its essence, the relational model describes how a given set of data should be presented to the user, rather than how it should be stored on disk or in memory. Key concepts of the relational model include:

- **Tuples**, an unordered set of **attribute** values. In an actual database system, a tuple corresponds to a row, and an attribute to a column value.

- A **relation**, which is a collection of distinct tuples and corresponds to a table in relational database implementations.

- **Constraints**, which enforce consistency of the database. Key constraints are used to identify tuples and relationships between tuples.

- **Operations** on relations such as joins, projections, unions, and so on. These operations always return relations. In practice, this means that a query on a table returns data in a tabular format.

A row in a table should be identifiable and efficiently accessed by a unique key value, and every column in that row must be dependent on that key value and no other identifier. Arrays and other structures that contain nested information are, therefore, not directly supported.

Levels of conformance to the relational model are described in the various "*normal forms.*" *Third normal form* is the most common level. Database practitioners typically remember the definition of third normal form by remembering that all non-key attributes must be dependent on "the key, the whole key, and nothing but the key—So Help Me Codd"![2]

Figure 1-4 provides an example of normalization: the data on the left represents a fairly simple collection of data. However, it contains redundancy in student and test names, and the use of a repeating set of attributes for the test answers is dubious (while possibly within relational form, it implies that each test has the same number of questions and makes certain operations difficult). The five tables on the right represent a normalized representation of this data.

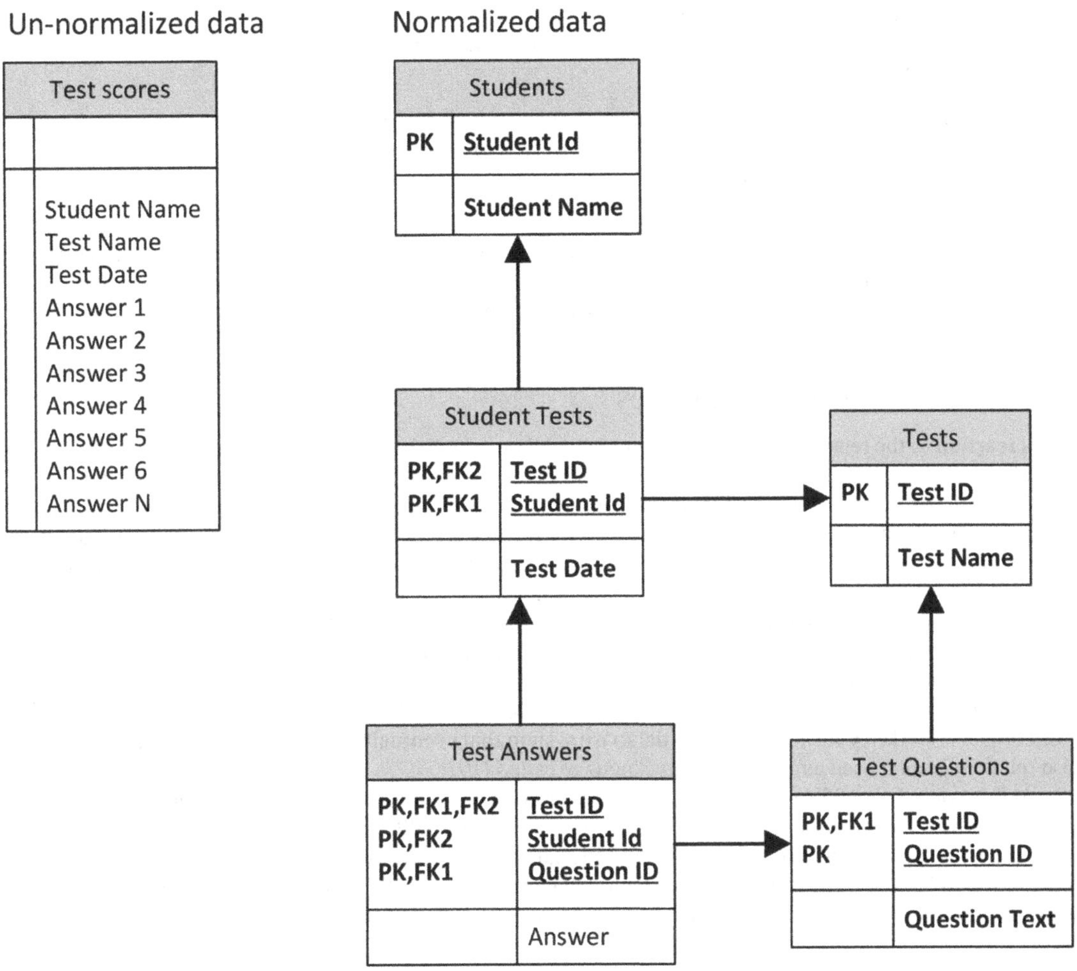

Un-normalized data   Normalized data

Figure 1-4. *Normalized and un-normalized data*

Transaction Models

The relational model does not itself define the way in which the database handles concurrent data change requests. These changes—generally referred to as database *transactions*—raise issues for all database systems because of the need to ensure consistency and integrity of data.

Jim Gray defined the most widely accepted transaction model in the late 1970s. As he put it, "A transaction is a transformation of state which has the properties of atomicity (all or nothing), durability (effects survive failures) and consistency (a correct transformation)."[3] This soon became popularized as *ACID transactions*: Atomic, Consistent, Independent, and Durable. An ACID transaction should be:

- **Atomic**: The transaction is indivisible—either all the statements in the transaction are applied to the database or none are.

- **Consistent**: The database remains in a consistent state before and after transaction execution.

- **Isolated**: While multiple transactions can be executed by one or more users simultaneously, one transaction should not see the effects of other in-progress transactions.

- **Durable**: Once a transaction is saved to the database (in SQL databases via the COMMIT command), its changes are expected to persist even if there is a failure of operating system or hardware.

ACID transactions became the standard for all serious database implementations, but also became most strongly associated with the relational databases that were emerging at about the time of Gray's paper.

As we will see later, the restriction on scalability beyond a single data center implied by the ACID transaction model has been a key motivator for the development of new database architectures.

The First Relational Databases

Initial reaction to the relational model was somewhat lukewarm. Existing vendors including IBM were disinclined to accept Codd's underlying assumption: that the databases of the day were based on a flawed foundation. Furthermore, many had sincere reservations about the ability of a system to deliver adequate performance if the data representation was not fine-tuned to the underlying access mechanisms. Would it be possible to create a high-performance database system that allowed data to be accessed in any way the user could possibly imagine?

IBM did, however, initiate a research program to develop a prototype relational database system in 1974, called System R. System R demonstrated that relational databases could deliver adequate performance, and it pioneered the *SQL language*. (Codd had specified that the relational system should include a query language, but had not mandated a specific syntax.) Also during this period, Mike Stonebraker at Berkeley started work on a database system that eventually was called *INGRES*. INGRES was also relational, but it used a non-SQL query language called *QUEL*.

At this point, Larry Ellison enters our story. Ellison was more entrepreneurial than academic by nature, though extremely technically sophisticated, having worked at Amdahl. Ellison was familiar both with Codd's work and with System R, and he believed that relational databases represented the future of database technology. In 1977, Ellison founded the company that would eventually become Oracle Corporation and which would release the first commercially successful relational database system.

Database Wars!

It was during this period that minicomputers challenged and eventually ended the dominance of the mainframe computer. Compared with today's computer hardware, the minicomputers of the late '70s and early '80s were hardly "mini". But unlike mainframes, they required little or no specialized facilities, and they allowed mid-size companies for the first time to own their own computing infrastructure. These new hardware platforms ran new operating systems and created a demand for new databases that could run on these operating systems.

By 1981, IBM had released a commercial relational database called SQL/DS, but since it only ran on IBM mainframe operating systems, it had no influence in the rapidly growing minicomputer market. Ellison's *Oracle* database system was commercially released in 1979 and rapidly gained traction on the minicomputers provided by companies such as Digital and Data General. At the same time, the Berkeley INGRES project had given birth to the commercial relational database *Ingres*. Oracle and Ingres fought for dominance in the early minicomputer relational database market.

By the mid-'80s, the benefits of the relational database—if not the nuances of relational theory— had become widely understood. Database buyers appreciated in particular that the SQL language, now adopted by all vendors including Ingres, provided massive productivity gains for report writing and analytic queries. Furthermore, a next generation of database development tools—known at the time as 4GLs—were becoming increasingly popular and these new tools typically worked best with relational database servers. Finally, minicomputers offered clear price/performance advantages over mainframes especially in the midmarket, and here the relational database was pretty much the only game in town.

Indeed, relational databases became so dominant in terms of mindshare that the vendors of the older database systems became obliged to describe their offerings as also being relational. This prompted Codd to pen his famous 12 rules (actually 13 rules, starting at rule 0) as a sort of acid test to distinguish legitimate relational databases from pretenders.

During the succeeding decades many new database systems were introduced. These include *Sybase*, Microsoft *SQL Server, Informix, MySQL,* and *DB2*. While each of these systems attempts to differentiate by claiming superior performance, availability, functionality, or economy, they are virtually identical in their reliance on three key principles: Codd's relational model, the SQL language, and the ACID transaction model.

■ **Note**   When we say RDBMS, we generally refer to a database that implements the relational data model, supports ACID transactions, and uses SQL for query and data manipulation.

Client-server Computing

By the late 1980s, the relational model had clearly achieved decisive victory in the battle for database mindshare. This mindshare dominance translated into market dominance during the shift to *client-server computing*.

Minicomputers were in some respects "little mainframes": in a minicomputer application, all processing occurred on the minicomputer itself, and the user interacted with the application through dumb "green screen" terminals. However, even as the minicomputer was becoming a mainstay of business computing, a new revolution in application architecture was emerging.

The increasing prevalence of microcomputer platforms based on the IBM PC standard, and the emergence of graphical user interfaces such as Microsoft Windows, prompted a new application paradigm: client-server. In the client-server model, presentation logic was hosted on a PC terminal typically running Microsoft Windows. These PC-based client programs communicated with a database server typically running on a minicomputer. Application logic was often concentrated on the client side, but could also be located within the database server using the *stored procedures*—programs that ran inside the database.

Client-server allowed for a richness of experience that was unparalleled in the green-screen era, and by the early '90s, virtually all new applications aspired to the client-server architecture. Practically all client-development platforms assumed an RDBMS backend—indeed, usually assumed SQL as the vehicle for all requests between client and server.

Object-oriented Programming and the OODBMS

Shortly after the client-server revolution, another significant paradigm shift impacted mainstream application-development languages. In traditional "procedural" programming languages, data and logic were essentially separate. Procedures would load and manipulate data within their logic, but the procedure itself did not contain the data in any meaningful way. *Object-oriented (OO) programming* merged attributes and behaviors into a single object. So, for instance, an employee object might represent the structure of employee records as well as operations that can be performed on those records—changing salary, promoting, retiring, and so on. For our purposes, the two most relevant principles of object-oriented programming are:

- **Encapsulation**: An object class encapsulates both data and actions (methods) that may be performed on that data. Indeed, an object may restrict direct access to the underlying data, requiring that modifications to the data be possible only via an objects methods. For instance, an employee class might include a method to retrieve salary and another method to modify salary. The salary-modification method might include restrictions on minimum and maximum salaries, and the class might allow for no manipulation of salary outside of these methods.

- **Inheritance**: Object classes can inherit the characteristics of a parent class. The employee class might inherit all the properties of a people class (DOB, name, etc.) while adding properties and methods such as salary, employee date, and so on.

Object-oriented programming represented a huge gain in programmer productivity, application reliability, and performance. Throughout the late '80s and early '90s, most programming languages converted to an object-oriented model, and many significant new languages— such as Java—emerged that were natively object-oriented.

The object-oriented programming revolution set the stage for the first serious challenge to the relational database, which came along in the mid-1990s. Object-oriented developers were frustrated by what they saw as an impedance mismatch between the object-oriented representations of their data within their programs and the relational representation within the database. In an object-0riented program, all the details relevant to a logical unit of work would be stored within the one class or directly linked to that class. For instance, a customer object would contain all details about the customer, with links to objects that contained customer orders, which in turn had links to order line items. This representation was inherently nonrelational; indeed, the representation of data matched more closely to the network databases of the CODASYL era.

When an object was stored into or retrieved from a relational database, multiple SQL operations would be required to convert from the object-0riented representation to the relational representation. This was cumbersome for the programmer and could lead to performance or reliability issues. Figure 1-5 illustrates the problem.

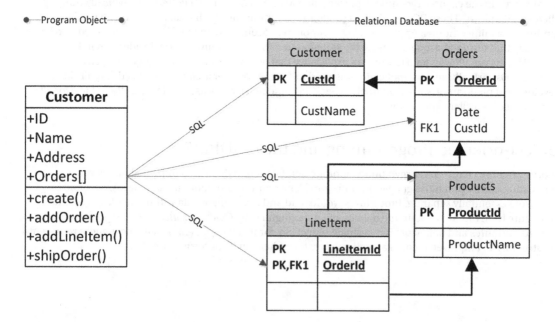

Figure 1-5. *Storing an object in an RDBMS requires multiple SQL operations*

Advocates of object-oriented programming began to see the relational database as a relic of the procedural past. This led to the rather infamous quote: "A relational database is like a garage that forces you to take your car apart and store the pieces in little drawers."

The rapid success of object-oriented programming led almost inevitably to the proposition that an *Object Oriented Database Management System* (OODBMS) was better suited to meet the demands of modern applications. An OODBMS would store program objects directly without normalization, and would allow applications to load and store their objects easily. The object-oriented database movement created a manifesto outlining the key arguments for and properties of OODBMS.[4] In implementation, OODBMS resembles the navigational model from the pre-relational era—pointers within one object (a customer, for instance) would allow navigation to related objects (such as orders).

Advocacy for the OODBMS model grew during the mid-'90s, and to many it did seem natural that the OODBMS would be the logical successor to the RDBMS. The incumbent relational database vendors—at this point, primarily Oracle, Informix, Sybase, and IBM—rapidly scrambled to implement OODBMS features within their RDBMS. Meanwhile, some pure OODBMS systems were developed and gained initial traction.

However, by the end of the decade, OODBMS systems had completely failed to gain market share. Mainstream database vendors such as Oracle and Informix had successfully implemented many OODBMS features, but even these features were rarely used. OO programmers became resigned to the use of RDBMS systems to persist objects, and the pain was somewhat alleviated by *Object-Relational Mapping* (ORM) frameworks that automated the most tedious aspects of the translation.

There are competing and not necessarily contradictory explanations for the failure of the OO database. For my part, I felt the advocates of the OODBMS model were concentrating on only the advantages an OODBMS offered to the application developer, and ignoring the disadvantages the new model had for those who wished to consume information for business purposes. Databases don't exist simply for the benefit of programmers; they represent significant assets that must be accessible to those who want to mine the information for decision making and business intelligence. By implementing a data model that could only be used by the programmer, and depriving the business user of a usable SQL interface, the OODBMS failed to gain support outside programming circles.

However, as we shall see in Chapter 4, the motivations for an OODBMS heavily influenced some of today's most popular nonrelational databases.

The Relational Plateau

Once the excitement over object-oriented databases had run its course, relational databases remained unchallenged until the latter half of the 2000s. In fact, for a period of roughly 10 years (1995–2005), no significant new databases were introduced: there were already enough RDBMS systems to saturate the market, and the stranglehold that the RDBMS model held on the market meant no nonrelational alternatives could emerge. Considering that this period essentially represents a time when the Internet grew from geeky curiosity to an all-pervasive global network, that no new database architectures emerged during this period is astonishing, and it is a testament to the power of the relational model.

The Third Database Revolution

By the middle of the 2000s, the relational database seemed completely entrenched. Looking forward from 2005, it seemed that although we would see continuing and significant innovation within the relational database systems of the day, there were no signs of any radical changes to come. But in fact, the era of complete relational database supremacy was just about to end.

In particular, the difference in application architectures between the client-server era and the era of massive web-scale applications created pressures on the relational database that could not be relieved through incremental innovation.

Google and Hadoop

By 2005, Google was by far the biggest website in the world—and this had been true since a few years after Google first launched. When Google began, the relational database was already well established, but it was inadequate to deal with the volumes and velocity of the data confronting Google. The challenges that enterprises face with "big data" today are problems that Google first encountered almost 20 years ago. Very early on, Google had to invent new hardware and software architectures to store and process the exponentially growing quantity of websites it needed to index.

In 2003, Google revealed details of the distributed file system *GFS* that formed a foundation for its storage architecture,[5] and in 2004 it revealed details of the distributed parallel processing algorithm *MapReduce,* which was used to create World Wide Web indexes.[6] In 2006, Google revealed details about its *BigTable* distributed structured database.[7]

These concepts, together with other technologies, many of which also came from Google, formed the basis for the *Hadoop* project, which matured within Yahoo! and which experienced rapid uptake from 2007 on. The Hadoop ecosystem more than anything else became a technology enabler for the Big Data ecosystem we'll discuss in more detail in Chapter 2.

The Rest of the Web

While Google had an overall scale of operation and data volume way beyond that of any other web company, other websites had challenges of their own. Websites dedicated to online e-commerce—Amazon, for example—had a need for a transactional processing capability that could operate at massive scale. Early social networking sites such as MySpace and eventually Facebook faced similar challenges in scaling their infrastructure from thousands to millions of users.

Again, even the most expensive commercial RDBMS such as Oracle could not provide sufficient scalability to meet the demands of these sites. Oracle's scaled-out RDBMS architecture (Oracle RAC) attempted to provide a roadmap for limitless scalability, but it was economically unattractive and never seemed to offer the scale required at the leading edge.

Many early websites attempted to scale open-source databases through a variety of do-it-yourself techniques. This involved utilizing distributed object cases such as Memcached to offload database load, database replication to spread database read activity, and eventually—when all else failed—"Sharding."

Sharding involves partitioning the data across multiple databases based on a key attribute, such as the customer identifier. For instance, in Twitter and Facebook, customer data is split up across a very large number of MySQL databases. Most data for a specific user ends up on the one database, so that operations for a specific customer are quick. It's up to the application to work out the correct shard and to route requests appropriately.

Sharding at sites like Facebook has allowed a MySQL-based system to scale up to massive levels, but the downsides of doing this are immense. Many relational operations and database-level ACID transactions are lost. It becomes impossible to perform joins or maintain transactional integrity across shards. The operational costs of sharding, together with the loss of relational features, made many seek alternatives to the RDBMS.

Meanwhile, a similar dilemma within Amazon had resulted in development of an alternative model to strict ACID consistency within its homegrown data store. Amazon revealed details of this system, "Dynamo," in 2008.[8]

Amazon's Dynamo model, together with innovations from web developers seeking a "webscale" database, led to the emergence of what came to be known as *key-value databases*. We'll discuss these in more detail in Chapter 3.

Cloud Computing

The existence of applications and databases "in the cloud"—that is, accessed from the Internet—had been a persistent feature of the application landscape since the late 1990s. However, around 2008, cloud computing erupted somewhat abruptly as a major concern for large organizations and a huge opportunity for startups.

For the previous 5 to 10 years, mainstream adoption of computer applications had shifted from rich desktop applications based on the client-server model to web-based applications whose data stores and application servers resided somewhere accessible via the Internet—"the cloud." This created a real challenge for emerging companies that needed somehow to establish sufficient hosting for early adopters, as well as the ability to scale up rapidly should they experience the much-desired exponential growth.

Between 2006 and 2008, Amazon rolled out *Elastic Compute Cloud* (*EC2*). EC2 made available virtual machine images hosted on Amazon's hardware infrastructure and accessible via the Internet. EC2 could be used to host web applications, and computing power could be relatively rapidly added on demand. Amazon added other services such as storage (S3, EBS), Virtual Private Cloud (VPC), a MapReduce service (EMR), and so on. The entire platform was known as *Amazon Web Services* (*AWS*) and was the first practical implementation of an *Infrastructure as a Service* (*IaaS*) cloud. AWS became the inspiration for cloud computing offerings from Google, Microsoft, and others.

For applications wishing to exploit the elastic scalability allowed by cloud computing platforms, existing relational databases were a poor fit. Oracle's attempts to integrate grid computing into its architecture had met with only limited success and were economically and practically inadequate for these applications, which needed to be able to expand on demand. That demand for elastically scalable databases fueled the demand generated by web-based startups and accelerated the growth of key-value stores, often based on Amazon's own Dynamo design. Indeed, Amazon offered nonrelational services in its cloud starting with *SimpleDB*, which eventually was replaced by *DynamoDB*.

Document Databases

Programmers continued to be unhappy with the impedance mismatch between object-oriented and relational models. Object relational mapping systems only relieved a small amount of the inconvenience that occurred when a complex object needed to be stored on a relational database in normal form.

Starting about 2004, an increasing number of websites were able to offer a far richer interactive experience than had been the case previously. This was enabled by the programming style known as *AJAX (Asynchronous JavaScript and XML)*, in which JavaScript within the browser communicates directly with a backend by transferring XML messages. XML was soon superseded by *JavaScript Object Notation* (*JSON*), which is a self-describing format similar to XML but is more compact and tightly integrated into the JavaScript language.

JSON became the de facto format for storing—serializing—objects to disk. Some websites started storing JSON documents directly into columns within relational tables. It was only a matter of time before someone decided to eliminate the relational middleman and create a database in which JSON could be directly stored. These became known as *document databases*.

CouchBase and *MongoDB* are two popular JSON-oriented databases, though virtually all nonrelational databases—and most relational databases, as well—support JSON. Programmers like document databases for the same reasons they liked OODBMS: it relieves them of the laborious process of translating objects to relational format. We'll look at document databases in some detail in Chapter 4.

The "NewSQL"

Neither the relational nor the ACID transaction model dictated the physical architecture for a relational database. However, partly because of a shared ancestry and partly because of the realities of the hardware of the day, most relational databases ended up being implemented in a very similar manner. The format of data on disk, the use of memory, the nature of locks, and so on varied only slightly among the major RDBMS implementations.

In 2007, Michael Stonebraker, pioneer of the Ingres and Postgres database systems, led a research team that published the seminal paper "The End of an Architectural Era (It's Time for a Complete Rewrite)."[9] This paper pointed out that the hardware assumptions that underlie the consensus relational architecture no longer applied, and that the variety of modern database workloads suggested a single architecture might not be optimal across all workloads.

Stonebraker and his team proposed a number of variants on the existing RDBMS design, each of which was optimized for a specific application workload. Two of these designs became particularly significant (although to be fair, neither design was necessarily completely unprecedented). *H-Store* described a pure in-memory distributed database while *C-Store* specified a design for a columnar database. Both these designs were extremely influential in the years to come and are the first examples of what came to be known as *NewSQL* database systems—databases that retain key characteristics of the RDBMS but that diverge from the common architecture exhibited by traditional systems such as Oracle and SQL Server. We'll examine these database types in Chapters 6 and 7.

The Nonrelational Explosion

As we saw in Figure 1-1, a huge number of relational database systems emerged in the first half of the 2000s. In particular, a sort of "Cambrian explosion" occurred in the years 2008-2009: literally dozens of new database systems emerged in this short period. Many of these have fallen into disuse, but some—such as MongoDB, Cassandra, and HBase—have today captured significant market share.

At first, these new breeds of database systems lacked a common name. "Distributed Non-Relational Database Management System" (DNRDBMS) was proposed, but clearly wasn't going to capture anybody's imagination. However, in late 2009, the term *NoSQL* quickly caught on as shorthand for any database system that broke with the traditional SQL database.

In the opinion of many, NoSQL is an unfortunate term: it defines what a database is not rather than what it is, and it focuses attention on the presence or absence of the SQL language. Although it's true that most nonrelational systems do not support SQL, actually it is variance from the strict transactional and relational data model that motivated most NoSQL database designs.

By 2011, the term *NewSQL* became popularized as a means of describing this new breed of databases that, while not representing a complete break with the relational model, enhanced or significantly modified the fundamental principles—and this included columnar databases, discussed in Chapter 6, and in some of the in-memory databases discussed in Chapter 7.

Finally, the term *Big Data* burst onto mainstream consciousness in early 2012. Although the term refers mostly to the new ways in which data is being leveraged to create value, we generally understand "Big Data solutions" as convenient shorthand for technologies that support large and unstructured datasets such as Hadoop.

■ **Note**   NoSQL, NewSQL, and Big Data are in many respects vaguely defined, overhyped, and overloaded terms. However, they represent the most widely understood phrases for referring to next-generation database technologies.

Loosely speaking, NoSQL databases reject the constraints of the relational model, including strict consistency and schemas. NewSQL databases retain many features of the relational model but amend the underlying technology in significant ways. Big Data systems are generally oriented around technologies within the Hadoop ecosystem, increasingly including Spark.

Conclusion: One Size Doesn't Fit All

The first database revolution arose as an inevitable consequence of the emergence of electronic digital computers. In some respect, the databases of the first wave were electronic analogs of pre-computer technologies such as punched cards and tabulating machines. Early attempts to add a layer of structure and consistency to these databases may have improved programmer efficiency and data consistency, but they left the data locked in systems to which only programmers held the keys.

The second database revolution resulted from Edgar Codd's realization that database systems would be well served if they were based on a solid, formal, and mathematical foundation; that the representation of data should be independent of the physical storage implementation; and that databases should support flexible query mechanisms that do not require sophisticated programming skills.

The successful development of the modern relational database over such an extended time —more than 30 years of commercial dominance—represents a triumph of computer science and software engineering. Rarely has a software theoretical concept been so successfully and widely implemented as the relational database.

The third database revolution is not based on a single architectural foundation. If anything, it rests on the proposition that a single database architecture cannot meet the challenges posed in our modern digital world. The existence of massive social networking applications with hundreds of millions of users and the emergence of *Internet of Things* (*IoT*) applications with potentially billions of machine inputs, strain the relational database—and particularly the ACID transaction model—to the breaking point. At the other end of the scale we have applications that must run on mobile and wearable devices with limited memory and computing power. And we are awash with data, much of which is of unpredictable structure for which rendering to relational form is untenable.

The third wave of databases roughly corresponds to a third wave of computer applications. IDC and others often refer to this as "the third platform." The first platform was the mainframe, which was supported by pre-relational database systems. The second platform, client-server and early web applications, was supported by relational databases. The third platform is characterized by applications that involve cloud deployment, mobile presence, social networking, and the Internet of Things. The third platform demands a third wave of database technologies that include but are not limited to relational systems. Figure 1-6 summarizes how the three platforms correspond to our three waves of database revolutions.

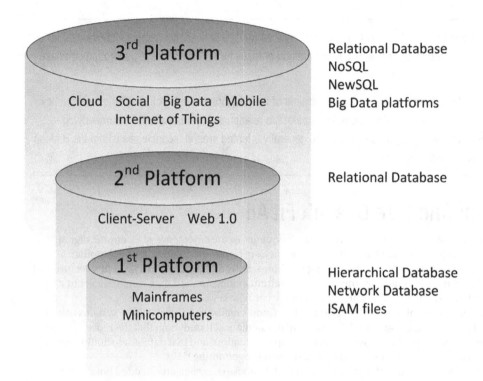

3rd Platform

Cloud   Social   Big Data   Mobile
Internet of Things

Relational Database
NoSQL
NewSQL
Big Data platforms

2nd Platform

Client-Server   Web 1.0

Relational Database

1st Platform

Mainframes
Minicomputers

Hierarchical Database
Network Database
ISAM files

Figure 1-6. *IDC's "three platforms" model corresponds to three waves of database technology*

It's an exciting time to be working in the database industry. For a generation of software professionals (and most of my professional life), innovation in database technology occurred largely within the constraints of the ACID-compliant relational databases. Now that the hegemony of the RDBMS has been broken, we are free to design database systems whose only constraint is our imagination. It's well known that failure drives innovation. Some of these new database system concepts might not survive the test of time; however, there seems little chance that a single model will dominate the immediate future as completely as had the relational model. Database professionals will need to choose the most appropriate technology for their circumstances with care; in many cases, relational technology will continue be the best fit—but not always.

In the following chapters, we'll look at each of the major categories of next-generation database systems. We'll examine their ambitions, their architectures, and their ability to meet the challenges posed by modern application systems.

Notes

1. http://www.seas.upenn.edu/~zives/03f/cis550/codd.pdf

2. William Kent, "A Simple Guide to Five Normal Forms in Relational Database Theory," 1983.

3. http://research.microsoft.com/en-us/um/people/gray/papers/ theTransactionConcept.pdf

4. https://www.cs.cmu.edu/~clamen/OODBMS/Manifesto/

5. http://research.google.com/archive/gfs.html

6. http://research.google.com/archive/mapreduce.html

7. http://research.google.com/archive/bigtable.html

8. http://queue.acm.org/detail.cfm?id=1466448

9. http://nms.csail.mit.edu/~stavros/pubs/hstore.pdf

■ ■ ■

CHAPTER 2

Google, Big Data, and Hadoop

Information is the oil of the 21st century, and analytics is the combustion engine.

—Peter Sondergaard, Gartner Research, 2011

Data creation is exploding. With all the selfies and useless files people refuse to delete on the cloud. . . . The world's data storage capacity will be overtaken. . . . Data shortages, data rationing, data black markets . . . data-geddon!

—Gavin Belson, HBOs Silicon Valley, 2015

In the history of computing, nothing has raised the profile of data processing, storage, and analytics as much as the concept of *Big Data*. We have considered ourselves to be an information-age society since the 1980s, but the concentration of media and popular attention to the role of data in our society have never been greater than in the past few years–thanks to Big Data.

Big Data technologies include those that allow us to derive more meaning from data–*machine learning*, for instance—and those that permit us to store greater volumes of data at higher granularity than ever before.

Google pioneered many of these Big Data technologies, and they found their way into the broader IT community in the form of *Hadoop*. In this chapter we review the history of Google's data management technologies, the emergence of Hadoop, and the development of other technologies for massive unstructured data storage.

The Big Data Revolution

Big Data is a broad term with multiple, competing definitions. For this author, it suggests two complementary significant shifts in the role of data within computer science and society:

- **More data**: We now have the ability to store and process *all* data—machine generated, multimedia, social networking, and transactional data—in its original raw format and maintain this data potentially in perpetuity.

- **To more effect**: Advances in machine learning, predictive analytics, and collective intelligence allow more value to be generated from data than ever before.

This is not a book about the Big Data revolution; there are enough of those already. However, we should spend a few pages articulating the significance of Big Data as a concept so as to put these technologies into context.

Big Data often seems like a meaningless buzz phrase to older database professionals who have been experiencing exponential growth in database volumes since time immemorial. There has never been a moment in the history of database management systems when the increasing volume of data has not been remarkable.

However, it is true that the nature of organizational data today is qualitatively different from that of the recent past. Some have referred to this paradigm shift as an "industrial revolution" in data, and indeed this term seems apt. Before the industrial revolution, all products were created essentially by hand, whereas after the industrial revolution, products were created in assembly lines that were in factories. In a similar way, before the industrial revolution of data, all data was generated "in house." Now, data comes in from everywhere: customers, social networks, and sensors, as well as all the traditional sources, such as sales and internal operational systems.

Cloud, Mobile, Social, and Big Data

Most would agree that the three leading information technology trends over the last decade have been in cloud, mobile, and social media. These three megatrends have transformed our economy, our society, and our everyday lives. The evolution of online retail over the past 15 years provides perhaps the most familiar example of these trends in motion.

The term *cloud computing* started to gain mindshare in 2008, but what we now call "The Cloud" was truly born in the e-commerce revolution of the late 1990s. The emergence of the Internet as a universal wide area network and the World Wide Web as a business-to-customer portal drove virtually all businesses "into the cloud" via the creation of web-based storefronts.

For some industries—music and books, for instance—the Internet rapidly became a significant or even dominant sales channel. But across the wider retail landscape, physical storefronts (brick-and-mortar stores) continued to dominate consumer interactions. Although retailers were fully represented in the cloud, consumers had only a sporadic and shallow presence. For most consumers, Internet connectivity was limited to a shared home computer or a desktop at work. The consumer was only intermittently connected to the Internet and had no online identity.

The emergence of *social networks* and *smartphones* occurred almost simultaneously. Smartphones allowed people to be online at all times, while social networks provided the motivation for frequent Internet engagement. Within a few years, the average consumer's Internet interactions accelerated: people who had previously interacted with the Internet just a few times a day were now continually online, monitoring their professional and social engagements through email and social networks.

Consumers now found it convenient to shop online whenever the impulse arose. Furthermore, retailers quickly discovered that they could leverage information from social networks and other Internet sources to target marketing campaigns and personalize engagement. Retailers themselves created social network presences that complemented their online stores and allowed the retailer to engage the consumer directly through the social network.

The synergy between the online business and the social network—mediated and enabled by the always connected mobile Internet—has resulted in a seismic shift in the retail landscape. The key to the effectiveness of the new retail model is data: the social-mobile-cloud generates masses of data that can be used to refine and enhance the online experience. This positive feedback loop drives the Big Data solutions that can represent success or failure for the next generation of retail operations.

Retail is a familiar example, but similar dynamics drive almost every other industry. In some cases the *Internet of Things* (*IoT*)—by hooking virtually every physical device that collects or consumes data into the Internet—plays the equivalent role as the smartphone in the retail context. New connected devices—Internet-enabled cars, wearable devices, home automation, and so on—propel the virtuous data cycle that generates and depends on data to drive competitive advantage. Figure 2-1 illustrates this cycle.

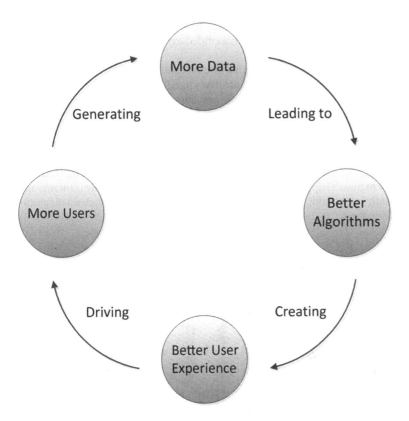

Figure 2-1. *The virtuous cycle of big data*

Google: Pioneer of Big Data

When Google was first created in 1996, the World Wide Web was already a network of unparalleled scale; indeed, it was that very large scale that made Google's key innovation—*PageRank*—such a breakthrough. Existing search engines simply indexed on keywords within webpages. This was inadequate, given the sheer number of possible matches for any search term; the results were primarily weighted by the number of occurrences of the search term within a page, with no account for usefulness or popularity. PageRank allowed the relevance of a page to be weighted based on the number of links to that page, and it allowed Google to immediately provide a better search outcome than its competitors.

PageRank is a great example of a data-driven algorithm that leverages the "wisdom of the crowd" (*collective intelligence*) and that can adapt intelligently as more data is available (*machine learning*). Google is, therefore, the first clear example of a company that succeeded on the web through what we now call *data science*.

Google Hardware

Google serves as a prime example of how better algorithm were forged by intelligently harnessing massive datasets. However, for our purposes, it is Google's innovations in data architecture that are most relevant.

Google's initial hardware platform consisted of the typical collection of off-the-shelf servers sitting under a desk that might have been found in any research lab. However, it took only a few years for Google to shift to masses of rack-mounted servers in commercial-grade data centers. As Google grew, it outstripped the capacity limits of even the most massive existing data center architectures. The economics and practicalities of delivering a hardware infrastructure capable of unbounded exponential growth required Google to create a new hardware and software architecture.

Google committed to a number of key tenants when designing its data center architecture. Most significantly—and at the time, uniquely—Google committed to massively parallelizing and distributing processing across very large numbers of commodity servers. Google also adopted a "Jedis build their own lightsabers" attitude: very little third party— and virtually no commercial—software would be found in the Google architecture. "Build" was considered better than "buy" at Google.

By 2005, Google no longer thought of individual servers as the fundamental unit of computing. Rather, Google constructed data centers around the *Google Modular Data Center*. The Modular Data Center comprises shipping containers that house about a thousand custom-designed Intel servers running Linux. Each module includes an independent power supply and air conditioning. Data center capacity is increased not by adding new servers individually but by adding new 1,000-server modules! Figure 2-2 shows a diagram of a module as described in Google's patent.[1]

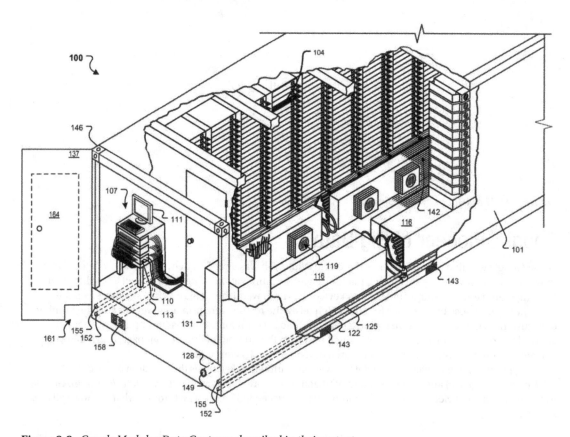

Figure 2-2. *Google Modular Data Center as described in their patent*

At this time, the prevailing architecture for data processing was to separate its storage to dedicated storage servers built by companies such as EMC. This storage would be made available to databases or other applications via Fibre Channel (or similar protocol) as a *storage area network* (*SAN*) or across TCP/IP as *network attached storage* (*NAS*). Google rejected these concepts; in the Google architecture, storage would be on directly attached disks within the same servers as would be providing computing power.

The Google Software Stack

There are many fascinating aspects to Google's hardware architecture. However, it's enough for our purposes to understand that the Google architecture at that time comprised hundreds of thousands of low-cost servers, each of which had its own directly attached storage.

It goes without saying that this unique hardware architecture required a unique software architecture as well. No operating system or database platform available at the time could come close to operating across such a huge number of servers. So, Google developed three major software layers to serve as the foundation for the Google platform. These were:

- **Google File System (GFS)**: a distributed cluster file system that allows all of the disks within the Google data center to be accessed as one massive, distributed, redundant file system.

- **MapReduce**: a distributed processing framework for parallelizing algorithms across large numbers of potentially unreliable servers and being capable of dealing with massive datasets.

- **BigTable**: a nonrelational database system that uses the Google File System for storage.

Google was generous enough to reveal the essential designs for each of these components in a series of papers released in 2003,[2] 2004,[3] and 2006.[4] These three technologies—together with other utilities and components—served as the foundation for many Google products.

A high level, very simplified representation of the architecture is shown in Figure 2-3. GFS abstracts the storage contained in the servers that make up Google's modular data centers. MapReduce abstracts the processing power contained within these servers, while BigTable allows for structured storage of massive datasets using GFS for storage.

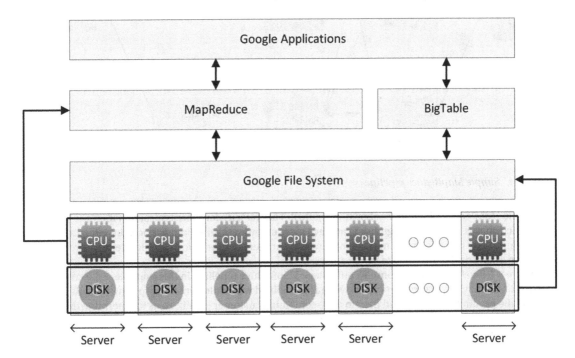

Figure 2-3. *Google software architecture*

More about MapReduce

MapReduce is a programming model for general-purpose parallelization of data-intensive processing. MapReduce divides the processing into two phases: a *mapping phase,* in which data is broken up into chunks that can be processed by separate threads—potentially running on separate machines; and a *reduce phase,* which combines the output from the mappers into the final result.

The canonical example of MapReduce is the word-count program, shown in Figure 2-4. For example, suppose we wish to count the occurrences of pet types in some input file. We break the data into equal chunks in the map phase. The data is then shuffled into groups of pet types. Finally, the reduce phase counts the occurrences to provide a total that is fed into the output.

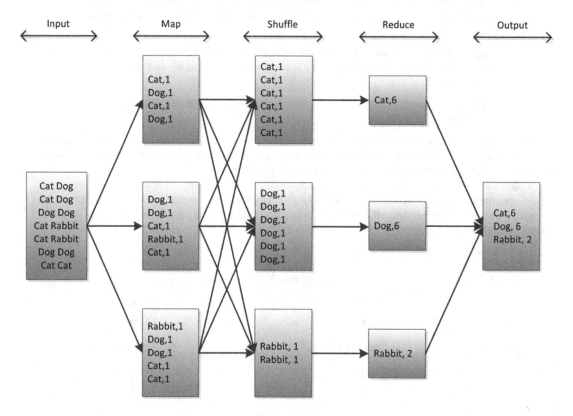

Figure 2-4. *Simple MapReduce pipeline*

Simple MapReduce pipelines as shown in Figure 2-4 are rare; it's far more typical that multiple MapReduce phases are chained together to achieve more complex results. For instance, there might be multiple input files that need to be merged in some way, or there may be some complex iterative processing to perform a statistical or machine learning analysis.

Figure 2-5 illustrates a more complex multistage MapReduce pipeline. In this example, a file containing information about visits to various product webpages is joined with a file containing product details—to obtain the product category—and then to a file containing customer details, so as to determine the customer's country. This joined data is then aggregated to provide a report of product categories, customer geographies, and page visits.

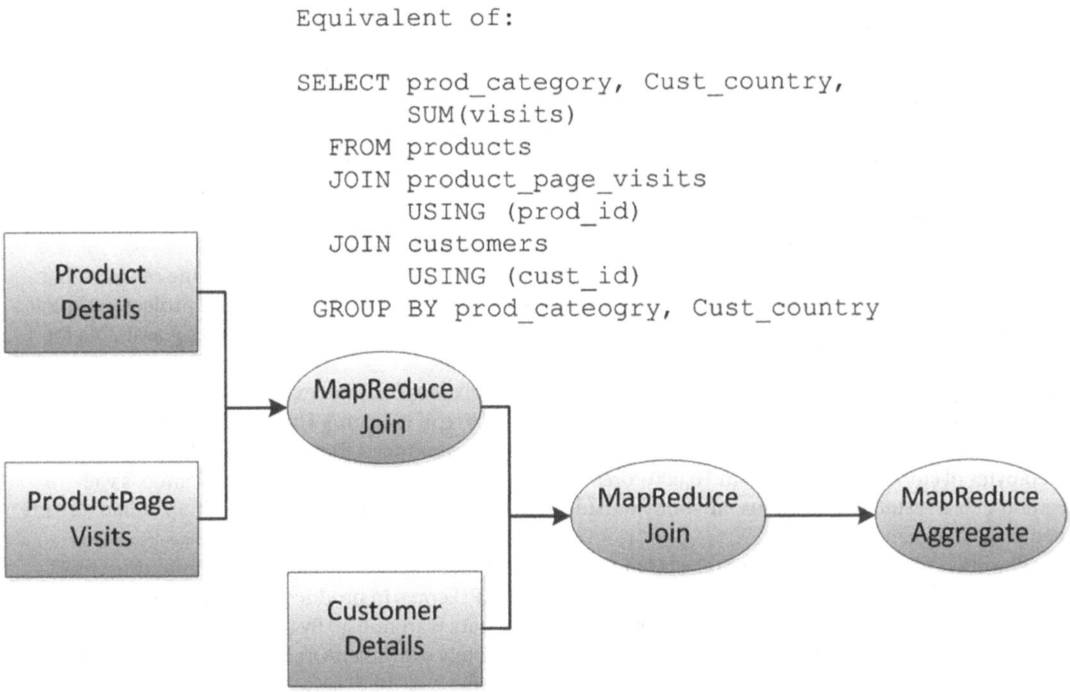
Equivalent of:
SELECT prod_category, Cust_country,
SUM(visits)
FROM products
JOIN product_page_visits
USING (prod_id)
JOIN customers
USING (cust_id)
GROUP BY prod_cateogry, Cust_country
Product Details
ProductPage Visits
MapReduce Join
Customer Details
MapReduce Join
MapReduce Aggregate

***Figure 2-5.** Multistage MapReduce*

MapReduce processes can be assembled into arbitrarily complex pipelines capable of solving a very wide range of data processing problems. However, in many respects, MapReduce represents a brute-force approach to processing, and is not always the most efficient or elegant solution. There also exist a category of computational problems for which MapReduce cannot offer scalable solutions. For all these reasons, MapReduce has been extended within and without Google by more sophisticated and specialized algorithms; we will look at some of these in Chapter 11. However, despite the increasing prevalence of alternative processing models, MapReduce remains a default and widely applicable paradigm.

Hadoop: Open-Source Google Stack

While the technologies outlined in the previous section underlie Google products that we have all used, they are not generally directly exposed to the public. However, they did serve as the inspiration for *Hadoop,* which contains analogs for each of these important technologies and which is available to all as an open-source Apache project.

No other single technology has had as great an influence on Big Data as Hadoop. Hadoop—by providing an economically viable means of mass unstructured data storage and processing— has bought Google-style Big Data processing within the reach of mainstream IT.

Hadoop's Origins

In 2004, Doug Cutting and Mike Cafarella were working on an open-source project to build a web search engine called Nutch, which would be on top of Apache Lucene. Lucene is a Java-based text indexing and searching library. The Nutch team aspired to use Lucene to build a scalable web search engine with the explicit intent of creating an open-source equivalent of the proprietary technologies used within Google.

Initial versions of Nutch could not demonstrate the scalability required to index the entire web. When Google published the GFS and MapReduce papers in 2003 and 2004, the Nutch team quickly realized that these offered a proven architectural foundation for solving Nutch's scalability challenges.

As the Nutch team implemented their GFS and MapReduce equivalents, it soon became obvious that these were applicable to a broad range of data processing challenges and that a dedicated project to exploit the technology was warranted. The resulting project was named Hadoop. Hadoop was made available for download in 2007, and became a top-level Apache project in 2008.

Many open-source projects start small and grow slowly. Hadoop was the exact opposite. Yahoo! hired Cutting to work on improving Hadoop in 2006, with the objective of maturing Hadoop to the point that it could contribute to the Yahoo! platform. In early 2008, Yahoo! announced that a Hadoop cluster with over 5 petabytes of storage and more than 10,000 cores was generating the index that resolved Yahoo!'s web searches. As a result, before almost anybody outside the IT community had heard of Hadoop, it had already been proven on a massive scale.

The other significant early adopter of Hadoop was Facebook. Facebook started experimenting with Hadoop in 2007, and by 2008 it had a cluster utilizing 2,500 CPU cores in production. Facebook's initial implementation of Hadoop supplemented its Oracle-based data warehouse. By 2012, Facebook`s Hadoop cluster had exceeded 100 petabytes of disk, and it had completely overtaken Oracle as a data warehousing solution, as well as powering many core Facebook products.

Hadoop has been adopted—at least in pilot form—by many of the Fortune 500 companies. As with all new technologies, some overhyping and subsequent disillusionment is to be expected. However, most organizations that are actively pursuing a Big Data solution use Hadoop in some form.

The degree to which Hadoop has become the de facto solution for massive unstructured data storage and processing can be illustrated by the positions taken by the top three database vendors: Microsoft, Oracle, and IBM. By 2012, each of these giants had ceased to offer any form of Hadoop alternative and instead were offering Hadoop within its product portfolio.

The Power of Hadoop

Hadoop provides an economically attractive storage solution for Big Data, as well as a scalable processing model for analytic processing. Specifically, it has:

- **An economical scalable storage model**. As data volumes increase, so does the cost of storing that data online. Because Hadoop can run on commodity hardware that in turn utilizes commodity disks, the price point per terabyte is lower than that of almost any other technology.

- **Massive scaleable IO capability**. Because Hadoop uses a large number of commodity devices, the aggregate IO and network capacity is higher than that provided by dedicated storage arrays in which smaller numbers of larger disks are provided by even smaller numbers of processors. Furthermore, adding new servers to Hadoop adds storage, IO, CPU, and network capacity all at once, whereas adding disks to a storage array might simply exacerbate a network or CPU bottleneck within the array.

- **Reliability**: Data in Hadoop is stored redundantly in multiple servers and can be distributed across multiple computer racks. Failure of a server does not result in a loss of data; in fact, a Hadoop job will continue even if a server fails—the processing simply switches to another server.

- **A scalable processing model**: MapReduce represents a widely applicable and scalable distributed processing model. While MapReduce is not the most efficient implementation for all algorithms, it is capable of brute-forcing acceptable performance for almost all.

- **Schema on read**: Data can be loaded into Hadoop without having to be converted to a highly structured normalized format. This makes it easy for Hadoop to quickly ingest data from various forms. The imposition of structure can be delayed until the data is accessed; this is sometimes referred to as *schema on read*, as opposed to the *schema on write* mode of relational data warehouses.

Hadoop's Architecture

Hadoop's architecture roughly parallels that of Google. Google File System capabilities are provided by the *Hadoop Distributed File System* (*HDFS*), which allows all the disk storage in the cluster to be accessed using familiar file system idioms.

There are currently two major iterations of Hadoop architecture. Hadoop 2.0 layers on top of the 1.0 architecture, so let's consider each in turn.

In Hadoop 1.0, the majority of servers in a Hadoop cluster function both as *data nodes* and as *task trackers*, which is to say that each server supplies both data storage and processing capacity (CPU and memory).

Specialized nodes within the Hadoop 1.0 architecture are also defined. The *job tracker* node coordinates the scheduling of jobs run on the Hadoop cluster, while the *name node* is a sort of directory that provides the mapping from blocks on data nodes to files on HDFS. Every piece of data will usually be replicated across three nodes, which can be located on separate server racks to avoid any single point of failure. Figure 2-6 illustrates the Hadoop 1.0 architecture.

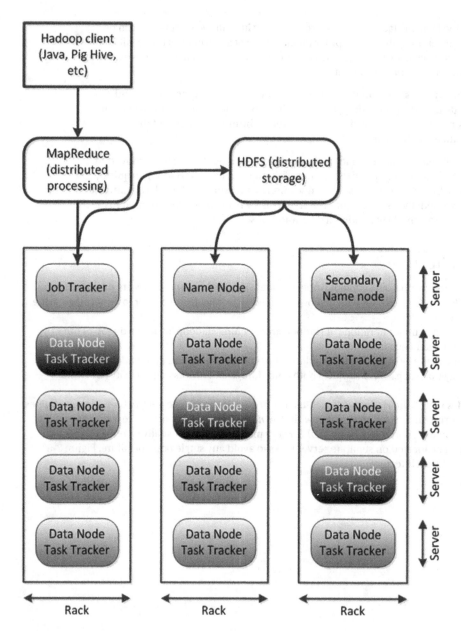

Figure 2-6. *Hadoop 1.0 architecture*

The Hadoop 1.0 architecture is powerful and easy to understand, but it is limited to MapReduce workloads and it provides limited flexibility with regard to scheduling and resource allocation. In the Hadoop 2.0 architecture, *YARN* (*Yet Another Resource Negotiator* or, recursively, *YARN Application Resource Negotiator*) improves scalability and flexibility by splitting the roles of the Task Tracker into two processes. A *Resource Manager* controls access to the clusters resources (memory, CPU, etc.) while the *Application Manager* (one per job) controls task execution.

YARN provides much more than just improved scalability. YARN treats traditional MapReduce as just one of the possible frameworks that can run on the cluster, allowing Hadoop to run tasks based on more complex processing models, some of which we'll discuss in Chapter 11.

Figure 2-7 illustrates the resource allocation and application execution aspects of YARN. For example, a Hadoop client submits an application execution request to the Resource Manager (1). The Resource Manager coordinates with the various Node Managers to determine which nodes have available resource (2). The Resource Manager then creates an Application Manager (3) on an available node. The Application Manager coordinates tasks that run in Containers on the selected nodes (4). The Containers control the amount of CPU and memory resource the application task may use.

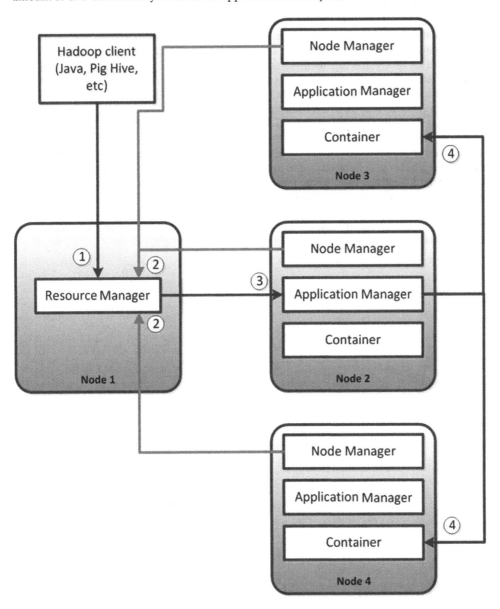

Figure 2-7. *Hadoop 2.0 YARN architecture*

HBase

As mentioned earlier in the chapter, Google published three key papers revealing the architecture of their platform between 2003 and 2006. The GFS and MapReduce papers served as the basis for the core Hadoop architecture. The third paper—on BigTable—served as the basis for one of the first formal NoSQL database systems: *HBase.*

HBase uses Hadoop HDFS as a file system in the same way that most traditional relational databases use the operating system file system. For instance, in a MySQL database using the MyISAM option, each table is represented as a file stored on the file system. By using Hadoop HDFS as its file system, HBase is able to create tables of truly massive size—way beyond the possible size for a system like MySQL, or even for Oracle. In addition, the fault tolerance of HDFS provides automatic redundancy for HBase tables. As we saw in Figure 2-6, each data item in an HDFS file system is replicated (by default) three times. Since HDFS provides this inherent redundancy, HBase need not store multiple copies of data to protect against data loss.

While HDFS allows a file of any structure to be stored within Hadoop, HBase does enforce structure on the data. The terminology of HBase objects seem pretty familiar—columns, rows, tables, keys. However, HBase tables vary significantly from the relational tables with which we are familiar.

First, in each cell—a column value for a particular row—there will usually be multiple versions of a data value. Each version of data within a cell is identified by a timestamp. This provides HBase tables with a sort of temporal "third dimension."

Second, HBase columns are more like the key values in a distributed Map of key : value pairs than the fixed and relatively small number of columns found in a relational database table. Each row can have a huge number of "sparse" columns. Each row in an HBase table can appear to consist of a unique set of columns.

To get a sense of how the HBase data model works, consider the data shown in Figure 2-8. First we see the raw data (1)—a list of users, websites, and the number of times each user visited the web site. The relational representation (2) involves three tables—sites, people, and visits—with foreign key relationships between sites and visits and people and visits.

① **Raw Data**

Name	Site	Visits
Dick	Ebay	507,018
Dick	Google	690,414
Jane	Google	716,426
Dick	Facebook	723,649
Jane	Facebook	643,261
Jane	ILoveLarry.com	856,767
Dick	MadBillFans.com	675,230

② **Relational representation**

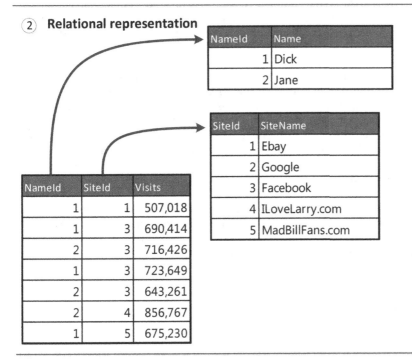

NameId	Name
1	Dick
2	Jane

SiteId	SiteName
1	Ebay
2	Google
3	Facebook
4	ILoveLarry.com
5	MadBillFans.com

NameId	SiteId	Visits
1	1	507,018
1	3	690,414
2	3	716,426
1	3	723,649
2	3	643,261
2	4	856,767
1	5	675,230

③ **HBase version**

Id	Name	Ebay	Google	Facebook	(other columns)	MadBillFans.com
1	Dick	507,018	690,414	723,649	....	675,230

Id	Name	Google	Facebook	(other columns)	ILoveLarry.com
2	Jane	716,426	643,261	....	856,767

Figure 2-8. *HBase data model compared to relational model*

In the HBase representation (3), each person's information is held in a single row. That row contains columns for every website visited by that person. The column name represents the site name and the column value represents the number of visits. Because people visit thousands to hundreds of thousands of sites, there can be potentially thousands or hundreds of thousands of columns in a row. And while there are some sites that almost everyone visits—Google.com, for instance—rows only have columns corresponding to websites that they actually visited. So for instance, if you have never visited dell.com, then there will be no dell.com column in your row.

The HBase data model and storage system is examined in more detail in Chapter 10.

Hive

The pioneers of Hadoop realized fairly early that the full value of the platform could not be realized if only people capable of coding MapReduce programs could access the system. Non-programmers needed flexible, powerful, and accessible query tools to extract data from the Hadoop system. Even for programmers, the laborious and tedious process of coding MapReduce to perform repetitive reporting tasks seemed terribly inefficient. Two solutions to this problem were independently developed at Facebook and Yahoo!: *Hive* and *Pig*, respectively.

Hive is usually thought of as "SQL for Hadoop," although Hive provides a catalog for the Hadoop system, as well as a SQL processing layer. The Hive metadata service contains information about the structure of registered files in the HDFS file system. This metadata effectively "schematizes" these files, providing definitions of column names and data types. The Hive client or server (depending on the Hive configuration) accepts SQL-like commands called *Hive Query Language* (*HQL*). These commands are translated into Hadoop jobs that process the query and return the results to the user. Most of the time, Hive creates MapReduce programs that implement query operations such as joins, sorts, aggregation, and so on. However, recent versions of Hive can employ more modern YARN-based processing paradigms such as *Tez*, a programming model designed to speed up operations of certain data processing patterns; we'll look more at Tez in Chapter 11.

Figure 2-9 illustrates the Hive architecture. The Hive metastore maps HDFS files to Hive tables (1). A Hive client or server (depending on the installation mode) accepts HQL commands that perform SQL operations on those tables. Hive translates HQL to Hadoop code (3)—usually MapReduce. This code operates against the HDFS files (4) and returns query results to Hive (5).

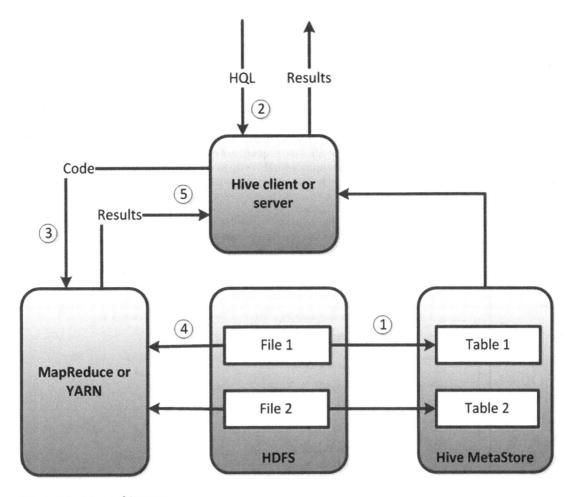

Figure 2-9. *Hive architecture*

It's hard to overstate the importance of Hive. Hive opened up Hadoop to anybody familiar with SQL, illustrated to the community at large that Hadoop could operate as a form of data warehouse, and set the stage for integration of Hadoop into Business Intelligence tools. However, by raising expectations that Hadoop could operate as a traditional database, Hive also contributed to some unrealistic expectations. SQL is generally used as a real-time query tool, but Hadoop's batch orientation means that even the simplest HQL query cannot run in a real-time mode.

The Hadoop community has attempted to deal with Hive performance issues in two ways. The predominant Hadoop vendor Cloudera has created an alternative proprietary SQL on the Hadoop framework called *Impala*, while others—including another major Hadoop vendor Hortonworks—have attempted to improve Hive's performance through incremental changes and better integration with post-MapReduce frameworks such as YARN and Tez. Meanwhile, traditional database vendors such as Oracle and Teradata have attempted to provide SQL on Hadoop functionality through their existing SQL engines. We'll spend some more time on SQL interfaces to Hadoop and NoSQL in Chapter 11.

Pig

Facebook created Hive to empower analysts wanting to access data in Hadoop. Yahoo!, in response to similar demands, independently created another solution: *Pig*.

Pig supports a procedural, high-level data flow language called *Pig Latin*. Like Hive, Pig Latin is compiled to MapReduce code. However, Pig is more of a scripting language than a SQL alternative. While it is possible to create Pig equivalents to virtually all Hive HQL queries, Pig is capable of expressing far more complex pipelines of operations than is HQL.

Figure 2-10 compares a Pig Latin script with an equivalent Hive HQL statement. Note that the Pig script is a procedural representation—it explicitly specifies the sequence of events that must be undertaken in order to achieve the result. Like SQL, HQL is nonprocedural: it's up to the Hive optimizer to determine the means of execution; the HQL only specifies the logical operations to be performed on the data.

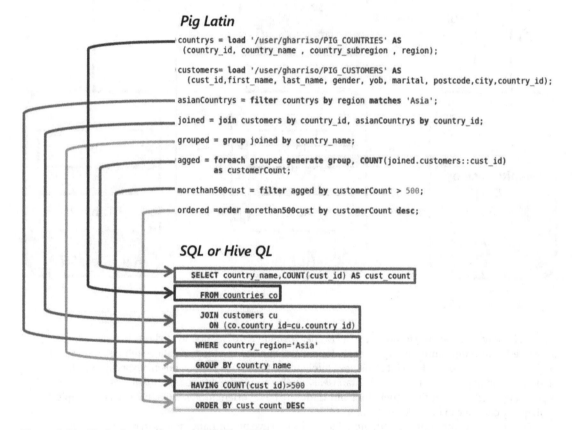

Figure 2-10. *Pig Latin as compared with Hive HQL*

The Hadoop Ecosystem

MapReduce, YARN, and HDFS represent the foundations of the Hadoop architecture. HBase, Pig, and Hive are built on top of those foundations. The Hadoop ecosystem includes an ever expanding family of utilities and applications built on top of or designed to work with core Hadoop. Some of the most significant are:

- **Flume**, a utility for loading file-based data into HDFS.

- **SQOOP**, a utility for exchanging data with relational databases, either by importing relational tables into HDFS files or by exporting HDFS files to relational databases.

- **Zookeeper**, which provides coordination and synchronization services within the cluster.

- **Oozie**, a workflow scheduler that allows complex workflows to be constructed from lower level jobs (for instance, running a Sqoop or Flume job prior to a MapReduce application).

- **Hue**, a graphical user interface that simplifies Hadoop administrative and development tasks.

In addition, there are many Apache and open-source projects that, while not entirely dependent on Hadoop, are often integrated into a Hadoop implementation. This includes the machine-learning framework *Mahout*, the distributed streaming messaging system *Kafka,* and many other significant Apache projects.

The most important addition to the Hadoop family in recent years has been *Spark* and other elements of the *Berkeley Data Analytics Stack* (*BDAS*) to which it belongs. If we think about Hadoop as a disk-oriented framework for running MapReduce-style programs, Spark represents a memory-oriented framework for running similar workloads. We'll look at Spark in more detail in Chapter 7.

Conclusion

Hadoop represents one of the most significant transformations in database architecture since the relational model. It provides economies of storage and processing that are beyond the reach of the traditional RDBMS, and it offers an ability for the storage and processing of unstructured and semi-structured data for which the RDBMS had no real solution. More than any other technology, Hadoop has rightfully been associated with the Big Data movement.

However, while Hadoop provides a framework for the mass processing of data, it doesn't have a framework for transactional and online operations. As we will see in the next chapter, bleeding-edge websites demanded not just a storage and batch processing solution but also an online transactional solution. These demands led to what we now call NoSQL, and that will be examined in the next chapter.

Notes

1. http://www.google.com/patents/US20100251629

2. http://research.google.com/arcHive/gfs.html

3. http://research.google.com/arcHive/mapreduce.html

4. http://research.google.com/arcHive/bigtable.html

■ ■ ■

CHAPTER 3

Sharding, Amazon, and the Birth of NoSQL

Step 1 - Shard database. Step 2 - shoot yourself.

—Twitter user @Dmitriy, 2009

"Bob: So, how do I query the database?

IT guy: It's not a database. It's a Key-Value store. . . .

You write a distributed map-reduce function in Erlang.

*Bob: Did you just tell me to go **** myself?*

IT guy: I believe I did, Bob."

—Fault Tolerance cartoon, @jrecursive, 2009

The last time we saw a major new brand of relational database was around 1995, with the first release of MySQL. In 1995, the World Wide Web in the United States was barely two years old—the Netscape browser had been released only the year before. In terms of computer systems, it was a different era.

In the 10 years between 1995 and 2005, the Internet was transformed from a dial-up curiosity to arguably the most important communication system in our civilization, a foundation for international commerce, and soon to be a centerpiece of our social lives. Despite that, the database systems used in 2005 had the same names as those used in 1995. Surveying the software landscape in 2005, you would be excused for thinking that there was nothing new under the database sun.

Behind the scenes, however, the ability of the relational database to sustain the needs of web applications had been stretched to the breaking point. Out of this pressure arose a new breed of web-scale transactional database systems—what we now call NoSQL.

Scaling Web 2.0

The World Wide Web was initially conceived and implemented as a global collection of linked static documents. Indeed, the vast majority of the web still consists of read-only static content. Google developed many of the technologies introduced in the last chapter to provide an index and search capability across these documents.

But to retailers and other businesses, the web promised to deliver much more than simply a place to store online catalogs and white papers. The idea of web-based retail outlets promised to revolutionize modern commerce. And although this concept of e-commerce resulted in the biggest boom and bust of our generation, the promise was eventually realized and today you can purchase virtually anything online.

The World Wide Web of static pages is often referred to as *Web 1.0*, and the World Wide Web of dynamically created content with transactional capability is referred to as *Web 2.0*. However, version 2.0 was not the result of a controlled architectural redevelopment; rather, it resulted from web developers scrambling to cope with ever-increasing demands for functionality, performance, and scale.

How Web 2.0 was Won

The first web servers provided accessed to hyperlink documents written in HTML. There were no database systems involved, and there was no ability to conduct business or any transactional activity.

Early websites that wanted to provide some form of user interaction—Amazon.com, for instance—used the *Common Gateway Interface* (*CGI*). CGI allowed an HTTP request to invoke a script rather than display a HTML page. Early dynamic webpages would then invoke scripts written in the Perl language, which would connect to a database and generate HTML code on the fly based on database contents. In this way, a website could display a catalog based on data held within a database or could personalize a page based on a user's profile.

CGI-based approaches gave way to more elegant and cohesive frameworks such as Java J2EE and ASP.NET, though huge numbers of websites based on the PHP language still follow the CGI model. However, regardless of the framework employed, the common pattern entailed a web application server displaying information dynamically generated from database content.

It's easy to scale up the web layer in this architecture. Just as there can be many clients for every database in the client/server architecture, there can be as many web servers as you like communicating with a single back-end database. So a bottleneck in the web server layer can be fixed simply by adding more web servers.

However, fixing bottlenecks at the database layer was not so simple. While there were a few database clustering solutions available at the beginning of the twenty-first century, it was generally difficult to achieve linear scalability with these solutions, and none had ever demonstrated scalability at the level required by the larger e-commerce sites.

During the early stages of Web 2.0, the solution to database performance was simply to buy a more powerful database server. Database servers were getting more capable every year, and storage servers could provide databases with massive IO capacity. So during the initial Internet bubble, companies like EMC and Oracle did very well, because it made sense for these early Web 2.0 companies to buy the most powerful database possible and thereby sustain the absurdly optimistic growth curves they expected.

Two factors led to the abandonment of this *scale-up* solution. First, the dot.com crash brought financial reality back into the equation, and the surviving web companies needed financially prudent solutions. Businesses wanted a solution that could start small and grow as required. Second, as Web 2.0 companies reached global scale, they found that even the most massive centralized database server could not meet their needs. Scaling up had run out of steam.

Furthermore, even if the scale-up solution had delivered the capacity required, it still represented a potential single point of failure, and it could not provide equitable response time across a global market.

The Open-source Solution

Following the dot.com crash, open-source software became increasingly valued within Web 2.0 operations. Linux supplanted proprietary UNIX as the operating system of choice, and the Apache web server became dominant. During this period, MySQL overtook Oracle as the Database Management System (DBMS) of choice for website development.

MySQL was then and is still now far less scalable than Oracle; it generally runs on less powerful hardware and is less able to take advantage of multicore processors. However, Web developers came up with a couple of tricks to get MySQL to go further.

First, they used a technology called *Memcached* to avoid database access as much is possible. Memcached is an open-source utility that provides a distributed object cache. Object-oriented languages could cache an object-oriented representation of database information across many servers. By reading from these servers rather than the database, the load on the database could be reduced.

Second, web developers took advantage of MySQL replication. Replication allows changes to one database to be copied to another database. Read requests could be directed to any one of these replica databases. Write operations still had to go to the master database however, because master-to-master replication was not possible. However, in a typical database application—and particularly in web applications—reads significantly outnumber writes, so the read replication strategy makes sense.

Figure 3-1 illustrates the transition from single web server and database server to multiple web servers, Memcached servers, and read-only database replicas.

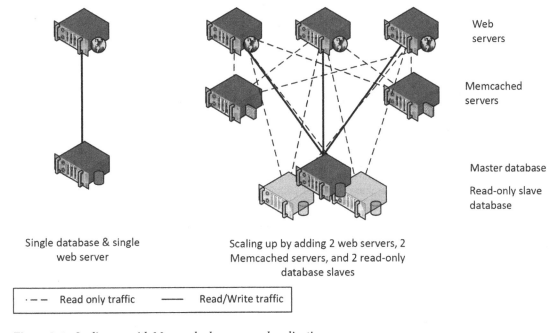

Figure 3-1. Scaling up with Memcached servers and replication

Memcached and read replication increase the overall capacity of MySQL-based web applications dramatically. However, both these techniques can only increase the read capability of the system. When the system reaches a bottleneck on database write activity, a more dramatic solution is required.

Sharding

Sharding allows a logical database to be partitioned across multiple physical servers.

In a sharded application, the largest tables are partitioned across multiple database servers. Each partition is referred to as a *shard*. This partitioning is based on a Key Value, such as a user ID. When operating on a particular record, the application must determine which shard will contain the data and then send the SQL to the appropriate server. Sharding is a solution used at the largest websites; Facebook and Twitter are the most well-known examples. At both of these websites, data that is specific to an individual user is concentrated in MySQL tables on a specific node.

Figure 3-2 illustrates the Memcached and replication configuration shown earlier in this chapter with sharding added. In this example, there are three shards, and for simplicity's sake, the shards are labeled by first letter of the primary key. As a result, we might imagine that rows with the key GUY are in shard 2, while key BOB would be allocated to shard 1. In practice, it is more likely that the primary key would be hashed to ensure even distribution of keys to servers.

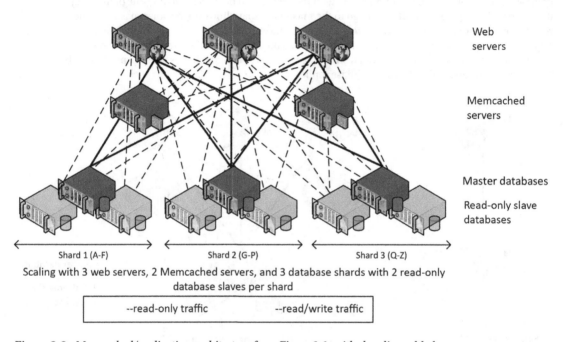

Figure 3-2. *Memcached/replication architecture from Figure 3-1, with sharding added*

The exact number of servers being used at Facebook is constantly changing and not always publicly disclosed, but in around 2011 they did reveal that they were using more than 4,000 shards of MySQL and 9,000 Memcached servers in their configuration. This sharded MySQL configuration supported 1.4 billion peak reads per second, 3.5 million row changes per second, and 8.1 million physical IOs per second. As we will see, sharding involves significant operational complexities and compromises, but it is a proven technique for achieving data processing on a massive scale.

Sharding is simple in concept but incredibly complex in practice. The application must contain logic that understands the location of any particular piece of data and the logic to route requests to the correct shard. Sharding is usually associated with rapid growth, so this routing needs to be dynamic. Requests that can only be satisfied by accessing more than one shard thus need complex coding as well, whereas on a nonsharded database a single SQL statement might suffice.

Death by a Thousand Shards

Sharding—together with caching and replication—is arguably the only way to scale a relational database to massive web use. However, the operational costs of sharding are huge. Among the drawbacks of a sharding strategy are:

- **Application complexity**. It's up to the application code to route SQL requests to the correct shard. In a statically sharded database, this would be hard enough; however, most massive websites are adding shards as they grow, which means that a dynamic routing layer must be implemented. This layer is often in addition to complex code being required to maintain Memcached object copies and to differentiate between the master database and read-only replicas.

- **Crippled SQL**. In a sharded database, it is not possible to issue a SQL statement that operates across shards. This usually means that SQL statements are limited to row-level access. Joins across shards cannot be implemented, nor can aggregate GROUP BY operations. This means, in effect, that only programmers can query the database as a whole.

- **Loss of transactional integrity**. ACID transactions against multiple shards are not possible—or at least not practical. It is possible in theory to implement transactions across databases in some database systems—those supporting *Two Phase Commit* (*2PC*)—but in practice this creates problems for conflict resolution, can create bottlenecks, has issues for MySQL, and is rarely implemented.

- **Operational complexity**. Load balancing across shards becomes extremely problematic. Adding new shards requires a complex rebalancing of data. Changing the database schema also requires a rolling operation across all the shards, resulting in transitory inconsistencies in the schema. In short, a sharded database entails a huge amount of operational effort and administrator skill.

Relational database vendors—Oracle, in particular—tried to create a relational database implementation that could provide the scalability of a sharded database without the ACID and relational compromises or operational headaches. Oracle's *Real Application Clusters* (*RAC*) is the most significant example of a transparently scalable, ACID compliant, relational cluster.

In Oracle RAC databases, each database node works with data located on shared storage devices. This *shared disk* clustering is in contrast to the *shared nothing* model employed by other clustered databases, which are more suited to data warehousing workloads. (We'll compare shared disk and shared nothing architectures in more detail in Chapter 8.)

New database nodes in RAC can be added without any data rebalancing, and a sort of distributed memory cache is implemented across these database nodes. Oracle RAC showed a lot of promise, and indeed is widely implemented. However, it failed as an alternative to the MySQL sharded model, for three reasons: First, it was too expensive. Second, it failed to demonstrate the level of scalability required at the biggest websites. Third, it became apparent that no ACID compliant database could ever satisfy the needs of the world's biggest websites. This last restriction was a sort of "laws of physics" constraint articulated in what has come to be known as *CAP theorem*.

CAP Theorem

In 2000, Eric Brewer outlined the "CAP" conjecture, which was later granted theorem status when a mathematical proof was provided. The CAP theorem says that in a distributed database system, you can have at most only two of Consistency, Availability, and Partition tolerance. *Consistency* means that every user of the database has an identical view of the data at any given instant. *Availability* means that in the event of a failure, the database remains operational. *Partition tolerance* means that the database can maintain operations in the event of the network's failing between two segments of the distributed system.

In 2000, the issue of partition tolerance was somewhat theoretical. Most systems resided in a single data center, and redundant network connectivity within that data center prevented any partition from ever occurring. If the data center failed, perhaps a failover data center would be bought online. However, there were almost no true multiple data center applications.

But as web systems became global in scope and aspired to continual availability, partition tolerance became a real issue. Consider the distributed application shown in Figure 3-3. In the event of the network partition shown, the system has two choices: either show each user a different view of the data, or shut down one of the partitions and disconnect one of the users.

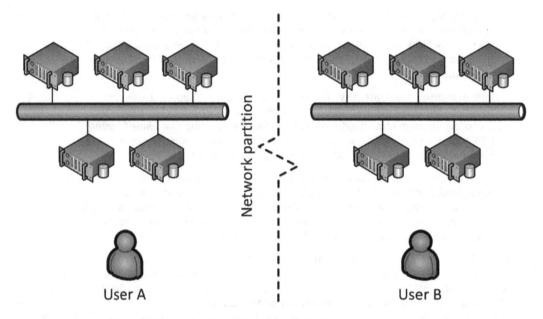

Figure 3-3. *Network partition in a distributed database application*

Oracle's RAC solution, which of course supported the ACID transactional model, would choose consistency. In the event of a network partition—known in Oracle circles as the "split brain" scenario—one of the partitions would choose to shut down. However, in the context of a global social network application, or a worldwide e-commerce system, the desired solution is to maintain availability even if some consistency between users is sacrificed.

Eventual Consistency

CAP theorem provides a stark choice: if you want your system to be undisturbed by network partitions, you must sacrifice strict consistency between partitions.

However, even without considerations of CAP theorem, ACID transactions were increasingly untenable in large-scale distributed websites. This relates more to performance than to availability. In any highly available database system, multiple copies of each data element must be maintained in order to allow the system to continue operating in the event of node failure. In a globally distributed system, it becomes increasingly desirable to distribute nodes around the world to reduce latency in various locations. To ensure strict consistency, though, it becomes necessary to ensure that a database change is propagated to multiple nodes synchronously and immediately. When one of those nodes is on the other side of the planet, this creates an unavoidable increase in latency.

For banks, this sort of latency penalty is unavoidable. However, for many websites, including social networks and certain e-commerce operations, this worldwide synchronous consistency is unnecessary. It doesn't matter if my friend in Australia can see my tweet a few seconds before my friend in America. As long as both friends can see the tweet eventually, I'm happy.

This concept of *eventual consistency* has become a key characteristic of many NoSQL databases. The concept was most notably outlined by Werner Vogels, CTO of Amazon, and was implemented in Amazon's *Dynamo* key-value store.

Amazon's Dynamo

Amazon had pioneered many of the web technologies used in early Web 2.0, particularly the use of the Perl language to glue together databases and web front ends. Early Amazon used Oracle databases as the primary repository for catalogs, customer details, and orders. The load placed on the Oracle database was tremendous, and several notable Amazon outages were associated with database failures.

Amazon tried splitting the website into multiple functional areas, each of which could have its own dedicated database. They were also very early adopters of *service-oriented architecture* (*SOA*), in which logical services such as get-product-details would be resolved not by SQL queries but by web service calls. This abstracted the database from the application layer and allowed Amazon to experiment with alternative database technologies.

In 2007, Amazon revealed details of an alternative nonrelational system that had been developed internally to address the requirements of their massive online website.[1] This system—called Dynamo—was built with the following requirements in mind:

- **Continuous availability**: Even the shortest application outage was incredibly costly for Amazon. The data store simply had to remain available under all foreseeable circumstances.

- **Network partition tolerant**: As a global e-commerce vendor with customers and data centers all around the world, Amazon was most concerned that a network partition should not force a loss of availability, even if that loss of availability was isolated to a particular geography.

- **No-loss conflict resolution**: Another of Amazon's key requirements was that no order or shopping cart update should ever be lost. So for instance, if the user added items to his or her shopping cart from two different computers, both items should show up in the final cart. Furthermore, there should be no circumstances under which someone was blocked from adding an item to his or her cart, which implied that there be no exclusive write locks on objects.

- **Efficiency**: The system needed to respond quickly, since it was well understood that even small delays in website response time resulted in a significant reduction in online sales. Online customers were notoriously fickle and impatient.

- **Economy**: This system needed to be able to run on commodity hardware.

- **Incremental scalability**: It should be possible to grow the system by adding servers in small increments without manual maintenance or downtime.

Amazon was willing to compromise on a lot of features of existing databases in order to achieve these goals.

Principally, the data store should relax consistency—within limits—if necessary in order to ensure availability. The phrase "within limits" is important here: the system should favor availability over consistency, but in a predictable, controllable, and manageable way. Also, the trade-off between consistency and availability should be configurable—the application should be able to choose what happens if there is a network partition, for instance.

Additionally, the data store need only support primary key-based access and need not support a data model: the values retrieved by a key lookup would be unstructured binary objects. Unlike Google's BigTable, which had the design goal of storing massive files, the assumption for Dynamo was that most objects would be small—under 1 MB.

Dynamo—and many of the systems that it inspired—explicitly attempted to achieve a different outcome in terms of CAP theorem. Rather than try to always achieve consistency at the expense of network partition tolerance, Dynamo would allow (though not require) consistency to be sacrificed instead. See Figure 3-4.

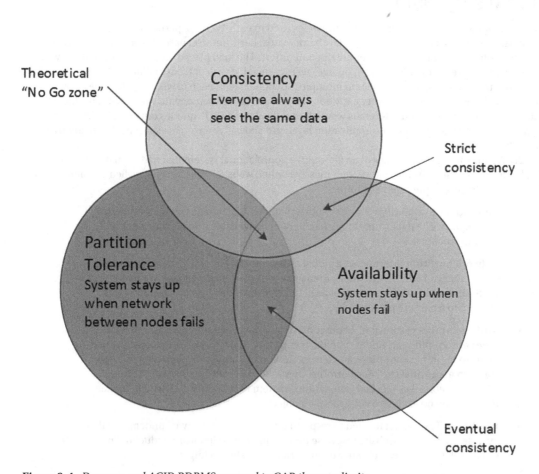

Figure 3-4. *Dynamo and ACID RDBMS mapped to CAP theorem limits*

Dynamo has served as an architectural model for quite a few nonrelational databases. (We'll look into the gory details of Dynamo internals in Chapters 8 and 9.) Some of the key architectural characteristics of Dynamo include:

- **Consistent hashing**: Consistent hashing is a scheme that uses the hash value of the primary key to determine the nodes in the cluster responsible for that key and that allows nodes to be added or removed from the cluster with minimal rebalancing overhead. See below for more details.

- **Tunable consistency**: The application can specify trade-offs between consistency, read performance, and write performance. It's possible in Dynamo to specify strong consistency, eventual consistency, or weak consistency. See below for more details.

- **Data versioning**: Since write operations will never be blocked, it is possible that there will be multiple versions of an object in the system. Sometimes these can be merged by the data store itself, but sometimes they will need to be resolved by the application or user. For instance, if the buyer updates his or her shopping cart from two computers, the resulting cart may have duplicate items that he or she may need to remove.

There are lots of complex design features in the Dynamo system; many of these will be discussed in Chapters 8 and 9. However, it would be remiss to continue without at least a little bit of elaboration on two of the key features: consistent hashing and tunable consistency.

Consistent Hashing

When we *hash* a key value, we perform a mathematical computation on the key value and use that computed value to determine where to store the data. One reason to use hashing is so that we are able to evenly distribute the data across a certain number of slots. The most simple example is to use the *modulo* function, which returns the remainder of a division. If we want to hash any number into 10 buckets, we can use modulo 10; then key 27 would map to bucket 7, key 32 would map to bucket 2, key 25 to bucket 5, and so on.

Using this method, we could map keys evenly across 10 servers. When we want to determine which node should store a particular item, we would calculate its modulo and use the result to locate the node. In practice, hashing functions are more complex than a simple modulo function, and a good hash function always distributes the hash values evenly across nodes, regardless of any skew in key values.

Hashing works great as a way of distributing data evenly across a fixed number of nodes. But we have a problem if we add or remove a node—we have to recalculate the hash values and redistribute all the data. For instance, if we wanted to add a new server in the modulo 10 example above, we would recalculate hashes using modulo 11 and then we would have to move almost every data item accordingly. *Consistent hashing* works by hashing key values and applying a consistent method for allocating those hashed values to specific nodes.

By convention and possibly federal law, consistent hashing schemes are represented as rings— because the hash values "loop around" to 0. Figure 3-5 shows what happens when a node is added to an existing cluster. Only those keys currently mapped to the "neighbors" of the new node need remapping.

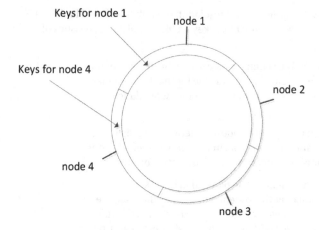

Split of keys in 4-node cluster

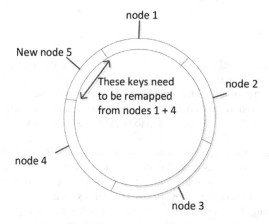

Adding a new node to the cluster

Figure 3-5. *Adding a new node to the consistent hashing scheme*

The remapping process when a new node is added is still an expensive operation, and in practice Dynamo-based databases often employ a "virtual nodes" workaround to further reduce the overhead. This mechanism is explained in detail in Chapter 8.

Tunable Consistency

Dynamo allows the application to choose the level of consistency applied to specific operations. *NWR notation* describes how Dynamo will trade off consistency, read performance, and write performance:

- **N** is the number of copies of each data item that the database will maintain.

- **W** is the number of copies of the data item that must be written before the write can complete.

- **R** is the number of copies that the application will access when reading the data item.

When W = N, Dynamo will always write every copy before returning control to the application—this is what ACID databases do when implementing synchronous replication. If the application is more concerned about write performance than read performance, then it could set W = 1, R = N. Then each read must access all copies to determine which is correct, but each write only has to touch a single copy of the data before returning control (other writes propagate to all copies as a background task).

Probably the most common configuration is N > W > 1. More than one write must complete, but not all nodes need to be updated immediately. Another common setting is W + R > N; this ensures that the latest value will always be included in a read operation, even if it is mixed in with "older" values. This is sometimes referred to as *quorum assembly*.

Figure 3-6 shows examples of various NWR settings. Depending on the settings, Dynamo can trade off consistency, reliability, and performance.

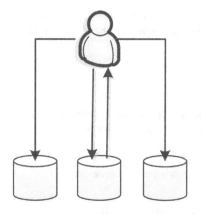

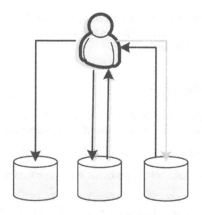

N=3 W=3 R=1
Slow writes, fast reads, consistent
There will be 3 copies of the data.
A write request only returns when all 3
have written to disk.
A read request only needs to read one
version.

N=3 W=2 R=2
Faster writes, still consistent (quorum
assembly)
There will be 3 copies of the data.
A write request returns when 2 copies
are written – the other can happen
later.
A read request reads 2 copies
make sure it has the latest version.

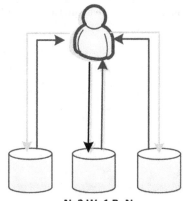

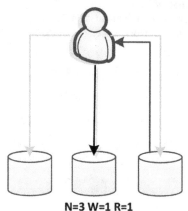

N=3 W=1 R=N
**Fastest write, slow but consistent
reads**
There will be 3 copies of the data.
A write request returns once the first
copy is written – the other 2 can
happen later.
A read request reads all copies to
make sure it gets the latest version.
Data might be lost if a node fails
before the second write.

N=3 W=1 R=1
Fast, but not consistent
There will be 3 copies of the data.
A write request returns once the first
copy is written – the other 2 can
happen later.
A read request reads a single version
only: it might not get the latest copy.
Data might be lost if a node fails
before the second write.

Figure 3-6. *Tunable consistency in Dynamo*

Dynamo and the Key-value Store Family

Systems that implement one of the primary characteristics of Dynamo—the idea of a binary value retrieved by primary key only—became generically known as *key-value stores*. Just as Google's GFS and MapReduce papers became the blueprint for Hadoop, Amazon's Dynamo paper became the blueprint for many key-value stores.

Web developers who were struggling with the operational complexity entailed by sharding and other heroic database techniques had already started experimenting with various nonrelational designs. However, with the release of Amazon's Dynamo paper, these developers had a proven architectural model to build on. The result was a relatively sudden burst of Dynamo-inspired systems in 2008–2009. These systems were the first recognizable NoSQL databases.

It's true that not all key-value stores were based explicitly on the Dynamo model. However, the list of Dynamo-inspired systems is impressive, and it includes active databases such as Riak, LinkedIn's Voldemort, Cassandra, and of course, Amazon's own DynamoDB. Some of these systems, such as Riak and Voldemort, are more or less exact copies of the Dynamo architecture, while others use Dynamo in conjunction with other concepts. For instance, Apache's Cassandra implements Dynamo's consistent hashing and tunable consistency models, combined with a variation on the BigTable data model.

Although Dynamo represents the most popular and well-articulated key-value store architecture, there are certainly key-value stores that owe little or nothing to the Dynamo design. These include systems such as Redis and Oracle NoSQL.

Conclusion

We've seen that the challenge of maintaining highly available global websites proved inconsistent with the ACID transaction model. Brewer's CAP theorem—as well as practical experience—argue that a system cannot aspire to both strong consistency and global availability in the event of an imperfect network like the Internet. For most massive websites, continual availability may be more important than perfect consistency.

Attempts to deploy relational databases on the scale required by the largest web properties involved the use of caching (Memcached, in particular), read-only replication, and sharding. This architectural pattern effectively broke both the relational and the ACID properties of the database: once a database has been sharded, ACID consistency and ad hoc SQL query access are lost. Nevertheless, the sharding solution has proved to be effective at sites such as Twitter and Facebook.

Amazon—the pioneer of Internet retailers—abandoned the RDBMS as the core database in favor of an internally developed, nonrelational key-value store called Dynamo. Dynamo implements eventual consistency rather than strict consistency; updates to data are eventually guaranteed to be propagated throughout the system, but may not be seen by every user instantaneously.

Dynamo has been a strong influence on the design of many other key-value stores, such as Riak and Cassandra, and is the basis for Amazon's cloud-based database DynamoDB. Systems such as Dynamo enforce no structure on their payload. This makes them impenetrable to all but programmers. As we will see in the next chapter, another class of databases—the document databases—extend the key-value concept by requiring that values be structured in a self-describing format such as XML or JSON.

Note

1. http://www.allthingsdistributed.com/files/amazon-dynamo-sosp2007.pdf

CHAPTER 4

■ ■ ■

Document Databases

A relational database is like a garage that forces you to take your car apart and store the pieces in little drawers

—Object-oriented data community, mid-1990s

An Object database is like a closet which requires that you hang up your suit with tie, underwear, belt, socks and shoes all attached.

—David Ensor, same period

A document database is a nonrelational database that stores data as structured documents, usually in XML or JSON formats. The "document database" definition doesn't imply anything specific beyond the document storage model: document databases are free to implement ACID transactions or other characteristics of a traditional RDBMS, though the dominant document databases provide relatively modest transactional support.

JSON-based document databases flourished after the nonrelational breakout of 2008, for three main reasons. First, they address the conflict between object-oriented programming and the relational database model that had frustrated software developers, and that motivated much of the object-oriented database movement of the mid-1990s. Second, because the self-describing document formats could be interrogated independently of the program that had created them, they supported ad hoc query access to the database that was absent in pure key-value stores. Third, they aligned well with the dominant web-based programming paradigms, particularly the AJAX programming model.

A document database, by allowing some form of data description without enforcing a schema, perhaps provides a happy medium between the rigid schema of the relational database and the completely schema-less key-value stores. Programmers remain free to change the data model as requirements shift within an application, but data consumers are still able to interrogate the data to determine its meaning.

The alignment with web-development programming practices has resulted in JSON document databases—and the MongoDB database in particular—becoming the default choice for many web developers.

■ **Note**   Describing something as a document database only tells us that it stores data in XML or JSON format. The term does not define any specific transaction or clustering model.

XML and XML Databases

The first document databases were built around the XML document standard. XML databases are interesting to us primarily as the architectural precursors to the modern JSON document database; XML databases today represent a significant but small niche in the overall database market.

XML (*eXtensible Markup Language*) arose as a result of the convergence of efforts to develop a generalized markup language as the successor to various specialized formats such as SGML and a realization that HTML—the foundation of Web 1.0—uncomfortably combined layout and data. XML was capable of representing almost any form of information and, together with *Cascading Style Sheets* (*CSS*) that controlled rendering, allowed second-generation websites to separate data and format.

XML was widely used beyond these Web 2.0 use cases and became a standard format for many document types, eventually including word processing documents and spreadsheets. XML is also the basis for many data interchange protocols and, in particular, was a foundation for web service specifications such as *SOAP* (*Simple Object Access Protocol*).

During the early 2000s, it was widely expected that most documents in an organization outside of a relational database would end up represented as XML. And while the momentum behind XML has slowed, today a huge variety of document types use XML under the hood.

XML Tools and Standards

XML is supported by a rich ecosystem that includes a variety of standards and tools to assist with authoring, validation, searching, and transforming XML documents. These include:

- **XPath**: A syntax for retrieving specific elements from an XML document. XPath provides a simple and convenient way to filter documents using wildcards and tag references.

- **XQuery**: A query language for interrogating XML documents. The related **XQuery Update** specification provides mechanisms for modifying a document. XQuery is sometimes referred to as "the SQL of XML."

- **XML schema**: A special type of XML document that describes the elements that may be present in a specified class of XML documents. XML schema can be used to validate that a document is in the correct format, or to assist programs that wish to interrogate XML documents that conform to that format.

- **XSLT** (**Extensible Stylesheet Language Transformations**): A language for transforming XML documents into alternative formats, including non-XML formats such as HTML.

- **DOM** (**Document Object Model**): An object-oriented API that programs can use to interact with XML, XHTML, and similarly structured documents.

As the "SQL for XML," XQuery figures prominently in most XML database architectures. Figure 4-1 shows a simple XQuery statement that searches for documents with an ADDRESS element that includes the string "Berlin" within an embedded CITY element.

```
query
1    xquery version "3.0";
2    collection("/db/apps/demo/data")//address[contains(city, "Berlin")]
3
```

```
↱  /db/query
◀◀    XML Output    ▼   ☐ Live Preview   ⊞                              ▶▶
1   <address id="0ff8612a-b998-4677-84a3-73e9ef84ba5f">
       <name>Biene Maja</name>
       <street>Wiesenweg 33</street>
       <city>Berlin</city>
    </address>
```

Figure 4-1. *Example of XQuery*

XML Databases

The increasing volume of XML documents within organizations provided a motivation for some form of XML document management system—or native *XML database.*

XML databases generally consist of a platform that implements the various XML standards such as XQuery and XSLT, and that provides services for the storage, indexing, security, and concurrent access of XML files. Figure 4-2 illustrates a simplified generic XML database architecture.

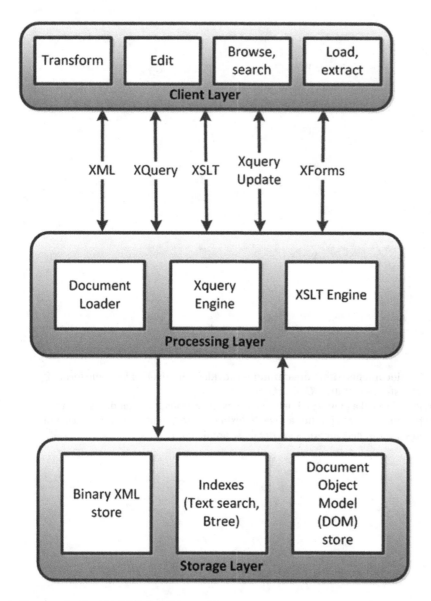

Figure 4-2. *Generic XML database architecture*

A variety of XML databases emerged during the first half of the 2000s, and they experienced a healthy uptake. However, they were not positioned as alternatives to the RDBMS but, rather, as a means of managing the XML document sprawl that had confronted many organizations.

Two of the more significant XML databases include the open-source XML database *eXist* and the commercial XML database *MarkLogic*.

XML Support in Relational Systems

Relational database vendors all introduced XML support within their core offerings, typically allowing XML documents to be stored within long/BLOB columns within database tables and providing support for the various XML standards such as DOM, XSLT, and XQuery. In addition, XML support was added to the ANSI SQL definition (SQL/XML), allowing XML manipulation within standard SQL language statements. Support for these SQL extensions appears in Oracle, Postgres, DB2, MySQL, and SQL Server.

JSON Document Databases

XML has many advantages as a standard format for file-based documents and for data interchange. But it has a number of drawbacks as a storage format for serious database applications. XML is justifiably criticized as being wasteful of space and computationally expensive to process. XML tags are verbose and repetitious, typically increasing the amount of storage required by several factors. Partly as a result, the XML language format is relatively expensive to parse.

XML has long been the predominant format for structured files, but for data interchange and for document databases themselves, a more recent format—*JavaScript Object Notation* (*JSON*)—promised greater benefits and has achieved far greater popularity than their XML predecessors.

JSON document-based databases and XML document-based databases share many similarities, not the least of which is the superficial similarity between XML and JSON formats. However, each is designed to support quite dissimilar use cases and significantly different applications. XML databases typically are used as content-management systems; that is, organizing and maintaining collections of text files in XML format—academic papers, business documents, and so on. JSON document databases, on the other hand, mostly support web-based operational workloads—storing and modifying the dynamic content and transactional data at the core of modern web-based applications.

▨ **Note** JSON and XML are similar formats, but XML document databases and JSON document databases generally support dissimilar applications. XML document databases excel for content management systems, JSON document databases generally aim to support operational web applications.

JSON and AJAX

JSON was created by JavaScript pioneer Douglas Crockford as part of an attempt to build a framework for more dynamic and interactive web applications. JSON was deliberately intended as a more lightweight substitute for XML, and it became a significant alternative to XML in the AJAX programming model that drove a revolution in web applications during the mid-2000s.

AJAX (Asynchronous JavaScript And XML) is a flexible programming pattern in which JavaScript on a web browser communicates with a back-end web server through asynchronous interchange of XML or JSON documents, rather than by the exchange of complete HTML pages. It was AJAX that enabled the rich and interactive experience provided by groundbreaking web applications such as Google Maps and Gmail.

Although the "X" in AJAX refers to XML, JSON documents can also be used as the medium of interaction with the web server. Indeed, because of its tight integration with JavaScript, JSON increasingly became more popular than XML for data interchange. Within a few years of the introduction of the AJAX approach, all serious web developers became familiar with JavaScript programming and with the JSON model.

Figure 4-3 compares the appearance of JSON and XML documents.

Figure 4-3. Comparison of XML and JSON file formats

JSON Databases

The emergence of key-value store databases such as Amazon's Dynamo, together with the growing popularity of JSON as a data interchange format, set the stage for the emergence of the JSON document database.

There is not a single specification or manifesto outlining the properties of a JSON-based document database. To be a JSON document database, all you need to do is store data in the JSON format.

In a JSON document database, the hierarchy of storage is typically as follows:

- A *document* is the basic unit of storage, corresponding approximately to a row in an RDBMS. A document comprises one or more key-value pairs, and may also contain nested documents and arrays. Arrays may also contain documents allowing for a complex hierarchical structure.

- A *collection* or *data bucket* is a set of documents sharing some common purpose; this is roughly equivalent to a relational table. The documents in a collection don't have to be of the same type, though it is typical for documents in a collection to represent a common category of information.

While a document database could theoretically implement a third normal form schema exactly as it would be used within a relational system, document databases more typically model data in a smaller number of collections, with nested documents representing master-detail relationships.

For instance, consider a database of movies and actors. In a relational data model, we would represent actors and films in separate tables, and create a join table that would indicate which actors appeared in which films, as shown in Figure 4-4.

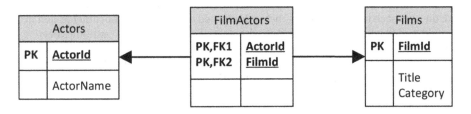

Figure 4-4. *Simple Relational movie database*

In a JSON document database, we could create three collections with key-value pairs corresponding to the columns in a relational schema—but to do so would be unnatural. Document databases do not generally provide join operations, and programmers generally like to have the JSON structure map closely to the object structure of their code. So it would be more natural to represent this data as shown in Figure 4-5.

```
{ "_id" : 97, "Title" : "BRIDE INTRIGUE",
            "Category" : "Action",
     "Actors" :
       [ { "actorId" : 65, "Name" : "ANGELA HUDSON" } ]
}

{ "_id": 115,"Title": "CAMPUS REMEMBER",
            "Category": "Action",
     "Actors" :
       [                    Actor document
         { "actorId": 8,"Name": "MATTHEW JOHANSSON" },
         { "actorId": 45,"Name": "REESE KILMER" },
         { "actorId": 168,"Name": "WILL WILSON" }
       ]
}

{ "_id" : 105, "Title" : "BULL SHAWSHANK",
            "Category" : "Action",
     "Actors" :
       [ { "actorId" : 2, "Name" : "NICK WAHLBERG" },
         { "actorId" : 23, "Name" : "SANDRA KILMER" } ]
}
```

Film Document

Array of actors

Collection

Figure 4-5. *JSON movie collection*

Data Models in Document Databases

In Figure 4-5, "actors" are nested as an array within the "films" documents. This pattern is often referred to as *document embedding*. The design pattern has the advantage of allowing a film and all its actors to be retrieved in a single operation, and it avoids the need to perform joins within the application code.

On the other hand, the approach results in "actors" being duplicated across multiple documents, and in a complex design this could lead to issues and possibly inconsistencies if any of the "actor" attributes need to be changed. The number of actors in a film is relatively small, but in other application scenarios, problems can also occur if the number of members in an embedded document increases without limit (because the size of a single JSON document is usually capped—64MB in MongoDB, for instance).

For these reasons, a database designer might choose instead to link multiple documents using document identifiers, much in the way a relational database relates rows via foreign keys. For instance, in Figure 4-6, we embed an array of actor IDs into the "films" document, which can be used to locate the actors who appear in a film.

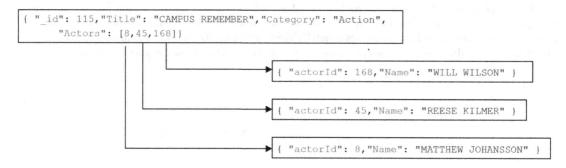

Figure 4-6. *Linking documents in a document database*

In Figure 4-7, we see another example of document linking. In this case, the design is in a relational style: a link document relates films to actors. Although this is somewhat an unnatural style for a document database, for some workloads it may provide the best balance between performance and maintainability.

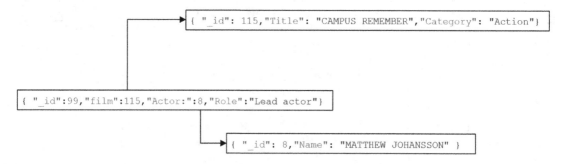

Figure 4-7. *Document linking can resemble relational third normal form*

Data modeling in document databases is less deterministic than for relational databases: there is no equivalent of third normal form that defines a "correct" model. Furthermore, while modeling in a relational database is driven primarily by the nature of the data to be stored, in a document database the nature of the queries to be executed is far more significant.

Early JSON Databases

CouchDB, created by Damien Katz, was the first notable JSON-based database system. Damien Katz had worked on Lotus Notes, a collaboration system with strong document-handling capabilities. In 2005, he decided to create a database system more closely aligned with web development and object-oriented programming models. The result was CouchDB.

Initially, CouchDB was written in C++ and it stored XML documents. Around 2007, a new architecture emerged that incorporated JSON as the primary storage format, a JavaScript command, and query interface and a core engine rewritten in the Erlang language.

As it matured, CouchDB embraced other paradigms that had inspired key-value stores and Hadoop, including a JavaScript implementation of MapReduce, an eventual consistency and multiple versioning model, and a hash-based clustering/sharding model to allow CouchDB to scale across nodes.

CouchDB became an Apache project in 2008 and was supported by IBM. In 2009, a commercial company couch.io (later CouchOne) was formed to maintain and promote the technology.

MemBase and CouchBase

When the interest in nonrelational databases exploded in 2009, CouchDB had already several years of active development and seemed well placed to benefit from the increasing buzz surrounding "NoSQL."

Membase was another nonrelational system experiencing significant uptake during this period. The Membase database provided a persistent variation on the extremely popular *Memcached* framework, which we discussed in Chapter 3. Memcached is a distributed read-only object cache that is commonly deployed in conjunction with MySQL to reduce database load. Objects are distributed across multiple Memcached nodes, and it can be located by a hash key lookup. If the data is in a Memcached server, a database read is avoided.

Membase provided a Memcached-compatible solution in which data could also be modified and persisted to disk. Membase was therefore particularly attractive for those who had an existing investment in Memcached technology, offering the possibility that an application could be converted to Membase from Memcached/MySQL. Membase was initially well known as the database underlying Zynga's incredibly popular Farmville online game.

Meanwhile, despite CouchDB's many technical achievements, the CouchDB database and the CouchOne company appeared to be struggling to establish a commercial niche; it lacked a viable scale-out architecture. In early 2011, a merger between Membase and CouchOne was announced. The resulting company was called CouchBase. CouchBase donated the existing CouchDB code to the Apache community, and it embarked on a new effort to merge the capabilities of CouchDB and MemBase. In the resulting Couchbase server, the JSON engine from CouchDB was merged with the Memcached-compatible key-value layer from MemBase.

Couchbase inherited CouchDB's MapReduce interface for creating queries and views, but Couchbase 4.0 introduced a SQL-like layer for document access called *N1QL* (*Non-first Normal Form Query Language*). See Chapter 11 for more details on this and other SQL-like NoSQL interfaces.

MongoDB

In 2007, founders and senior engineers from the online ad-serving company DoubleClick, which had just been acquired by Google, established a new startup called 10gen. The company aimed to create a PaaS (Platform as a Service) offering similar to Google App Engine. The platform required a scalable and elastic data storage engine; in the absence of a suitable existing candidate, the team created its own database, which they called MongoDB. In 2008, 10gen pivoted to focus exclusively on MongoDB, and in 2009, it released the product under an open-source license together with a commercial enterprise distribution.

MongoDB is a JSON-oriented document database, although internally it uses a binary encoded variant of JSON called BSON. The BSON format supports lower parse overhead than JSON, as well as richer support for data types such as dates and binary data.

MongoDB provides a JavaScript-based query capability that is reasonably easy to learn—at least when compared to MapReduce approaches such as were initially required in CouchDB. Figure 4-8 compares a MongoDB JavaScript query to retrieve films that feature a specific actor with the SQL equivalent in MySQL. We'll look at the MongoDB query language in detail in Chapter 11.

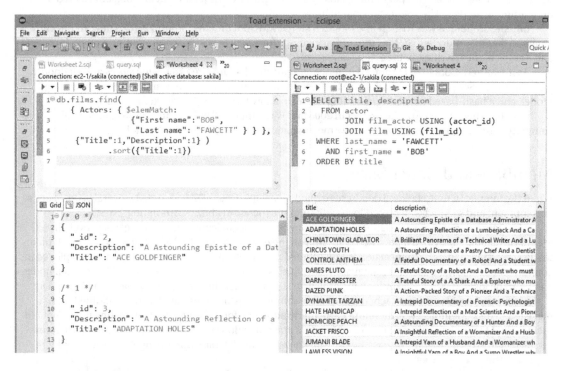

Figure 4-8. *MongoDB JavaScript query and SQL equivalent*

MongoDB established a strong lead in the NoSQL database space by providing a developer-friendly ecosystem and architecture. Developers looking for a nonrelational alternative—typically to MySQL or Oracle—found it relatively easy to get started with MongoDB. Developer-led adoption of MongoDB was robust, and today MongoDB can claim to be the most widely used nonrelational database.

In many respects, the rise of MongoDB today resembles the ascendance of MySQL in the last decade. In both cases these databases entered the organization not as a result of some sort of l strategic technology plan, but as the result of its popularity with developers. Just as MySQL became the default database for LAMP (Linux-Apache-MySQL-PHP) stack applications in the early 2000s, MongoDB seems to have achieved a similar position within the modern web-development community.

MongoDB may lack some of the scalability and throughput capabilities of other NoSQL offerings such as Cassandra or HBase, although the implementation of the WiredTiger storage engine in version 3.0 has provided the base engine with a significant increase in capability. Nevertheless, it has powered many high-end, large-scale websites, and it looks poised to be a leading NoSQL database for the immediate future.

JSON, JSON, Everywhere

The central role of JSON within modern document databases does not preclude the use of JSON in other systems.

Just as the relational world embraced XML and introduced XML features into the SQL standard, many RDBMS vendors are offering native support for JSON. For instance, Oracle and other relational vendors have introduced features in the SQL language to allow JSON documents stored within database tables to be manipulated within SQL statements. Indeed, as we'll see in Chapter 12, Oracle now provides a completely non-SQL access path for JSON.

It has, of course, always been possible and not unusual to store JSON documents within a key-value store object. However, pure key-value databases such as Riak have also introduced JSON-aware indexing schemes. Furthermore, the latest release of the Cassandra database allows JSON structures to be mapped directly to Cassandra table columns.

MarkLogic—the successful commercial XML database vendor mentioned earlier in this chapter—added support for native JSON storage in 2014. Based on its broad penetration as an XML database, MarkLogic can now claim to be a leading contender in the modern document database market, though it remains to be seen if MarkLogic can break out of its XML content management niche to compete directly with databases such as MongoDB and CouchBase for the hearts and minds of web application developers.

In any case, we can expect to see some level of JSON support in almost all database systems.

Conclusion

Document databases differentiate from other relational and nonrelational systems through their adoption of a document format—XML or JSON—as the data model. Document databases that support XML document formats have been primarily important as content management systems, providing a management repository for XML-based text files. JSON document databases, on the other hand, use JSON documents as the data layer for web-based applications—the sort of purpose to which MySQL would previously have been tasked. To some degree, XML-based document databases represent a previous generation of database system, while JSON databases can claim to be the next generation.

The popularity of JSON and the growing support for JSON within relational databases and key-value stores blur the lines that initially existed between databases like MongoDB and Dynamo-inspired databases such as Riak. In the near future, support for JSON may be a feature common to all databases, rather than one that differentiates a specific database technology segment.

However, today JSON document databases represent a distinct and important niche within next generation of database systems. They provide useful features beyond those of pure key-value stores, particularly in terms of programmer productivity and data accessibility.

The simplistic self-describing model of JSON and simple key-value access paths work well for web applications where simple CRUD (Create, Read, Update, Delete) access paths dominate. However, modern applications have increasingly generated data models that not only exceed the sophistication of document oriented key-value stores but also exceed the comfortable modeling capability of even the relational models. We'll consider these graph databases in the next chapter.

■ ■ ■

CHAPTER 5

Tables are Not Your Friends: Graph Databases

Google sought to gauge what people were thinking, and became what people were thinking. Facebook sought to map the social graph, and became the social graph

—George Dyson, Turing's Cathedral

Whenever someone gives you a problem, think graphs.

—Steve Yegge, Get That Job at Google (blog post)

Proponents of key-value stores, document databases, and relational systems disagree about practically every aspect of database design, but they do agree in one respect: databases are about storing information about "things," be those things represented by JSON, tables, or binary values. But sometimes it's the relationship between things, rather than the things themselves, that are of primary interest. This is where graph database systems shine.

Graph structures are most familiar to us from social networks such as Facebook. In Facebook, the information about individuals is important, but it's the network between people—the social graph—that provides the unique power of the platform. Similar graph-oriented datasets occur within network topologies, access-control systems, medical models, and elsewhere.

The relational database is completely capable of modeling such networks through the use of foreign keys and self-joins. Unfortunately, the RDBMS generally hits performance issues when working with very large graphs, and SQL lacks an expressive syntax to work with graph data.

The NoSQL solutions described so far do even a worse job with graph models than the relational database. In a key-value store or document database, a graph structure can be stored in a single document or object, but relationships between objects are not inherently supported (because there are no joins).

To efficiently process a data model in which complex networks of relationships between objects or entities are a primary focus, a different type of database is called for: the graph database.

What is a Graph?

Like the relational database, but unlike many nonrelational systems, graph databases are based on a strong theoretical foundation. Graph theory is a long-established branch of mathematics, with many practical applications in medicine, physics, and sociology, as well as in computer science.

Graph theory defines these major components of a graph:

- **Vertices,** or "nodes," represent distinct objects.
- **Edges,** or "relationships" or "arcs," connect these objects.
- Both vertices and edges can have **properties**.

While vertices and edges are the terms used most frequently in mathematical theory, we'll use "nodes" and "relationships" more often in this chapter because those terms lead to less convoluted and murky language.

Both nodes and relationships can have properties. The properties of nodes are not dissimilar to those you might find associated with a relational table or in a JSON document. Properties of relationships might include the type, strength, or history of the relationship.

Figure 5-1 illustrates a simple graph with four nodes (vertices) and three relationships (edges).

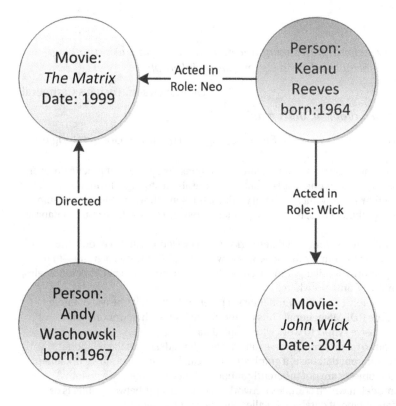

Figure 5-1. *Simple graph with four vertices (nodes) and three edges (relationships)*

Graph theory provides mathematical notation for defining or removing nodes or relationships from the graph, and for performing operations to find adjacent nodes. These primitive operations can be used to perform a *graph traversal*—walking through the graph to explore the network. To use a familiar example, Facebook sometimes performs a graph traversal to find the friends of your friends. In the example shown in Figure 5-1, we might perform a graph traversal to find all the actors that have ever appeared as a co-star in a movie starring Keanu Reeves.

RDBMS Patterns for Graphs

It's relatively easy to represent graph structures in the relational model. For instance, we might create the relational structure shown in Figure 5-2 to represent the graph shown in Figure 5-1.

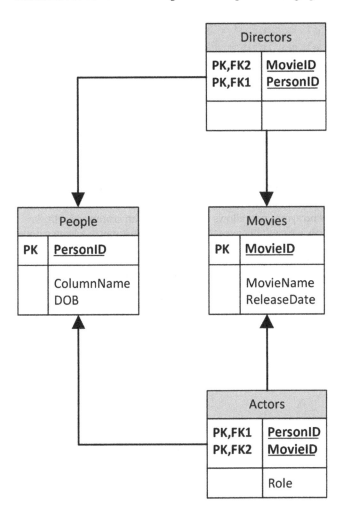

Figure 5-2. *Relational schema to represent our sample graph data*

While the relational model can easily represent the data that is contained in a graph model, we face two significant problems in practice:

1. SQL lacks the syntax to easily perform graph traversal, especially traversals where the depth is unknown or unbounded. For instance, using SQL to determine friends of your friends is easy enough, but it is hard to solve the "degrees of separation" problem (often illustrated using the example of the number of connections that separate you from Kevin Bacon).

2. Performance degrades quickly as we traverse the graph. Each level of traversal adds significantly to query response time.

For instance, consider the SQL needed to find all actors who have ever worked with Keanu Reeves. It might look something like that shown in Figure 5-3.

```
1⊖SELECT p2.personname, m1.movieName
2    FROM people p1
3           JOIN actors a1 ON (p1.personid = a1.personid)
4           JOIN movies m1 ON (a1.movieid = m1.movieid)
5           JOIN actors a2 ON (a2.movieid = m1.movieid)
6           JOIN people p2 ON (p2.personid = a2.personid)
7    WHERE p1.personname = 'Keanu Reeves';
8
```

Figure 5-3. *SQL to perform first-level graph traversal*

This SQL queries PEOPLE to find Keanu, then ACTORS and MOVIES to find the movies he has starred in, then ACTORS and PEOPLE again to find other actors who have been in those movies. A five-way join such as this is manageable, but as we traverse more we have to add another three joins each time we increase the search depth. Furthermore, there is no syntax that allows us to search to an arbitrary depth. So for instance, if we want to expand the whole graph, we can't because there is no way to know in advance how many levels we need to examine.

Performance in an RDBMS is also a potential issue. Providing that appropriate indexes are created, our sample query above will execute with acceptable overhead. But each join requires an index lookup for each actor and movie. Each index lookup adds overhead and performance that for deep graph traversals are often unacceptable. Sometimes the best solution is to load the tables in their entirety into map structures within application code and traverse the graph in memory. However, this assumes that there is enough memory in application code to cache all the data, which is not always the case.

Because key-value stores do not support joins, they offer even less graph traversal capability than the relational database. In a pure key-value store or document database, graph traversal logic must be implemented entirely in application code.

RDF and SPARQL

The *Resource Description Framework* (*RDF*) is a web standard developed in the late 1990s for the modeling of web resources and the relationships between them. It represents one of the earliest standards for representing and processing graph data.

Information in RDF is expressed in *triples,* conceptually of the form entity: attribute :value; for instance:

```
TheMatrix: is :Movie
Kenau: is :Person
Kenau: starred in: TheMatrix
```

RDF was intended as a means of creating a formal database of resources—particularly web services—on the web together with the dependencies that these resources relied on.

RDF graphs can be stored in a variety of formats including XML, or even within tables inside a relational database. However, native RDF databases—known as *triplestores*—have been implemented. These include AllegroGraph, Ontotext GraphDB, StarDog, and Oracle Spatial.

RDF supports a query language *SPARQL* (a recursive acronym: *SPARQL Protocol and RDF Query Language*), which is a SQL-like language for interrogating RDF data. Figure 5-4 shows a SPARQL query interrogating DBpedia (an RDF representation of selected Wikipedia data) to find all objects that have Edgar Codd as a topic.

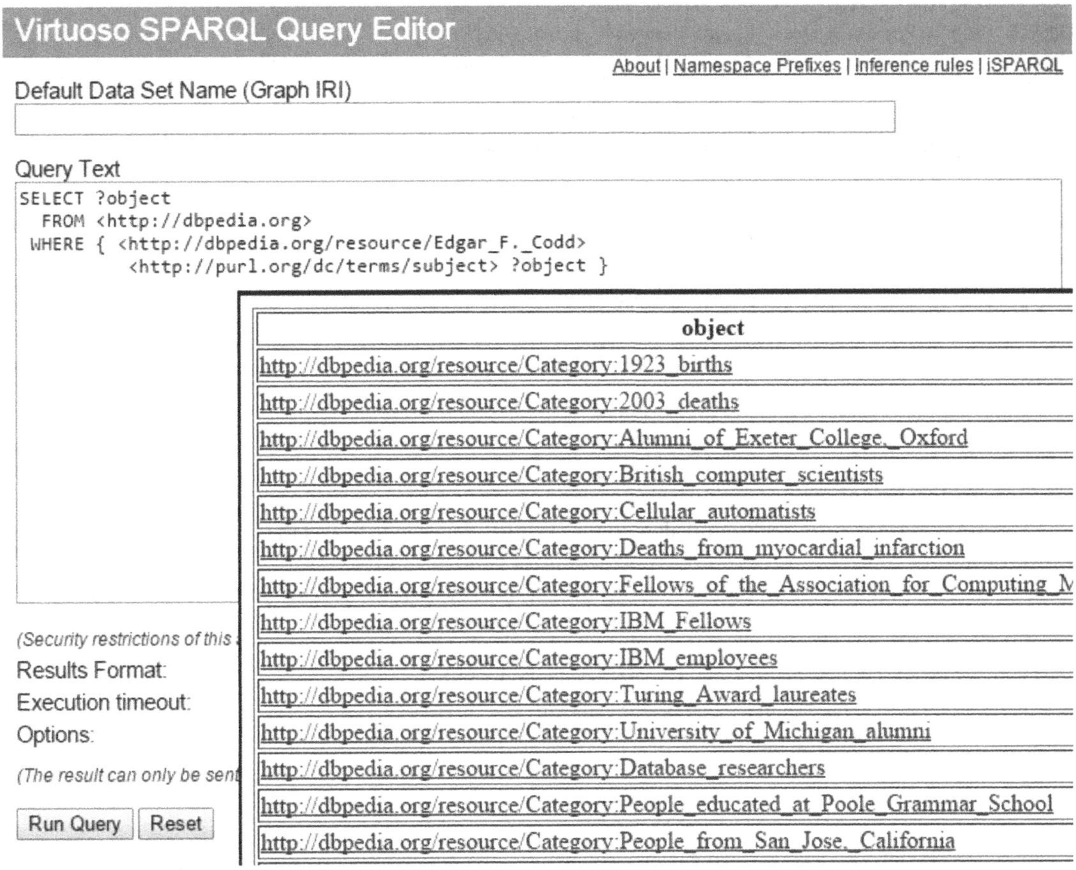

Figure 5-4. Interrogating Dbpedia using SPARQL

Property Graphs and Neo4j

While RDF is an important graph technology, the *Property Graph* model provides a richer model for representing complex data by associating both nodes and relationships with attributes.

The property graph model is the basis for *Neo4j,* which is the most widely adopted graph database. Neo4J is a Java-based graph database that can be easily embedded in any Java application or run as a standalone server. Neo4j supports billions of nodes, ACID compliant transactions, and multiversion consistency.

Neo4j implements a declarative graph query language *Cypher*. Cypher allows graphs to be queried using simple syntax somewhat comparable to SQL or SPARQL, but particularly optimized for graph traversals.

The following Cypher statements would create the graph structure shown in Figure 5-1 within Neo4J:

```
CREATE (TheMatrix:Movie {title:'The Matrix', released:1999,
        tagline:'Welcome to the Real World'})
CREATE (JohnWick:Movie {title:'John Wick', released:2014,
        tagline:'Silliest Keanu movie ever'})
CREATE (Keanu:Person {name:'Keanu Reeves', born:1964})
CREATE (AndyW:Person {name:'Andy Wachowski', born:1967})
CREATE
  (Keanu)-[:ACTED_IN {roles:['Neo']}]->(TheMatrix),
  (Keanu)-[:ACTED_IN {roles:['John Wick']}]->(JohnWick),
  (AndyW)-[:DIRECTED]->(TheMatrix)
```

The following Cypher query retrieves information for a single node in the graph:

```
neo4j-sh (?)$ MATCH (kenau:Person {name:"Keanu Reeves"})
>              RETURN kenau;
+-----------------------------------------+
| kenau                                   |
+-----------------------------------------+
| Node[1]{name:"Keanu Reeves",born:1964}  |
+-----------------------------------------+
```

The MATCH clause is roughly equivalent to the WHERE clause in SQL and the RETURN clause to a SELECT list.

MATCH supports a syntax for traversing relationships in the graph. For instance, the following query finds all the actors who have ever acted in the same movie as Keanu Reeves:

```
neo4j-sh (?)$ MATCH (kenau:Person {name:"Keanu Reeves"})
              -[:ACTED_IN]->(movie)<-[:ACTED_IN]-(coStar)
              RETURN coStar.name;
+----------------------+
| coStar.name          |
+----------------------+
| "Jack Nicholson"     |
| "Diane Keaton"       |
| "Dina Meyer"         |
| "Ice-T"              |
| "Takeshi Kitano"     |
```

In the above example, we specified the relationship type (ACTED_IN) and the node type (movie). We can also specify a wildcard to match all relationship or node types and can specify the depth of the traversal, as in the following query which matches all nodes within two traversals from "Keanu Reeves." This list will include all movies that he has starred in, together with all co-stars and directors.

```
neo4j-sh (?)$ MATCH (kenau:Person {name:"Keanu Reeves"})
              -[*1..2]-(related) RETURN distinct related;
+--------------------------------------------------------------------
| related
+--------------------------------------------------------------------
```

```
| Node[0]{title:"The Matrix",released:1999,
          tagline:"Welcome to the Real World"}
| Node[7]{name:"Joel Silver",born:1952}
| Node[5]{name:"Andy Wachowski",born:1967}
| Node[6]{name:"Lana Wachowski",born:1965}
```

Just as SQL queries generate result sets that are structured as tables, Cypher returns results that can themselves be graphs. For instance, in Figure 5-5, we generate a graph showing all nodes related to "Keanu Reeves" out to two levels.

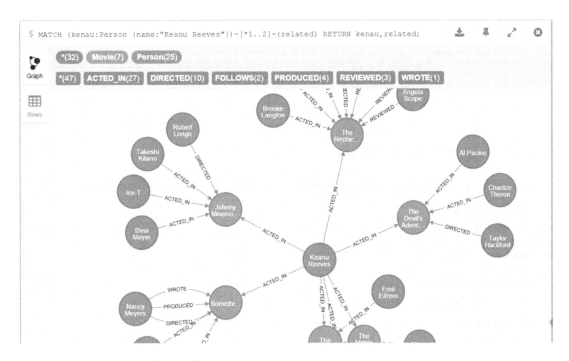

Figure 5-5. *Graph output from cypher query*

Gremlin

Although easy to use, Cypher was until recently specific to Neo4J. *Gremlin* is an alternative graph database query language that can be used with Neo4J and a variety of other graph engines, including Titan (now part of the Datastax Cassandra distribution) and OrientDB.

Compared to Cypher's nonprocedural SQL-like style, Gremlin is a more procedurally oriented language. Using Gremlin, the programmer declares the specific traversal operations to be performed—possibly in multiple statements.

Figure 5-6 illustrates the Gremlin "toy" sample database. The database contains six vertices (nodes) which define four people and two projects. Some people have created projects, and some people know other people.

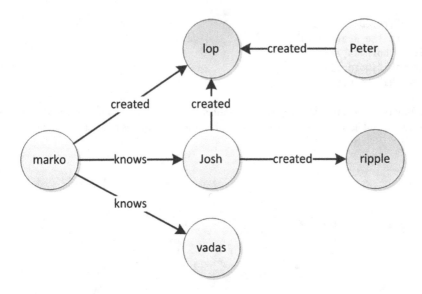

Figure 5-6. *Gremlin sample graph database*

In Gremlin notation, V represents the vertices/nodes while E represents edges/relationships:

```
gremlin> myGraph.V.map
==>{name=marko, age=29}
==>{name=vadas, age=27}
==>{name=lop, lang=java}
==>{name=josh, age=32}
==>{name=ripple, lang=java}
==>{name=peter, age=35}

gremlin> myGraph.E
==>e[11][4-created->3]
==>e[12][6-created->3]
==>e[7][1-knows->2]
==>e[8][1-knows->4]
==>e[9][1-created->3]
==>e[10][4-created->5]
```

This command displays the people "known" by Marko:

```
gremlin> marko=myGraph.v(1)
==>v[1]
gremlin> marko.out('knows').name
==>vadas
==>josh
```

This command walks the tree to find the projects created by people whom Marko knows:

```
gremlin> marko.out('knows').out('created').name
==>lop
==>ripple
```

In late 2015, Neo technology announced an open-source version of the Cypher language. Oracle and Databricks—the Spark company—and several other vendors have announced support for this *openCypher* language. Given the popularity of Neo4j and the arguably more accessible syntax offered by Cypher, it's quite possible that the motivation for Gremlin as an alternative language will be diminished.

Graph Database Internals

Graph processing can be performed on databases irrespective of their internal storage format. The logical model of a graph database outlined at the beginning of the chapter can be implemented on almost any database system; indeed, relational systems can implement the logical relationships within a graph without compromise. However, as we discussed earlier, performance on relational systems—even with optimal indexing—degrades as the depth of the graph traversal increases. Enabling efficient real-time graph processing in practice requires a way to move through the graph structure without index lookups. This index-free navigation is referred to as *index-free adjacency*.

For example, to implement a graph in a relational model such as we saw in Figure 5-2, a join table is used to navigate between two rows—possibly in the same table—that represent adjacent nodes. Indexes allow the logical key value of the adjacent row to be translated to a physical address within the database. This physical address can then be quickly accessed. In a typical implementation, three or four logical IO operations are required to traverse the B-Tree index, and a further lookup to retrieve the value. These IO operations may be satisfied in cache memory, but usually some physical IO is required.

As we discussed earlier, index lookups are typically adequate for shallow traversals, but they contribute to performance degradation as the traversals become deeper. The exact implementation varies depending on the type of database, but the need to create an index to facilitate a graph traversal is common to all nongraph databases.

In a native graph database utilizing index-free adjacency, each node knows the physical location of all adjacent nodes. There is, therefore, no need to use indexes to efficiently navigate the graph, because each node "points" to all adjacent nodes.

Not surprisingly, native graph databases massively outperform alternative implementations for graph traversal operations. However, the architecture presents challenges for distributing the graph across multiple servers. While a node can, of course, point to an adjacent node located on another machine, the overhead of routing the traversal across multiple machines eliminates the advantages of the graph database model, because inter-server communication is far more time consuming than local access. For this reason, many pure graph databases like Neo4j do not currently support a distributed deployment—the graph database can run on a single server only.

Graph Compute Engines

Graph-only databases excel at graph processing, of course, but they are rarely optimal for all the workloads in a typical application. Conversely, many applications—even if their predominant workloads are satisfied by a nongraph database technology—sometimes need to be able to perform efficient graph traversals.

Furthermore, as we discussed previously, the pure graph model has difficulties coping with massive distributed datasets, because it is inefficient to perform graph based traversals across multiple physical machines.

Graph compute engines provide a solution for databases that want to merge graph processing with other data models and for graph processing that needs to work across massive distributed datasets. A graph compute engine implements efficient graph processing algorithms and exposes graph APIs, but it does not assume or require that the data be stored in the index free *adjacency* graph format we discussed previously; the underlying datasets may be held in a relational database, a NoSQL system, or Hadoop. Graph compute engines don't always offer the efficient real-time graph traversal offered by pure graph databases; instead, they tend to excel at batch operations that process all or large parts of the graph.

Significant graph compute engines include:

- **Apache Giraph:** A graph processing system designed to run over Hadoop data using MapReduce.

- **GraphX:** A graph processing system that is part of the *Berkeley Data Analytic Stack* (*BDAS*), which includes Spark (see Chapter 7). It uses Spark as the foundation for graph processing just as Giraph uses MapReduce.

- **Titan:** A graph database that can be layered on top of Big Data storage engines, including Hbase and Cassandra. Datastax—the commercial vendor of Cassandra—acquired Auerlius, the commercial sponsor of Titan, in 2014.

Conclusion

Graph databases occupy a specific and important niche in database technology. Unlike advocates of key-value stores and document databases, the proponents of graph databases do not claim to be on a mission to replace the venerable RDBMS; rather, they correctly describe graph databases as an important alternative when the analysis of relationships between objects is of as much significance as the objects themselves.

The logical model of a graph database is conceptually quite simple. Nodes (or "vertices") are connected to each other by relationships (or "edges"). Both nodes and relationships may have properties—sets of name : value pairs.

Languages such as SPARQL, Cypher, and Gremlin are optimized for graph traversal operations, offering a syntax that allows us to walk the graph without requiring the recursive joins necessitated by relational databases.

Pure graph databases such as Neo4J store data in a format that is optimized for real-time graph processing, but that is not always suitable for other purposes. These databases store the data in a physical format that matches the logical relationships of the graph.

Graph compute engines perform graph processing over data held in other formats, often in Hadoop but potentially in a relational format. A graph compute engine is typically optimized to perform batch processing over an entire graph, while a native graph database is optimized toward real-time graph processing.

Modifying the physical organization of data to suit a particular processing workload is not unique to graph databases. As we will see in the next chapter, columnar databases turn the traditional physical organization of database storage on its side so as to optimize analytic workloads.

- - -

CHAPTER 6

Column Databases

I wish I could find a witty quote about column databases

—Guy Harrison, Next Generation Databases

Those of us raised in Western cultures have been conditioned to think of data as arranged in rows. The way data is presented in ledgers, tables, spreadsheets, and even in the left to right, top to bottom organization of European languages has programmed us to visualize data in row format. It's not surprising, therefore, that the first digital files were created with each record represented as a row. But no matter how convenient and familiar this format may be, it is not always the best way to organize data physically.

When the first digital files were created, the data for each record was kept together in a way we think of as "row formatted." The first databases that attempted to implement the relational model were created during a period in which OLTP processing—essentially, record at a time processing—was the most important type of database workload. This sort of workload is primarily record oriented, and the row-oriented physical structure of early digital files provided good performance.

However, as we progressed beyond OLTP processing into the realm of data warehousing and analytic workloads, row-oriented physical organization became less ideal. In a data warehouse you rarely want to process all the columns of a single row, but you often want to process the values of a single column across all rows. Column-oriented databases address this requirement by storing columns physically together on disk.

Data Warehousing Schemas

At the time that Edgar Codd published his seminal paper on the relational database model, database workloads were dominated by record-based processing: so-called CRUD operations (Create, Read, Update, Delete) were the most time-critical ones, while report programs typically iterated through entire tables and were run in a background batch mode where query response time was not a critical issue. However, during the late 1980s and 1990s, an increasing number of relational databases were tasked with supporting analytic and decision support applications that often demanded interactive response times. These systems became known as *data warehouses,* and increasingly were operated parallel to the OLTP system that had generated the original data. The acronym *OLAP* (*Online Analytic Processing*) was coined by Edgar Codd to differentiate these workloads from those of OLTP systems.

Separating OLTP and OLAP workloads was important for maintaining service-level response times for the OLTP systems: sudden IO intensive aggregate queries would generally cause an unacceptable response-time degradation in the OLTP system. But equally important, the OLAP system demanded a different schema from the OLTP system.

Star schemas were developed to create data warehouses in which aggregate queries could execute quickly and which would provide a predictable schema for Business Intelligence (BI) tools. In a star schema, central large *fact* tables are associated with numerous smaller *dimension* tables. When the dimension tables implement a more complex set of foreign key relationships, then the schema is referred to as a *snowflake schema.*

Figure 6-1 shows an example of a simplified star schema.

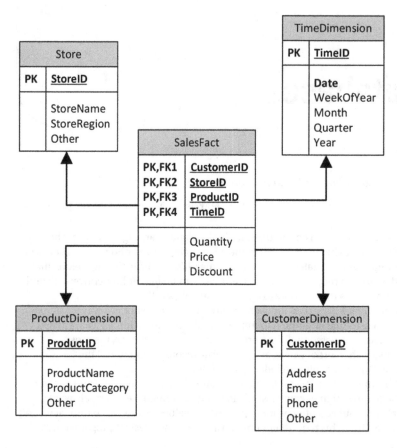

Figure 6-1. *Star schema*

■ **Note**   although star schemas are typically found in relational databases, they do not represent a fully normalized relational model of data. Both the dimension tables and the fact tables usually contain redundant information, or information depended only partly on the primary key. In some respects, widespread adoption of the star schema was a step away from full compliance with Codd's relational model.

Almost all data warehouses adopted some variation on the star schema paradigm, and almost all relational databases adopted indexing and SQL optimization schemes to accelerate queries against star schemas. These optimizations allowed relational data warehouses to serve as the foundation for management dashboards and popular BI products. However, despite these optimizations, star schema processing in data warehouses remained severely CPU and IO intensive. As data volumes grew and user demands for interactive response times continued, there was increasing discontent with traditional data warehousing performance.

The Columnar Alternative

The idea that it might be better to store data in columnar format dates back to the 1970s, although commercial columnar databases did not appear until the mid-1990s.

The essence of the columnar concept is that data for columns is grouped together on disk. Figure 6-2 compares columnar and row-oriented storage for some simple data: in a columnar database, values for a specific column become co-located in the same disk blocks, while in the row-oriented model, all columns for each row are co-located.

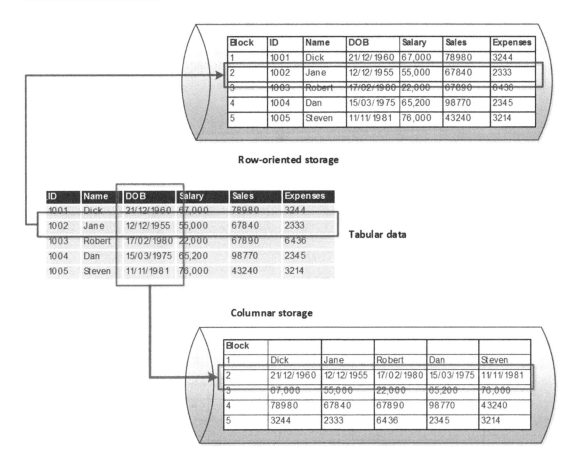

Figure 6-2. *Comparison of columnar and row-oriented storage*

There are two big advantages to the columnar architecture. First, in a columnar architecture, queries that seek to aggregate the values of specific columns are optimized, because all of the values to be aggregated exist within the same disk blocks. Figure 6-3 illustrates this phenomenon for our sample database; retrieving the sum of salaries from the row store must scan five blocks, while a single block access suffices in the column store.

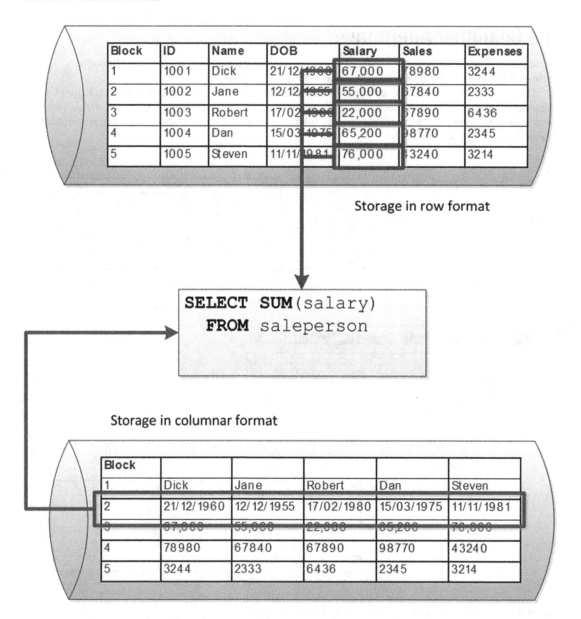

Figure 6-3. *Aggregate operations in columnar stores require fewer IOs*

The exact IO and CPU optimizations delivered by a column architecture vary depending on workload, indexing, and schema design. In general, queries that work across multiple rows are significantly accelerated in a columnar database.

Columnar Compression

The second key advantage for the columnar architecture is compression. Compression algorithms work primarily by removing redundancy within data values. Data that is highly repetitious—especially if those repetitions are localized—achieve higher compression ratios than data with low repetition. Although the total amount of repetition is the same across the entire database, regardless of row or column orientation, compression schemes usually try to work on localized subsets of the data; the CPU overhead of compression is far lower if it can work on isolated blocks of data. Since in a columnar database the columns are stored together on disk, achieving a higher compression ratio is far less computationally expensive.

Furthermore, in many cases a columnar database will store column data in a sorted order. In this case, very high compression ratios can be achieved simply by representing each column value as a "delta" from the preceding column value. The result is extremely high compression ratios achieved with very low computational overhead.

Columnar Write Penalty

The key disadvantage of the columnar architecture—and the reason it is a poor choice for OLTP databases—is the overhead it imposes on single row operations. In a columnar database, retrieving a single row involves assembling the row from each of the column stores for that table. Read overhead can be partly reduced by caching and multicolumn projections (storing multiple columns together on disk). However, when it comes to DML operations—particularly inserts—there is virtually no way to avoid having to modify all the columns for each row.

Figure 6-4 illustrates the insert overhead for a column store on our simple example database. The row store need only perform a single IO to insert a new value, while the column store must update as many disk blocks as there are columns.

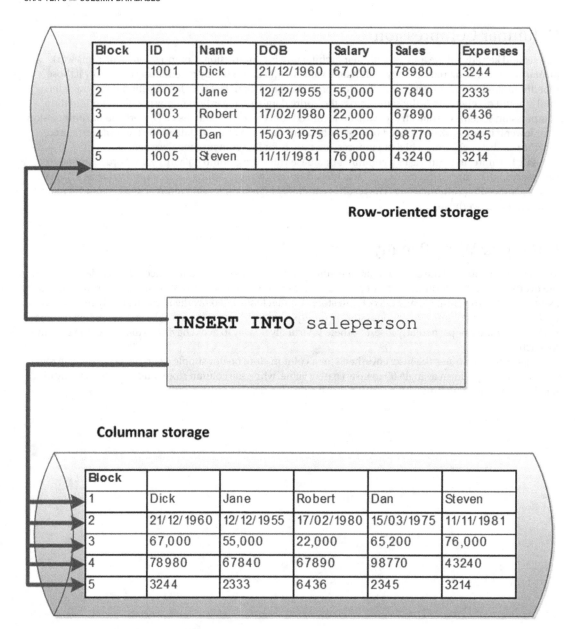

Block	ID	Name	DOB	Salary	Sales	Expenses
1	1001	Dick	21/12/1960	67,000	78980	3244
2	1002	Jane	12/12/1955	55,000	67840	2333
3	1003	Robert	17/02/1980	22,000	67890	6436
4	1004	Dan	15/03/1975	65,200	98770	2345
5	1005	Steven	11/11/1981	76,000	43240	3214

Row-oriented storage

INSERT INTO saleperson

Columnar storage

Block					
1	Dick	Jane	Robert	Dan	Steven
2	21/12/1960	12/12/1955	17/02/1980	15/03/1975	11/11/1981
3	67,000	55,000	22,000	65,200	76,000
4	78980	67840	67890	98770	43240
5	3244	2333	6436	2345	3214

Figure 6-4. *Insert overhead for a column store*

In real-world row stores (e.g., traditional RDBMS), inserts require more than a single IO because of indexing overhead, and real-world column stores implement mitigating schemes to avoid the severe overhead during single-row modifications. However, the fundamental principle—that column stores perform poorly during single-row modifications—is valid.

Sybase IQ, C-Store, and Vertica

In the mid-1990s, Sybase—one of the top four relational database vendors of the day— acquired Expressway. Expressway had developed what was arguably the first significant commercial column-oriented database. Expressway technology became the basis of *Sybase IQ* ("Intelligent Query"), which became Sybase's flagship data warehousing platform. However, although Sybase IQ gained significant traction during the succeeding decade, and despite its leading-edge technology, Sybase IQ failed to dominate the data warehousing market. Industry recognition of the significance of columnar technology remained low.

In 2005, relational pioneer and Ingres inventor Mike Stonebraker and colleagues published a paper outlining a formal database system that they called *C-store*.[1] C-store shared many characteristics with existing columnar systems, as well as having some significant innovations to improve write performance. Stonebraker's paper included TPC-H benchmark results that demonstrated the C-Store architecture was able to outperform existing row-based DBMS for data warehousing workloads.

Stonebraker formed a company *Vertica*—to build a commercial implementation of C-Store. Vertica was acquired by HP in 2011.

Timing is everything, and while Sybase IQ had delivered a successful commercial columnar database almost a decade earlier, C-Store and Vertica arrived just as cracks were emerging in the "one size fits all" relational edifice. C-Store and Vertica became emblematic of a new wave of systems that—while not rejecting the relational model or SQL—departed significantly from the traditional RDBMS architecture. Vertica became the poster child for a "NewSQL" database.

Subsequent to the release of the C-Store model, several other significant column-based systems entered the market, including InfoBright, VectorWise, and MonetDB. Columnar technology also became an important element within many significant commercial relational databases, including Oracle Exadata, Microsoft SQL Server, and SAP HANA. (We'll look at Oracle's implementation later in this chapter and at HANA in the next chapter.)

Column Database Architectures

As we noted earlier, insert and update overhead for single rows is a key weakness of a columnar architecture. Many data warehouses were bulk-loaded in daily batch jobs—a classic overnight ETL scenario. However, it became increasingly important for data warehouses to provide real-time "up-to-the-minute" information, which implied that the data warehouse should be able to accept a constant trickle feed of changes. The simplistic columnar architecture outlined above would be unable to cope with this constant stream of row-level modifications.

To address this issue, columnar databases generally implement some form of *write-optimized delta store* (we'll call this the *delta store* for short). This area of the database is optimized for frequent writes. You can think simplistically of the data in the delta store as being in a row format, although in practice the internal format might still be columnar or a row/column hybrid. Regardless of the internal format of the data, the delta store is generally memory resident, the data is generally uncompressed, and the store can accept high-frequency data modifications.

Data in the delta store is periodically merged with the main columnar-oriented store. In Vertica, this process is referred to as the *Tuple Mover* and in Sybase IQ as the *RLV (Row Level Versioned) Store Merge*. The merge will occur periodically, or whenever the amount of data in the delta store exceeds a threshold. Prior to the merge, queries might have needed to access both the delta store and the column store in order to return complete and accurate results.

Figure 6-5 shows a generic columnar database architecture. The database contains a primary column store that contains highly compressed columnar data backed by disk storage. A smaller write-optimized delta store contains data that is minimally compressed, memory resident, and possibly row oriented.

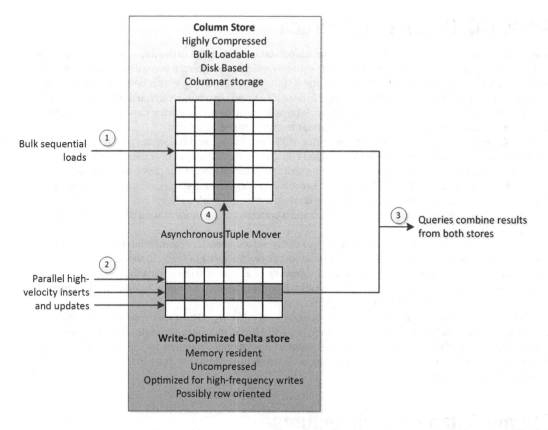

Figure 6-5. *Write optimization in column store databases*

Large-scale bulk sequential loads—such as nightly ETL jobs—will generally be directed to the column store (1). Incremental inserts and updates will be directed to the write-optimized store (2). Queries may need to read from both stores in order to get complete and consistent results (3). Periodically, or as required, a process will shift data from the write-optimized store to the column store (4).

Projections

In the simplistic description of a columnar database earlier, we showed each column stored together. For queries that access only a single column, storing each column in its own region on disk may be sufficient, but in practice complex queries need to read combinations of column data. It therefore sometimes makes sense to store combinations of columns together on disk.

To achieve this, columnar databases such as Vertica store tables physically as a series of *projections*, which contain combinations of columns that are frequently accessed together.

For instance, in Figure 6-6 we see a single logical table with three projections. In Vertica, each table has a default *superprojection* that includes all the columns in the table (1). Additional projections are created to support specific queries. In this case, a projection is created to support sales aggregated by customer (2) and another projection created for sales aggregated by region and product (3).

Region	Customer	Product	Sales
A	G	C	789
B	C	C	743
D	F	D	675
C	C	A	23
A	R	B	654

Logical Table
Table appears to user in relational normal form

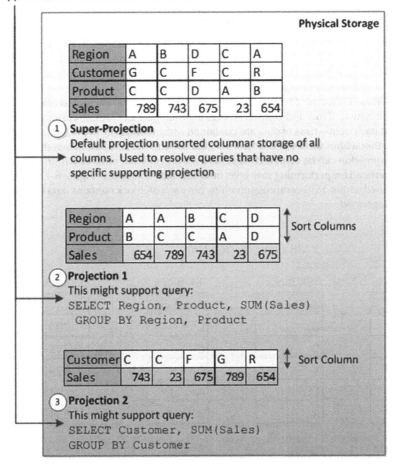

Figure 6-6. Columnar database table with three projections

In Vertica, projections may be sorted on one or more columns. This decreases processing time for sort and aggregate operations, and also increases compression efficiency. Vertica also supports *pre-join projections* that materialize columns from multiple tables based on a join criterion. Pre-join projections serve a similar function to materialized views that are created to support specific join operations in traditional relational systems.

Projections may be created manually by the database administrator, on the fly by the query optimizer in response to a specific SQL, or in bulk based on historical workloads. Creating the correct set of projections is of critical importance to columnar store performance—roughly equivalent to the importance of correct indexing in a row store.

Sybase IQ refers to its query optimization structures as "indexes"; however, these indexes bear more resemblance to Vertica projections than to B-Tree indexes in Oracle or SQL Server. Indeed, the Sybase IQ default index—which is automatically created on all columns during table creation—is called the *fast projection index*. Sybase also supports other indexing options based on traditional bitmap and B-Tree indexing schemes.

Columnar Technology in Other Databases

Variations on the columnar paradigm have been implemented within both traditional relational systems and other "NewSQL" systems. For instance the in-memory database SAP HANA provides support for column or row orientation on a table-by-table basis. The Oracle 12c "Database in Memory" also implements a column store. We'll touch on these architectures in Chapter 7.

Oracle's *Enhanced Hybrid Columnar Compression* (*EHCC*) is an interesting attempt to achieve a best-of-both-worlds combination of row and column storage technologies. In EHCC— currently only available in Oracle's Exadata system—rows of data are contained within *compression units* of about 1 MB, with columns stored together within smaller 8K blocks. Because the columns are stored together within blocks, high levels of compression can be achieved. Because rows are guaranteed to be within a 1 MB compression unit, the overhead for performing row-level modifications is reduced. Figure 6-7 illustrates the concept. Rows are contained within 1MB compression units, but each 8K block contains data for a specific column that is highly compressed.

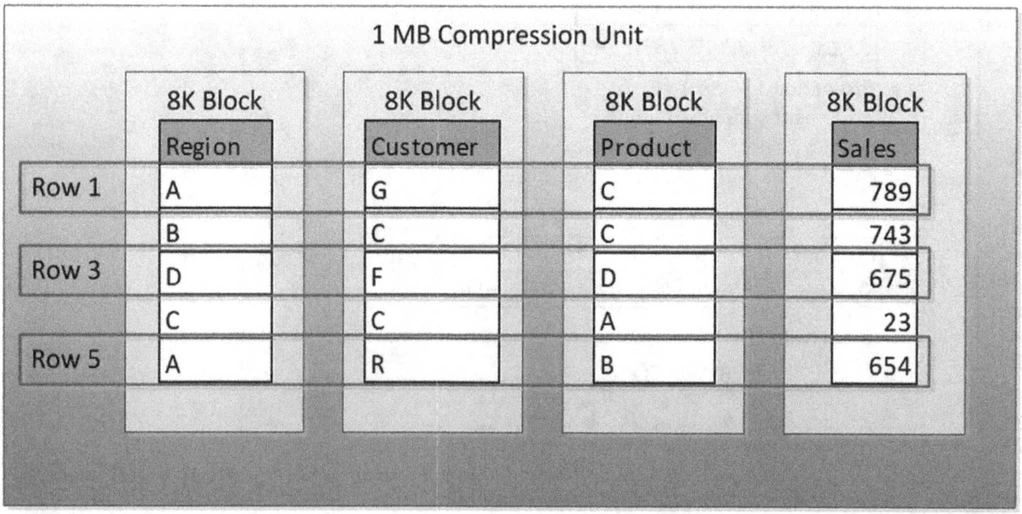

1 MB Compression Unit

	8K Block	8K Block	8K Block	8K Block
	Region	Customer	Product	Sales
Row 1	A	G	C	789
	B	C	C	743
Row 3	D	F	D	675
	C	C	A	23
Row 5	A	R	B	654

Figure 6-7. *Oracle's hybrid columnar compression scheme*

Column-oriented storage is common in modern nonrelational systems as well. *Apache Parquet* is a column-oriented storage mechanism for Hadoop files that allows Hadoop systems to take advantage of columnar performance advantages and compression. *Apache Kudu* uses both row and column storage formats to bridge the perceived performance gap between HDFS row-based processing and Hadoop file scans.

Conclusion

It's easy to think of columnar architecture as a physical tweak to storage that has only a minor impact on the overall design of database systems. However, the columnar storage paradigm is incredibly influential in the evolution of both existing relational systems that aspire to perform data warehousing roles and "new SQL" systems such as Vertica.

Understanding columnar architecture is also important when examining the new breed of in-memory databases; as we will see in the next chapter, many of these adopt a columnar architecture internally in order to optimize and compress memory-resident data for analytical purposes.

Note

1. *C-Store: A Column-oriented DBMS*, Proceedings of the 31st VLDB Conference, Trondheim, Norway, 2005; http://db.lcs.mit.edu/projects/cstore/vldb.pdf

■ ■ ■

CHAPTER 7

The End of Disk? SSD and In-Memory Databases

640K of memory should be enough for anybody.

—attributed (without foundation) to Bill Gates, 1981

I've said some stupid things and some wrong things, but not that.

—Bill Gates, 2001

Ever since the birth of the first database systems, database professionals have strived to avoid disk IO at all costs. IO to magnetic disk devices has always been many orders of magnitude slower than memory or CPU access, and the situation has only grown worse as Moore's law accelerated the performance of CPU and memory while leaving mechanical disk performance behind.

The emergence of affordable *solid state disk* (*SSD*) technology has allowed for a quantum leap in database disk performance. Over the past few years, SSD technology has shifted from an expensive luxury to a mainstream technology that has a place in almost every performance-critical database system. However, SSDs have some unique performance characteristics and some database systems have been developed to exploit these capabilities.

While SSDs allow IO to be accelerated, the increasing capacity and economy of server memory sometimes allows us to avoid IO altogether. Many smaller databases can now fit entirely within the memory capacity of a single server, and certainly within the memory capacity of a cluster. For these databases, an in-memory solution may be even more attractive than an SSD architecture.

The End of Disk?

The magnetic disk device has been a pervasive presence within digital computing since the 1950s. The essential architecture has changed very little over that time: one or more *platters* contain magnetic charges that represent bits of information. These magnetic charges are read and written by an *actuator arm*, which moves across the disk to a specific position on the radius of the platter and then waits for the platter to rotate to the appropriate location. These mechanical operations are inherently slow and do not benefit from the exponential improvement described by Moore's law. This is simple physics—if disk rotational speed had increased in line with increases in CPU processing capabilities, then by now the velocity on the outside of the disk would be about 10 times the speed of light!

Figure 7-1 illustrates that while the size and density of these devices has improved over the years, the architecture remains fundamentally unchanged. While Moore's law drives exponential growth in CPU, memory, and disk density, it does not apply to the mechanical aspects of disk performance. Consequently, magnetic disks have become an increasing drag on database performance.

Figure 7-1. *Disk devices over the years*

Solid State Disk

In contrast to a magnetic disk, solid state disks contain no moving parts and provide tremendously lower IO latencies. Commercial SSDs are currently implemented using either DDR RAM—effectively a battery-backed RAM device—or NAND flash. NAND flash is an inherently nonvolatile storage medium and almost completely dominates today's SSD market.

Performance of flash SSD is on orders of magnitude superior to magnetic disk devices, especially for read operations. A random read from a high-end solid state disk may complete in as little as 25 microseconds, while a read from a magnetic disk may take up to 4,000 microseconds (4 milliseconds or 4/1000 of a second)—over 150 times slower.

While SSDs are certainly faster than magnetic disks, the speed improvement is not proportionate for all workloads. In particular, it costs more—takes longer—to modify information in an SSD than to read from it.

SSDs store bits of information in *cells*. A *single-level cell* (*SLC*) SSD contains one bit of information per cell, while a *multi-level cell* (*MLC*) SSD contains more than one bit— usually only two but sometimes three—in each cell. Cells are arranged in *pages* of about 4K and pages are arranged in *blocks* that typically contain 256 pages.

Read operations, and initial write operations, require only a single-page IO. However, changing the contents of a page requires an erase and overwrite of a complete block. Even the initial write can be significantly slower than a read, but the block erase operation is particularly slow—around two milliseconds. Figure 7-2 shows the approximate times for a page seek, page write, and block erase.

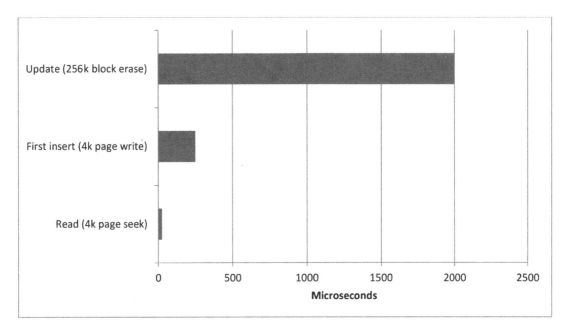

Figure 7-2. *Flash SSD performance characteristics*

Commercial SSD manufacturers go to great efforts to avoid the performance penalty of the erase operation and the reliability concerns raised by the "wear" that occurs on an SSD when a cell is modified. Sophisticated algorithms are used to ensure that erase operations are minimized and that writes are evenly distributed across the device. However, these algorithms create a *write amplification* effect in which each write operation is associated with multiple physical IOs on the SSD as data is moved and storage is reclaimed.

■ **Note** Regardless of whatever sophisticated algorithms and optimizations that an SSD vendor might implement, the essential point remains: **flash SSD is significantly slower when performing writes than when performing reads**.

The Economics of Disk

The promise of SSD has led some to anticipate a day when all magnetic disks are replaced by SSD. While this day may come, in the near term the economics of storage and the economics of I/O are at odds: magnetic disk technology provides a more economical medium per unit of storage, while flash technology provides a more economical medium for delivering high I/O rates and low latencies. And although the cost of a solid state disk is dropping rapidly, so is the cost of a magnetic disk. An examination of the trend for the cost per gigabyte for SSD and HDD is shown in Figure 7-3.

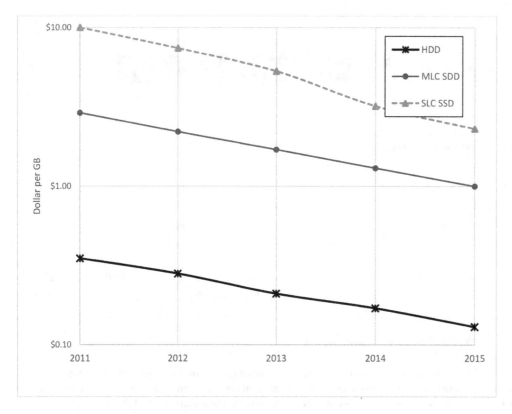

Figure 7-3. *Trends in SSD and HDD storage costs (note logarithmic scale)*

While SSD continues to be an increasingly economic solution for small databases or for performance-critical systems, it is unlikely to become a universal solution for massive databases, especially for data that is infrequently accessed. We are, therefore, likely to see combinations of solid state disk, traditional hard drives, and memory providing the foundation for next-generation databases.

SSD-Enabled Databases

A couple of next-generation database systems have engineered architectures that are specifically designed to take advantage of the physics of SSD.

Many traditional relational databases perform relatively poorly on SSD because critical IO has been isolated to sequential write operations for which hard disk drives perform well, but that represent the worst possible workload for SSD. When a transaction commits in an ACID-compliant relational database, the transaction record is usually written immediately to a sequential transaction log (called a *redo log* in some databases). IO to this transaction log might not improve when the log is moved to SSD because of lesser SSD write performance and the write amplification effect we discussed earlier. In this scenario, users may be disappointed with the performance improvement achieved when a write-intensive RDBMS is moved to SSD.

Many nonrelational systems (Cassandra, for instance) utilize *log-structured* storage engines— often based on the *log-structured merge tree* (*LSM*) architecture—see Chapter 10 for details. These tend to avoid updating existing blocks and perform larger batched write operations, which are friendlier to solid state disk performance characteristics.

Aerospike is a NoSQL database that attempts to provide a database architecture that can fully exploit the IO characteristics of flash SSD. Aerospike implements a log-structured file system in which updates are physically implemented by appending the new value to the file and marking the original data as invalid. The storage for the older values are recovered by a background process at a later time.

Aerospike also implements an unusual approach in its use of main memory. Rather than using main memory as a cache to avoid physical disk IO, Aerospike uses main memory to store indexes to the data while keeping the data always on flash. This approach represents a recognition that, in a flash-based system, the "avoid IO at all costs" approach of traditional databases may be unnecessary.

In-Memory Databases

The solid state disk may have had a transformative impact on database performance, but it has resulted in only incremental changes for most database architectures. A more paradigm-shifting trend has been the increasing practicality of storing complete databases in main memory.

The cost of memory and the amount of memory that can be stored on a server have both been moving exponentially since the earliest days of computing. Figure 7-4 illustrates these trends: both the cost of memory per unit storage and the amount of storage that can fit on a single memory chip have been increasing over many decades (note the logarithmic scale—the relatively straight lines indicate exponential trends).

Source: http://www.jcmit.com/memoryprice.htm

Figure 7-4. Trends for memory cost and capacity for the last 40 years (note logarithmic scale)

The size of the average database—particularly in light of the Big Data phenomenon—has been growing exponentially as well. For many systems, database growth continues to outpace memory growth. But many other databases of more modest size can now comfortably be stored within the memory of a single server. And many more databases than that can reside within the memory capacity of a cluster.

Traditional relational databases use memory to cache data stored on disk, and they generally show significant performance improvements as the amount of memory increases. But there are some database operations that simply must write to a persistent medium. In the traditional database architecture, COMMIT operations require a write to a transaction log on a persistent medium, and periodically the database writes "checkpoint" blocks in memory to disk. Taking full advantage of a large memory system requires an architecture that is aware the database is completely memory resident and that allows for the advantages of high-speed access without losing data in the event of a power failure.

There are two changes to traditional database architecture an in-memory system should address:

- **Cache-less architecture**: Traditional disk-based databases almost invariably cache data in main memory to minimize disk IO. This is futile and counterproductive in an in-memory system: there is no point caching in memory what is already stored in memory!

- **Alternative persistence model**: Data in memory disappears when the power is turned off, so the database must apply some alternative mechanism for ensuring that no data loss occurs.

In-memory databases generally use some combination of techniques to ensure they don't lose data. These include:

- Replicating data to other members of a cluster.

- Writing complete database images (called *snapshots* or *checkpoints*) to disk files.

- Writing out transaction/operation records to an append-only disk file (called a *transaction log* or *journal*).

TimesTen

TimesTen is a relatively early in-memory database system that aspires to support workloads similar to a traditional relational system, but with better performance. TimesTen was founded in 1995 and acquired by Oracle in 2005. Oracle offers it as a standalone in-memory database or as a caching database supplementing the traditional disk-based Oracle RDBMS.

TimesTen implements a fairly familiar SQL-based relational model. Subsequent to the purchase by Oracle, it implemented ANSI standard SQL, but in recent years the effort has been to make the database compatible with the core Oracle database—to the extent of supporting Oracle's stored procedure language PL/SQL.

In a TimesTen database, all data is memory resident. Persistence is achieved by writing periodic snapshots of memory to disk, as well as writing to a disk-based transaction log following a transaction commit.

In the default configuration, all disk writes are asynchronous: a database operation would normally not need to wait on a disk IO operation. However, if the power fails between the transaction commit and the time the transaction log is written, then data could be lost. This behavior is not ACID compliant because transaction durability (the "D" in ACID) is not guaranteed. However, the user may choose to configure synchronous writes to the transaction log during commit operations. In this case, the database becomes ACID compliant, but some database operations will wait on disk IO.

Figure 7-5 illustrates the TimesTen architecture. When the database is started, all data is loaded from checkpoint files into main memory (1). The application interacts with TimesTen via SQL requests that are guaranteed to find all relevant data inside that main memory (2). Periodically or when required database data is written to checkpoint files (3). An application commit triggers a write to the transaction log (4), though by default this write will be asynchronous so that the application will not need to wait on disk. The transaction log can be used to recover the database in the event of failure (5).

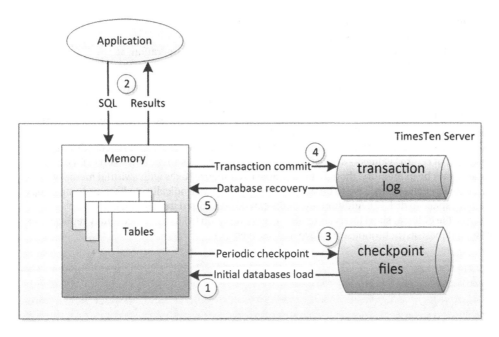

Figure 7-5. *TimesTen Architecture*

TimesTen is significant today primarily as part of Oracle's enterprise solutions architecture. However, it does represent a good example of an early memory-based transactional relational database architecture.

Redis

While TimesTen is an attempt to build an RDBMS compatible in-memory database, *Redis* is at the opposite extreme: essentially an in-memory key-value store. Redis (*Remote Dictionary Server*) was originally envisaged as a simple in-memory system capable of sustaining very high transaction rates on underpowered systems, such as virtual machine images.

Redis was created by Salvatore Sanfilippo in 2009. VMware hired Sanfilippo and sponsored Redis development in 2010. In 2013, Pivotal software—a Big Data spinoff from VMware's parent company EMC—became the primary sponsor.

Redis follows a familiar key-value store architecture in which keys point to objects. In Redis, objects consist mainly of strings and various types of collections of strings (lists, sorted lists, hash maps, etc.). Only primary key lookups are supported; Redis does not have a secondary indexing mechanism.

Although Redis was designed to hold all data in memory, it is possible for Redis to operate on datasets larger than available memory by using its virtual memory feature. When this is enabled, Redis will "swap out" older key values to a disk file. Should the keys be needed they will be brought back into memory. This option obviously involves a significant performance overhead, since some key lookups will result in disk IO.

Redis uses disk files for persistence:

- **The Snapshot** files store copies of the entire Redis system at a point in time. Snapshots can be created on demand or can be configured to occur at scheduled intervals or after a threshold of writes has been reached. A snapshot also occurs when the server is shut down.

- The **Append Only File** (AOF) keeps a journal of changes that can be used to "roll forward" the database from a snapshot in the event of a failure. Configuration options allow the user to configure writes to the AOF after every operation, at one-second intervals, or based on operating-system-determined flush intervals.

In addition, Redis supports asynchronous master/slave replication. If performance is very critical and some data loss is acceptable, then a replica can be used as a backup database and the master configured with minimal disk-based persistence. However, there is no way to limit the amount of possible data loss; during high loads, the slave may fall significantly behind the master.

Figure 7-6 illustrates these architectural components. The application interacts with Redis through primary key lookups that return "values"—strings, sets of strings, hashes of strings, and so on (1). The key values will almost always be in memory, though it is possible to configure Redis with a virtual memory system, in which case key values may have to be swapped in or out (2). Periodically, Redis may dump a copy of the entire memory space to disk (3). Additionally, Redis can be configured to write changes to an append-only journal file either at short intervals or after every operation (4). Finally, Redis may replicate the state of the master database asynchronously to slave Redis servers (5).

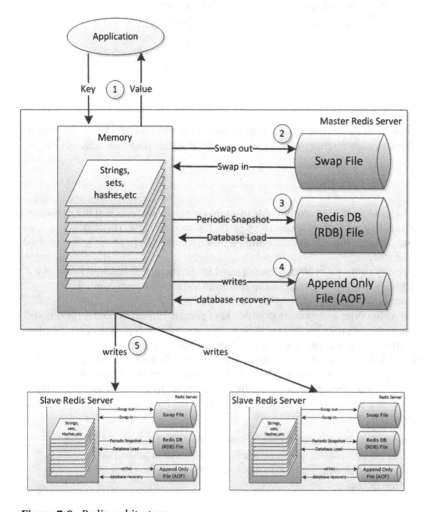

Figure 7-6. *Redis architecture*

Although Redis was designed from the ground up as in an in-memory database system, applications may have to wait for IO to complete under the following circumstances:

- If the Append Only File is configured to be written after every operation, then the application needs to wait for an IO to complete before a modification will return control.

- If Redis virtual memory is configured, then the application may need to wait for a key to be "swapped in" to memory.

Redis is popular among developers as a simple, high-performance key-value store that performs well without expensive hardware. It lacks the sophistication of some other nonrelational systems such as MongoDB, but it works well on systems where the data will fit into main memory or as a caching layer in front of a disk-based database.

SAP HANA

SAP introduced HANA in 2010, positioning it as a revolutionary in-memory database designed primary for Business Intelligence (BI), but also capable of supporting OLTP workloads.

SAP HANA is a relational database designed to provide breakthrough performance by combining in-memory technology with a columnar storage option, installed on an optimized hardware configuration. Although SAP do not ship HANA hardware, they do provide detailed guidelines for HANA-certified servers, including a requirement for fast SSD drives.

Tables in HANA can be configured for row-oriented or columnar storage. Typically, tables intended for BI purposes would be configured as columnar, while OLTP tables are configured as row oriented. The choice of row or columnar formats provides HANA with its ability to provide support for both OLTP and analytic workloads.

Data in the row store is guaranteed to be in memory, while data in the column store is by default loaded on demand. However, specified columns or entire tables may be configured for immediate loading on database startup.

The persistence architecture of HANA uses the snapshot and journal file pattern found in Redis and TimesTen. HANA periodically snapshots the state of memory to *Savepoint* files. These Savepoints are periodically applied to the master database files.

ACID transactional consistency is enabled by the *transaction "redo" log*. As with most ACID-compliant relational databases, this log is written upon transaction commit, which means that applications will wait on the transaction log IO to complete before the commit can return control. To minimize the IO waits, which might slow down HANA's otherwise memory-speed operations, the redo log is placed on solid state disk in SAP-certified HANA appliances.

HANA's columnar architecture includes an implementation of the write-optimized delta store pattern discussed in Chapter 6. Transactions to columnar tables are buffered in this delta store. Initially, the data is held in row-oriented format (the *L1 delta*). Data then moves to the *L2 delta* store, which is columnar in orientation but relatively lightly compressed and unsorted. Finally, the data migrates to the main column store, in which data is highly compressed and sorted.

Figure 7-7 illustrates these key aspects of the HANA architecture. On start-up, row-based tables and selected column tables are loaded from the database files (1). Other column tables will be loaded on demand. Reads and writes to row-oriented tables can be applied directly (2). Updates to column-based tables will be buffered in the delta store (3), initially to the L1 row-oriented store. Data in the L1 store will consequently be promoted to the L2 store, and finally to the column store itself (4). Queries against column tables must read from both the delta store and the main column store (5).

Busy little Figure 7-7 also illustrates the persistence architecture. Images of memory are copied to save points periodically (6) and these save points are merged with the data files in due course (7). When a commit occurs, a transaction record is written to the redo log (8). The HANA reference architecture specifies that this redo log be on fast SSD.

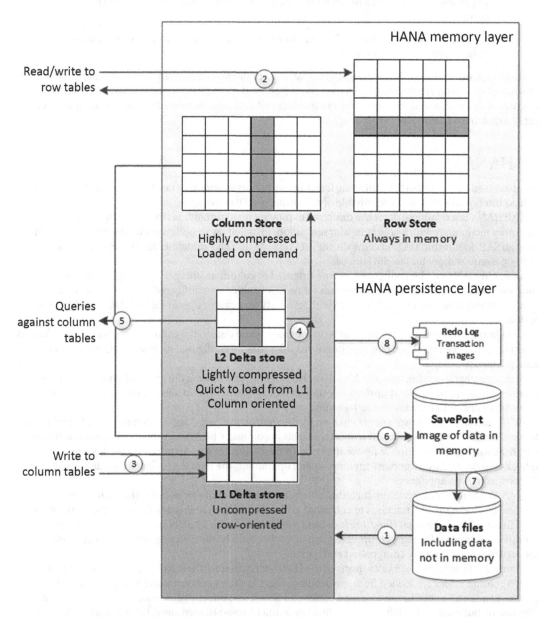

Figure 7-7. SAP HANA architecture

Again, we see that although HANA is described as an in-memory database, there are situations in which an application will need to wait for IO from a disk device; that is, on commit, and when column tables are loaded on demand into memory.

VoltDB

Redis, HANA, and TimesTen are legitimate in-memory database systems: designed from the ground up to use memory as the primary—and usually exclusive—source for all data. However, as we have seen, applications that use these systems still often need to wait for disk IO. In particular, there will often be a disk IO to some form of journal or transaction log when a transaction commits.

VoltDB is a commercial implementation of the *H-store* design. H-store was one of the databases described in Michael Stonebraker's seminal 2007 paper, which argued that no single database architecture was suitable for all modern workloads.[1] H-store describes an in-memory database designed with the explicit intention of not requiring disk IO during normal transactional operations—it aspires to be a pure in-memory solution.

VoltDB supports the ACID transactional model, but rather than guaranteeing data persistence by writing to a disk, persistence is guaranteed through replication across multiple machines. A transaction commit only completes once the data is successfully written to memory on more than one physical machine. The number of machines involved depends on the *K-safety level* specified. For instance, a K-safety level of 2 guarantees no data loss if any two machines fail; in this case, the commit must successfully be propagated to three machines before completing.

It is also possible to configure a *command log* that records transaction commands in a disk-based log. This log may be synchronous—written to at every transaction commit —or asynchronous. Because VoltDB supports only deterministic stored procedure-based transactions, the log need only record the actual command that drove the transaction, rather than copies of modified blocks, as is common in other database transaction logs. Nonetheless, if the synchronous command logging option is employed, then VoltDB applications may experience disk IO wait time.

VoltDB supports the relational model, though its clustering scheme works best if that model can be partitioned hierarchically across common keys. In VoltDB, tables must either be *partitioned* or *replicated*. Partitions are distributed across nodes of the cluster while replicated tables are duplicated in each partition. Tables that are replicated may incur additional overhead during OLTP operations, since the transactions must be duplicated in each partition; this is in contrast to partitioned tables, which incur additional overhead if data must be collated from multiple partitions. For this reason, replicated tables are usually smaller reference-type tables, while the larger transactional tables are partitioned.

Partitions in VoltDB are distributed not just across physical machines but also within machines that have multiple CPU cores. In VoltDB, each partition is dedicated to a single CPU that has exclusive single-threaded access to that partition. This exclusive access reduces the overhead of locking and latching, but it does require that transactions complete quickly to avoid serialization of requests.

Figure 7-8 illustrates how partitioning and replication affect concurrency in VoltDB. Each partition is associated with a single CPU core, and only one SQL statement will ever be active against the partition at any given moment (1). In this example, ORDERS and CUSTOMERS have been partitioned using the customer ID, while the PRODUCTS table is replicated in its entirety in all partitions. A query that accesses data for a single customer need involve only a single partition (2), while a query that works across customers must access—exclusively, albeit for a short time—all partitions (3).

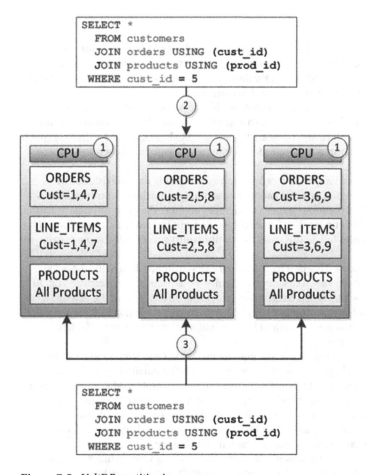

Figure 7-8. *VoltDB partitioning*

VoltDB transactions are streamlined by being encapsulated into a single Java stored procedure call, rather than being represented by a collection of separate SQL statements. This ensures that transaction durations are minimized (no think-time or network time within transactions) and further reduces locking issues.

Oracle 12c "in-Memory Database"

Oracle RDBMS version 12.1 introduced the "Oracle database in-memory" feature. This wording is potentially misleading, since the database as a whole is not held in memory. Rather, Oracle has implemented an in-memory column store to supplement its disk-based row store.

Figure 7-9 illustrates the essential elements of the Oracle in-memory column store architecture. OLTP applications work with the database in the usual manner. Data is maintained in disk files (1), but cached in memory (2). An OLTP application primarily reads and writes from memory (3), but any committed transactions are written immediately to the transaction log on disk (4). When required or as configured, row data is loaded into a columnar representation for use by analytic applications (5). Any transactions that are committed once the data is loaded into columnar format are recorded in a journal (6), and analytic queries will consult the journal to determine if they need to read updated data from the row store (7) or possibly rebuild the columnar structure.

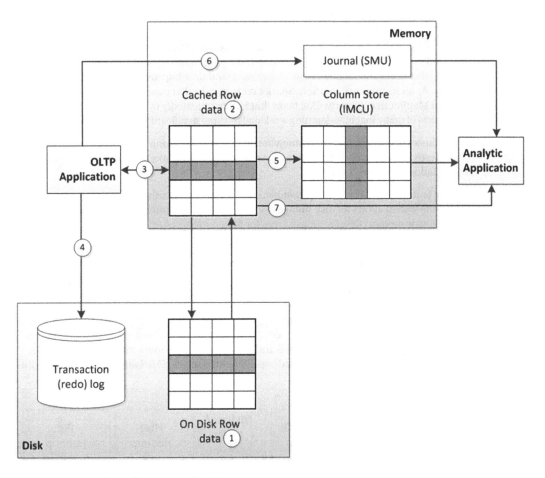

Figure 7-9. *Oracle 12c "in-memory" architecture*

Berkeley Analytics Data Stack and Spark

If SAP HANA and Oracle TimesTen represent in-memory variations on the relational database theme, and if Redis represents an in-memory variation on the key-value store theme, then *Spark* represents an in-memory variation on the Hadoop theme.

Hadoop became the de facto foundation for today's Big Data stack by providing a flexible, scalable, and economic framework for processing massive amounts of structured, unstructured, and semi-structured data. The Hadoop 1.0 MapReduce algorithm represented a relatively simple but scalable approach to parallel processing. MapReduce is not the most elegant or sophisticated approach for all workloads, but it can be adapted to almost any problem, and it can usually scale through the brute-force application of many servers.

However, it's long been realized that MapReduce—particularly when working on disk-based storage—is not a sufficient solution for emerging Big Data analytic challenges. MapReduce excels at batch processing, but falls short in real-time scenarios. Even the simplest MapReduce task takes a significant ramp-up time, and for some machine-learning algorithms the execution time is simply inadequate.

In 2011, the *AMPlab* (Algorithms, Machines, and People) was established at University of California, Berkeley, to attack the emerging challenges of advanced analytics and machine learning on Big Data. The resulting *Berkeley Data Analysis Stack* (*BDAS*)—and in particular the *Spark* processing engine—has shown rapid uptake.

BDAS consists of a few core components:

- **Spark** is an in-memory, distributed, fault-tolerant processing framework. Implemented in the Java virtual-machine-compatible programming language Scala, it provides higher-level abstractions than MapReduce and thus improves developer productivity. As an in-memory solution, Spark excels at tasks that cause bottlenecks on disk IO in MapReduce. In particular, tasks that iterate repeatedly over a dataset—typical of many machine-learning workloads—show significant improvements.

- **Mesos** is a cluster management layer somewhat analogous to Hadoop's YARN. However, Mesos is specifically intended to allow multiple frameworks, including BDAS and Hadoop, to share a cluster.

- **Tachyon** is a fault-tolerant, Hadoop-compatible, memory-centric distributed file system. The file system allows for disk storage of large datasets, but promotes aggressive caching to provide memory-level response times for frequently accessed data.

Other BDAS components build on top of this core. *Spark SQL* provides a Spark-specific implementation of SQL for ad hoc queries, and there is also an active effort to allow Hive— the SQL implementation in the Hadoop stack—to generate Spark code.

Spark streaming provides a stream-oriented processing paradigm using the Spark foundation, and *GraphX* delivers a graph computation engine build on Spark. BDAS also delivers machine-learning libraries at various levels of abstraction in the *MLBase* component.

Spark is sometimes referred to as a successor to Hadoop, but in reality Spark and other elements of the BDAS were designed to work closely with Hadoop HDFS and YARN, and many Spark implementations use HDFS for persistent storage. Figure 7-10 shows how Hadoop elements such as YARN and HDFS interact with Spark and other elements of the BDAS.

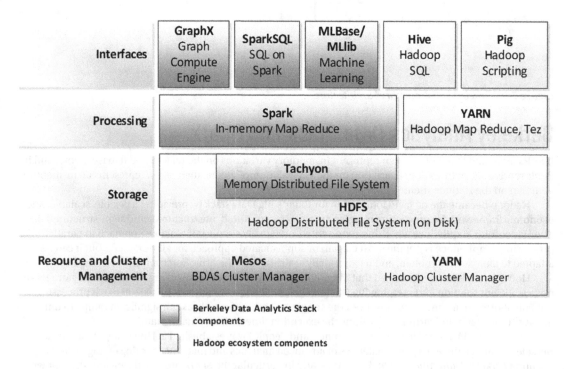

Figure 7-10. Spark, Hadoop, and the Berkeley Data Analytics Stack

Spark is incorporated into many other data management stacks; it is a core part of the three major organizational distributions of Hadoop (Cloudera, Hortonworks, and MapR). Spark is also a component of the Datastax distribution of Cassandra.

Spark Architecture

In Spark, data is represented as *resilient distributed datasets* (*RDD*). RDDs are collections of objects that can be partitioned across multiple nodes of the cluster. The partitioning and subsequent distribution of processing are handled automatically by the Spark framework.

RDDs are described as immutable: Spark operations on RDDs return new RDDs, rather than modifying the original RDD. So, for instance, sorting an RDD creates a new RDD that contains the sorted data.

The Spark API defines high-level methods that perform operations on RDDs. Operations such as joining, filtering, and aggregation, which would entail hundreds of lines of Java code in MapReduce, are expressed as simple method calls in Spark; the level of abstraction is similar to that found with Hadoop's Pig scripting language.

The data within an RDD can be simple types such as strings or any other Java/Scala object type. However, it's common for the RDD to contain key-value pairs, and Spark provides specific data manipulation operations such as aggregation and joins that work only on key-value oriented RDDs.

Under the hood, Spark RDD methods are implemented by *directed acyclic graph* (*DAG*) operations. Directed acyclic graphs provide a more sophisticated and efficient processing paradigm for data manipulation than MapReduce. We discuss directed acyclic graph operations in Chapter 11.

Although Spark expects data to be processed in memory, Spark is capable of managing collections of data that won't fit entirely into main memory. Depending on the configuration, Spark may page data to disk if the data volumes exceed memory capacity.

Spark is not an OLTP-oriented system, so there is no need for the transaction log or journal that we've seen in other in-memory databases. However, Spark can read from or write to local or distributed file systems, and in particular it integrates with the standard Hadoop methods for working with HDFS or external data. RDDs may be represented on disk as text files or JSON documents.

Spark can also access data held in any JDBC-compliant database (in practice, almost every relational system), as well as from HBase or Cassandra.

Figure 7-11 illustrates some of the essential features of Spark processing. Data can be loaded into resilient distributed datasets (RDD) from external sources including relational databases (1) or a distributed file system such as HDFS (2). Spark provides high-level methods for operating on RDDs and which output new RDDs. These operations include joins (3) or aggregations (4). Spark data may be persisted to disk in a variety of formats (5).

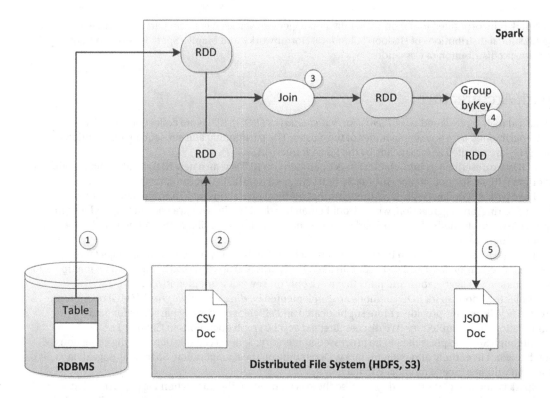

Figure 7-11. *Elements of Spark processing*

Conclusion

It's definitely premature to predict the end of magnetic disks in database systems: magnetic disks still offer the best economics for storage of massive amounts of "cold" or "warm" data, and in the age of Big Data the economics of storage still matter. However, solid state disk provides better economics for datasets where the speed of retrieval is more important than the cost of long-term storage. And all significant database systems are adapting to the unique physical characteristics of SSD. Some databases are being built from the ground up to exploit SSD processing characteristics.

As memory reduces in price, and the amount of memory that can be housed in a single database server increases, in-memory architectures grow ever more attractive for databases of smaller size or where latency or transaction processing speed are more important than economics of mass storage. When a database cannot fit into the memory of a single server, a distributed in-memory system may offer a compelling high-performance solution.

We've seen how in-memory database designs have arisen in each category of database system: relational, key-value, and Big Data. There are also an increasing number of hybrid designs such as Oracle's, which attempt to merge the processing benefits of an in-memory approach with the storage economics that are still only provided by traditional disk devices.

Note

1. *The End of an Architectural Era (It's Time for a Complete Rewrite),*
    http://nms.csail.mit.edu/~stavros/pubs/hstore.pdf

PART II

The Gory Details

CHAPTER 8

■ ■ ■

Distributed Database Patterns

The manager is to be blamed who distributes parts to his players which they are unable to act.

—Franz Schubert

The speed of communications is wondrous to behold. It is also true that speed can multiply the distribution of information that we know to be untrue.

—Edward R. Murrow

Administrators of web applications have traditionally had two choices when the application demand exceeds database capacity: *scaling up* by increasing the power of individual servers, or *scaling out* by adding more servers. For most of the relational database era, scaling up was the more practical option. Early relational databases did not provide a clustering option, whereas the CPU and memory supplied by a single server was constantly and exponentially increasing in line with Moore's law. Consequently, scaling out was neither practical nor necessary.

However, as database workloads shifted from client-server applications running behind the firewall to web applications with potentially global scope, it became increasingly difficult to support workload and availability requirements on a single server. Furthermore, Internet applications were often subject to unpredictable and massive growth in workload: it became possible for an application to "go viral" and to suddenly experience exponential growth in demand. The economic sweet spot for computer hardware and the imperatives of growth increasingly encouraged clusters of servers rather than single, monolithic proprietary servers. A scale-out solution for databases became imperative.

To address the demands of web-scale applications, a new generation of distributed nonrelational databases emerged. In this chapter, we'll dive deep into the architectures of these distributed database systems.

Distributed Relational Databases

The first database systems were designed to run on a single computer. Indeed, prior to the client-server revolution, all components of early database applications—including all the application code—would reside on a single system: the *mainframe*.

In this centralized model, all program code runs on the server, and users communicate with the application code through dumb terminals (the terminals are "dumb" because they contain no application code). In the client-server model, presentation and business logic were implemented on workstations—usually Windows PCs—that communicated with a single back-end database server. In early Internet applications, business logic was implemented on one or more web application servers, while presentation logic was shared between the web browser and the application server, which still almost always communicated with a single database server.

Figure 8-1 Illustrates the three architectures, showing how each pattern continued to rely on a single, monolithic database server.

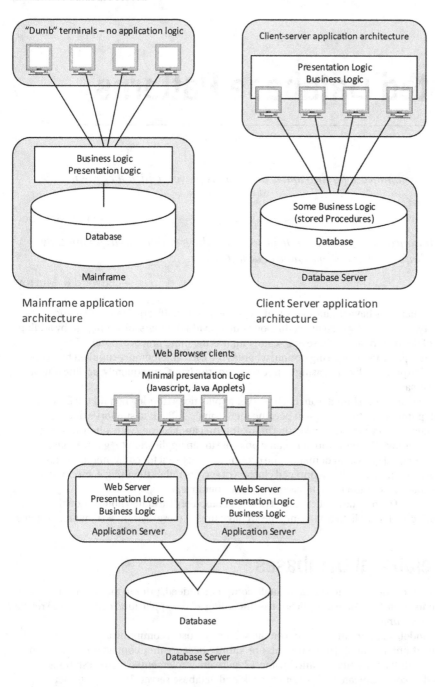

Figure 8-1. Mainframe, client-server, and early web architectures relied on single, monolithic database servers

Replication

Database replication was initially adopted as a means of achieving high availability. Using replication, database administrators could configure a *standby database* that could take over for the primary database in the event of failure.

Database replication often took advantage of the *transaction log* that most relational databases used to support ACID transactions. We introduced the transaction log pattern in the context of in-memory databases in Chapter 7. When a transaction commits in an ACID-compliant database, the transaction record is immediately written to the transaction log so that it is preserved in the event of failure. A replication process monitoring the transaction log can apply changes to a backup database, thereby creating a replica.

Figure 8-2 illustrates the log-based replication approach. Database transactions are written in an asynchronous "lazy" manner to the database files (1), but a database transaction immediately writes to the transaction log upon commit (2). The replication process monitors the transaction log and applies transactions as they are written to the read-only slave database (3). Replication is usually asynchronous, but in some databases the commit can be deferred until the transaction has been replicated to the slave.

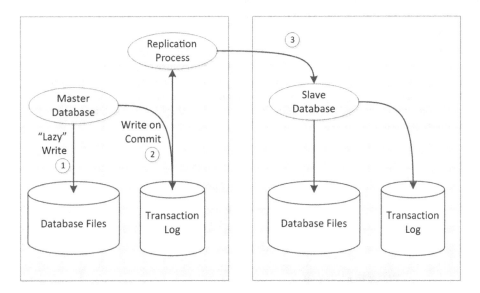

Figure 8-2. *Log-based replication*

As we saw in Chapter 3, replication is typically a first step toward distributing the database load across multiple servers. Using replication, the read workload can be distributed in a scale-out fashion, although database transactions must still be applied to the master copy.

Shared Nothing and Shared Disk

The replication pattern for distributing database workloads works well to distribute read activity across multiple servers, but it does not distribute transactional write loads, which still must be directed exclusively to the master server.

Replication is also of limited value for distributing data warehousing workloads. An OLTP workload typically consists of large numbers of short-duration requests. However, in a data warehousing environment, the workload usually consists of smaller numbers of data-intensive queries. In high-end database servers, these massive queries are executed by multiple processes or threads, each of which can leverage a separate CPU core and take advantage of multiple IO channels.

Parallelizing a query across multiple database servers requires a new approach. Data warehousing vendors provided a solution to this problem by implementing a *shared-nothing* clustered database architecture. Like so many concepts in the relational world, the shared-nothing idea was most notably outlined by Michael Stonebraker in the 1980s. A database server may be classified as:

- **Shared-everything**: In this case, every database process shares the same memory, CPU, and disk resources. Sharing memory implies that every process is on the same server and hence this architecture is a single-node database architecture.

- **Shared-disk**: In this case, database processes may exist on separate nodes in the cluster and have access to the CPU and memory of the server on which they reside. However, every process has equal access to disk devices, which are shared across all nodes of the cluster.

- **Shared-nothing**: In this case, each node in the cluster has access not only to its own memory and CPU but also to dedicated disk devices and its own subset of the database. We've seen several examples of shared-nothing architecture in this book already, including the sharded MySQL design in Chapter 3 and the VoltDB partitioning scheme in Chapter 7.

The shared-nothing model became the basis for several early clustered database systems, such as Teradata. It provides an attractive model for data warehousing workloads because queries can easily be parallelized across the multiple nodes based on the data they wish to access. For a system that wishes to maximize read-centric workloads, it is significantly easier to implement. Databases implementing the shared-nothing model often refer to themselves as *massively parallel processing (MPP)* databases. Figure 8-3 illustrates the shared-nothing model.

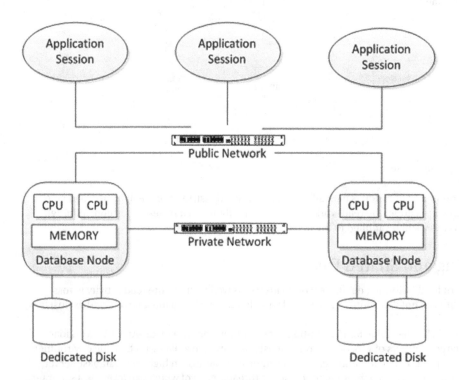

Figure 8-3. *Shared-nothing database architecture*

The shared-nothing architecture tends to break down in transactional scenarios, because of the need to coordinate transactions that may touch data on multiple nodes. Since ACID transactions are "all or nothing," it's necessary for all nodes in the transaction to coordinate closely on transaction execution. This coordination, known as *two-phase commit,* is notoriously difficult to implement and may result in "in doubt" transactional outcomes and poor transactional performance.

The other drawback of the shared-nothing architecture is that without careful partitioning, the cluster workload becomes unbalanced. Maintaining correct partitioning becomes a major operational activity. When nodes are added or removed from the cluster, expensive rebalancing is required.

A *shared-disk* architecture theoretically allows for greater and more elastic scalability, and it removes the need for rebalancing operations. It also provides a more economical high-availability solution, since no node has exclusive responsibility for any particular set of data. In shared-nothing, a node failure results in a portion of the database being unavailable, while in shared-disk, the remaining nodes are able to take over responsibility for the failed node.

The challenge for the shared-disk architecture is the need to coordinate cached data across nodes. Without an in-memory cache, performance for all operations will degrade to disk speed. But to maintain a consistent view of data across all nodes, each node needs to maintain a consistent cache. Maintaining this *cache coherency* puts a strain on the network between the nodes and is difficult to successfully implement.

To date, the only surviving commercially successful shared-disk RDBMS is Oracle's *Real Application Clusters (RAC)* cluster database. RAC is the basis for Oracle's Exadata database machine and cloud database offerings. Figure 8-4 illustrates the shared-disk model.

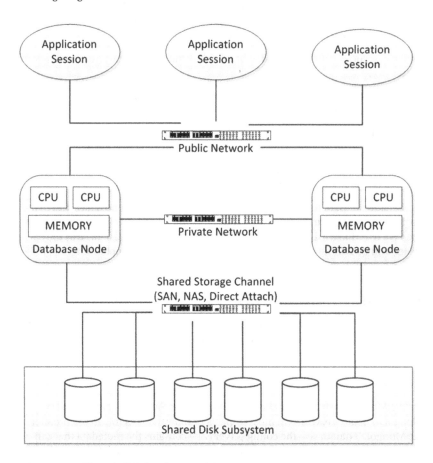

Figure 8-4. *Shared-disk database architecture*

Nonrelational Distributed Databases

Maintaining ACID transactional integrity across multiple nodes in a distributed relational database is a significant challenge. However, in nonrelational database systems, ACID compliance is often not provided. For nonrelational distributed databases, the following considerations become more significant:

- **Balancing availability and consistency**: As we saw in Chapter 3, Brewer's CAP theorem argues that a distributed database that aims to scale beyond a single local network must choose between availability and consistency in the event of a network partition. An ACID-compliant database is obliged to favor consistency over all other factors. However, a nonrelational database without the constraint of strict ACID compliance can strike a different balance.

- **Hardware economics**: Even small differences in the cost of individual servers multiply quickly when a system scales to thousands or hundreds of thousands of nodes. Therefore, an economical database architecture will better leverage commodity hardware so as to take advantage of the best price/performance ratios available. Furthermore, it may become necessary to be able to cope with disparities between server configurations, so that new hardware can be added to the database cluster without requiring all existing nodes to be upgraded to the latest hardware specification.

- **Resilience**:In a massive database cluster, nodes will fail from time to time. In the event of these failures, there can be no data loss, interruption to availability, or maybe even failure at the transaction level.

There have been three broad categories of distributed database architecture adopted by next-generation databases. The three models are:

- Variations on **traditional sharding architecture,** in which data is segmented across nodes based on the value of a "shard key."

- Variations on the Hadoop HDFS/HBase model, in which an **"omniscient master"** determines where data should be located in the cluster, based on load and other factors

- The Amazon Dynamo **consistent hashing model**, in which data is distributed across nodes of the cluster based on predictable mathematical hashing of a key value.

Replication may be inherent within each of these architectures in order to ensure that no data is lost in the event of a server failure, although the replication strategies vary. We look at examples of each of these approaches in the remainder of this chapter. We use MongoDB as an example of a sharding architecture, HBase as the example of an omniscient master, and Cassandra as an example of Dynamo-style consistent hashing.

MongoDB Sharding and Replication

MongoDB supports sharding to provide scale-out capabilities and replication for high availability. Although each can be implemented independently of the other, they are usually both present in a production scenario.

Sharding

A high-level representation of the MongoDB sharding architecture is shown in Figure 8-5. Each shard is implemented by a distinct MongoDB database, which in most respects is unaware of its role in the broader sharded server (1). A separate MongoDB database—the config server (2)—contains the metadata that can be used to determine how data is distributed across shards. A router process (3) is responsible for routing requests to the appropriate shard server.

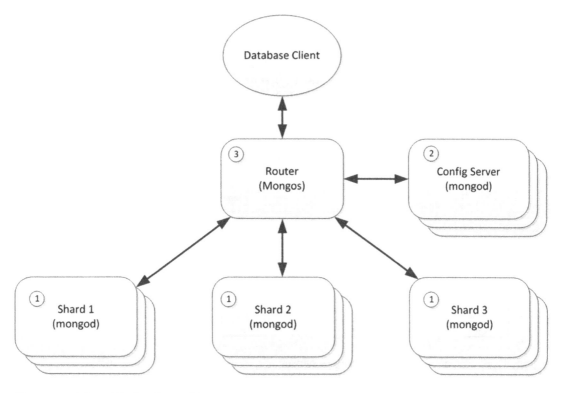

Figure 8-5. *MongoDB sharding architecture*

You may recall that in MongoDB, a collection is used to store multiple JSON documents that usually have some common attributes. To shard a collection, we choose a *shard key,* which is one or more indexed attributes that will be used to determine the distribution of documents across shards. The B-tree structure of the MongoDB index contains the information necessary to distribute keys evenly across shards.

Sharding Mechanisms

Distribution of data across shards can be either *range based* or *hash based*. In range-based partitioning, each shard is allocated a specific range of shard key values. MongoDB consults the distribution of key values in the index to ensure that each shard is allocated approximately the same number of keys. In hash-based sharding, the keys are distributed based on a hash function applied to the shard key.

There are advantages and compromises involved in each scheme. Figure 8-6 illustrates the performance trade-offs inherent in range and hash sharding for inserts and range queries.

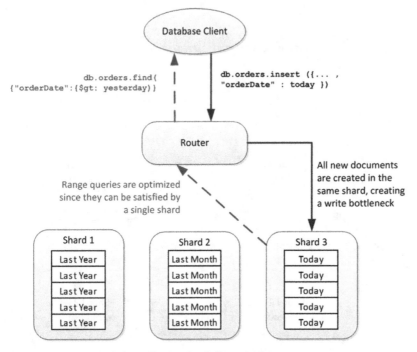

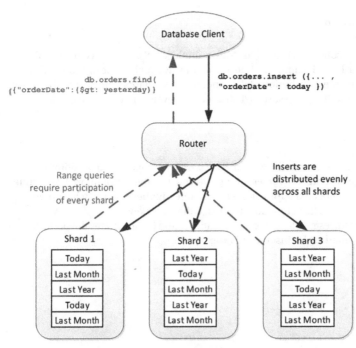

Figure 8-6. *Comparison of range and hash sharding in MongoDB*

Range-based partitioning allows for more efficient execution of queries that process ranges of values, since these queries can often be resolved by accessing a single shard. Hash-based sharding requires that range queries be resolved by accessing all shards. On the other hand, hash-based sharding is more likely to distribute "hot" documents (unfilled orders or recent posts, for instance) evenly across the cluster, thus balancing the load more effectively.

However, when range partitioning is enabled and the shard key is continuously incrementing, the load tends to aggregate against only one of the shards, thus unbalancing the cluster. With hash-based partitioning new documents are distributed evenly across all members of the cluster. Furthermore, although MongoDB tries to distribute shard keys evenly across the cluster, it may be that there are hotspots within particular shard key ranges which again unbalance the load. Hash-based sharding is more likely to evenly distribute the load in this scenario.

Tag-aware sharding allows the MongoDB administrator to fine-tune the distribution of documents to shards. By associating a shard with the tag, and associating a range of keys within a collection with the same tag, the administrator can explicitly determine the shard on which these documents will reside. This can be used to archive data to shards on cheaper, slower storage or to direct particular data to a specific data center or geography.

Cluster Balancing

When hash-based sharding is implemented, the number of documents in each shard tends to remain balanced in most scenarios. However, in a range-based sharding scenario, it is easy for the shards to become unbalanced, especially if the shard key is based on a continuously increasing value, such as an auto-incrementing primary key ID.

For this reason, MongoDB will periodically assess the balance of shards across the cluster and perform rebalance operations, if needed. The unit of rebalance is the *shard chunk*. Shards consist of chunks—typically 64MB in size—that contain contiguous values of shard keys (or of hashed shard keys). If a shard is added or removed from the cluster, or if the balancer determines that a shard has become unbalanced, it can move chunks from one shard to another. The chunks themselves will be split if they grow too large.

Replication

Sharding is almost always combined with replication so as to ensure both availability and scalability in a production MongoDB deployment.

In MongoDB, data can be replicated across machines by the means of *replica sets*. A replica set consists of a primary node together with two or more secondary nodes. The primary node accepts all write requests, which are propagated asynchronously to the secondary nodes.

The primary node is determined by an election involving all available nodes. To be eligible to become primary, a node must be able to contact more than half of the replica set. This ensures that if a network partitions a replica set in two, only one of the partitions will attempt to establish a primary.

The successful primary will be elected based on the number of nodes to which it is in contact, together with a priority value that may be assigned by the system administrator. Setting a priority of 0 to an instance prevents it from ever being elected as primary. In the event of a tie, the server with the most recent *optime*— the timestamp of the last operation—will be selected.

The primary stores information about document changes in a collection within its local database, called the *oplog*. The primary will continuously attempt to apply these changes to secondary instances.

Members within a replica set communicate frequently via heartbeat messages. If a primary finds it is unable to receive heartbeat messages from more than half of the secondaries, then it will renounce its primary status and a new election will be called. Figure 8-7 illustrates a three-member replica set and shows how a network partition leads to a change of primary.

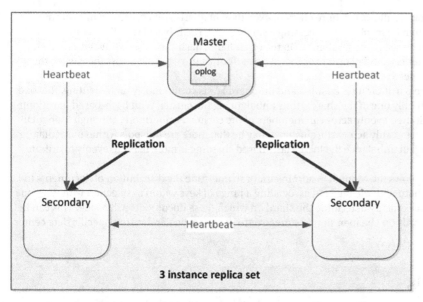

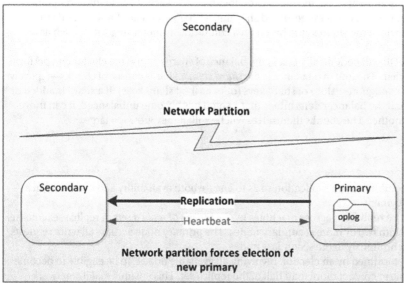

Figure 8-7. *MongoDB replica set and primary failover*

Arbiters are special servers that can vote in the primary election, but that don't hold data. For large databases, these arbiters can avoid the necessity of creating otherwise unnecessary extra servers to ensure that a quorum is available when electing a primary.

Write Concern and Read Preference

A MongoDB application has some control over the behavior of read and write operations, providing a degree of tunable consistency and availability.

- The **write concern** setting determines when MongoDB regards a write operation as having completed. By default, write operations complete once the primary has received the modification. This means that if the primary should fail irrecoverably, then data might be lost. To ensure that write operations have been propagated beyond the primary, the client can issue a blocking call, which will wait until the write has been received by all secondaries, a majority of secondaries, or a specified number of secondaries.

- The **read preference** determines where the client sends read requests. By default, all read requests are sent to the primary. However, the client driver can request that read requests be routed to the secondary if the primary is unavailable, or to secondaries, or to whichever server is "nearest." The latter setting is intended to favor low latency over consistency.

The default settings for read preference and write concern result in MongoDB behaving as a strictly consistent system: everybody will see the same version of a document. Allowing reads to be satisfied from a secondary node results in a more eventually consistent behavior, unless the write concern is configured to block writes until they reach secondary nodes.

We'll look more at MongoDB consistency in the next chapter.

HBase

HBase can be thought of both as the "Hadoop database" and as "open-source BigTable." That is, we can describe HBase as a mechanism for providing random access database services on top of the Hadoop HDFS file system, or we can think of HBase as an open-source implementation of Google's BigTable database that happens to use HDFS for data storage. Both of these descriptions are accurate: although HBase theoretically can be implemented on top of any distributed file system—or, indeed, even a nondistributed file system—it's almost always implemented on top of Hadoop HDFS, and many of HBase's architectural assumptions reflect this. On the other hand, HBase implements real-time random access database functionality, which is essentially distinct from the base capabilities of Hadoop.

In the discussion that follows, we are going to concentrate on the HBase architecture as it is most commonly encountered: as implemented on top of HDFS. The implementation of HBase over HDFS creates a sort of hybrid, a mix of shared-nothing and shared-disk clustering patterns. On the one hand, every HBase node can access any element of data in the database because all data is accessible via HDFS. On the other hand, it is typical to co-locate HBase servers with HDFS DataNodes, which means that in practice each node tends to be responsible for an exclusive subset of data stored on local disk.

In either case, HDFS provides the reliability guarantees for data on disk: the HBase architecture is not required to concern itself with write mirroring or disk failure management, because these are handled automatically by the underlying HDFS system.

We introduced HDFS and Hadoop architecture in Chapter 2; please refer to that chapter if you need a refresher. HDFS implements a distributed file system using disks that are directly attached to the servers— *DataNodes*—that constitute a Hadoop cluster. HDFS automatically manages redundancy of data: by default, data is replicated across three DataNodes, one of which (if possible) is located on a separate server rack.

Tables, Regions, and RegionServers

HBase implements a wide column store based on Google's BigTable specification. We touched on that data model in Chapter 2, and we'll talk more about it in Chapter 10. For now, we can consider HBase tables as potentially massive tabular datasets that are implemented on disk by a variable number of HDFS files called *Hfiles*.

All rows in an HBase table are identified by a unique *row key*. A table of nontrivial size will be split into multiple horizontal partitions called *regions*. Each region consists of a contiguous, sorted range of key values. This resembles the MongoDB range-based sharding scheme we described earlier in this chapter.

Read or write access to a region is controlled by a *RegionServer*. Each RegionServer normally runs on a dedicated host, and is typically co-located with the Hadoop DataNode.

There will usually be more than one region in each RegionServer. As regions grow, they split into multiple regions based on configurable policies. Regions may also be split manually. We'll discuss this more a little later in this chapter.

Each HBase installation will include a Hadoop *Zookeeper* service that is implemented across multiple nodes. Hbase may share this Zookeeper ensemble with the rest of the Hadoop cluster or use a dedicated service.

When an HBase client wishes to read or write to a specific key value, it will ask Zookeeper for the address of the RegionServer that controls the HBase catalog. This catalog consists of the tables -ROOT- and .META., which identify the RegionServers that are responsible for specific key ranges. The client will then establish a connection with that RegionServer and request to read or write the key value concerned.

The HBase *master server* performs a variety of housekeeping tasks. In particular, it controls the balancing of regions among RegionServers. If a RegionServer is added or removed, the master will organize for its regions to be relocated to other RegionServers.

Figure 8-8 illustrates some of these architectural elements. An HBase client consults Zookeeper to determine the location of the HBase catalog tables (1), which can be then be interrogated to determine the location of the appropriate RegionServer (2). The client will then request to read or modify a key value from the appropriate RegionServer (3). The RegionServer reads or writes to the appropriate disk files, which are located on HDFS (4).

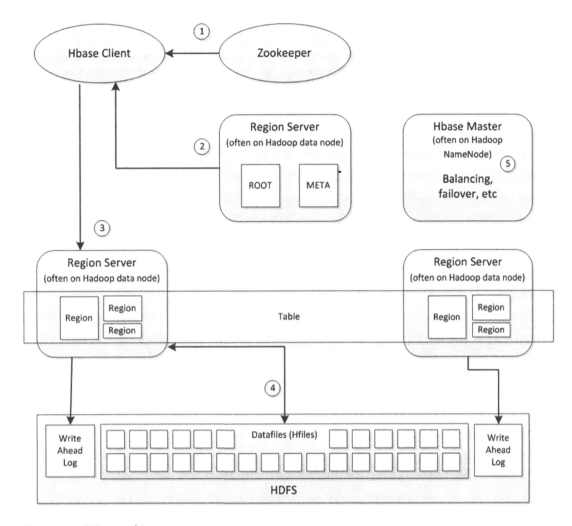

Figure 8-8. *HBase architecture*

Caching and Data Locality

The RegionServer includes a *block cache* that can satisfy many reads from memory, and a *MemStore*, which writes in memory before being flushed to disk. However, to ensure durability of the writes, each RegionServer has a dedicated *write ahead log* (*WAL*), which journals all writes to HDFS. This architecture is an implementation of the *log-structured merge tree* (*LSM*) pattern that is more fully described in Chapter 10.

The RegionServer can act as a generic HDFS client, communicating with the HDFS NameNode to perform read and write operations to files. In the most typical production deployment scenario, each RegionServer is located on a Hadoop NameNode, and as a result, region data will be co-located with the RegionServer, providing good *data locality*. This data locality will be disrupted by rebalance operations and RegionServer failovers, but compactions—which merge HDFS disk files as described in Chapter 10—will restore data locality.

Hadoop and HBase support a mode known as *short-circuit reads,* in which the RegionServer can read directly from local disk, bypassing the NameNode. This, of course, is only possible when the data is stored on a DataNode that also hosts the RegionServer.

The three levels of data locality are shown in Figure 8-9. In the first configuration, the RegionServer and the DataNode are located on different servers and all reads and writes have to pass across the network. In the second configuration, the RegionServer and the DataNode are co-located and all reads and writes pass through the DataNode, but they are satisfied by the local disk. In the third scenario, short-circuit reads are configured and the RegionServer can read directly from the local disk.

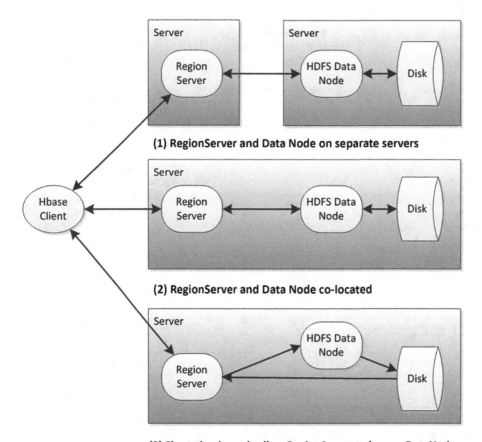

Figure 8-9. *Data locality in HBase*

Rowkey Ordering

The HBase region partitioning scheme requires that regions consist of contiguous ranges of *rowkeys*. This range-based partitioning has a significant impact on performance when the rowkey contains some form of monotonically incrementing value, such as a timestamp or a incrementing counter. In this event, all write operations will be directed to a specific region and hence to a single RegionServer. This can create a bottleneck on write throughput.

HBase offers no internal mechanisms to mitigate this issue. It's up to the application designer to construct a key that is either randomized—a hash of the timestamp, for instance—or is prefixed in some way with a more balanced attribute. In the HBase time series database *OpenTSDB*, the timestamp is prefixed by a metric identifier variable that has a large number of values. Data for a single metric will be located in a specific RegionServer, but data for a specific timestamp will be distributed across all the RegionServers.

RegionServer Splits, Balancing, and Failure

As regions grow, they will be split by the RegionServer as required. The new regions will remain controlled by the original RegionServer—at least initially—but they are eligible for relocation during load-balancing operations. The default region-split policy results in regions of incrementally greater size, with the first split occurring after as little as 128M, while the tenth region will be approximately 10GB in size. However, it is possible to split regions manually or to override the split policy with custom code.

One of the most important responsibilities of the HBase *master node* is to balance regions across RegionServers. The master will periodically evaluate the balance of regions across all RegionServers, and should it detect an imbalance, it will migrate regions to another server. This is a "soft" rebalance—the region's data remains in its original location on HDFS disk, but the responsibility for managing that data is moved to a different RegionServer.

As noted earlier, rebalancing tends to result in a loss of data locality: when the RegionServer acquires responsibility for a new region, that region will probably be located on a remote data node—at least until the next major compaction.

Region Replicas

In earlier versions of HBase, a failure of a RegionServer would require a failover to a new RegionServer. Because the RegionServers don't actually store the data for a region (the data is in HDFS), a failure is not catastrophic. The master would detect the failure and allocate the regions concerned to other RegionServers in a similar way to the balancing operation. However, some interruption of service would result.

Region replicas allow for redundant copies of regions to be stored on multiple RegionServers. Should a RegionServer fail, these replicas can be used to service client requests.

The original RegionServer serves as the master copy of the region. Read-only replicas of the region are distributed to other RegionServers—located in other racks, if possible—which then "follow" the primary RegionServer. Writes to these replicas are asynchronous to primary RegionServer writes, so data in the replicas will not always be up to date. We'll see in the next chapter how the configuration of HBase region replicas affects consistency and availability.

HBase also supports a replication facility that can be used to stand up a duplicated HBase database. This is typically used to duplicate an entire HBase database in another data center.

Cassandra

In Chapter 3, we introduced Amazon's Dynamo database and the concept of consistent hashing. A number of open-source systems have implemented the Dynamo model. In this chapter, we consider the Cassandra implementation.

Gossip

In HBase and MongoDB, we encountered the concept of master nodes—nodes which have a specialized supervisory function, coordinate activities of other nodes, and record the current state of the database cluster. In Cassandra and other Dynamo databases, there are no specialized master nodes. Every node is equal and every node is capable of performing any of the activities required for cluster operation.

Nodes in Cassandra do, however, have short-term specialized responsibilities. For instance, when a client performs an operation, a node will be allocated as the *coordinator* for that operation. When a new member is added to the cluster, a node will be nominated as the *seed node* from which the new node will seek information. However, these short-term responsibilities can be performed by any node in the cluster.

One of the advantages of a master node is that it can maintain a canonical version of cluster configuration and state. In the absence of such a master node, Cassandra requires that all members of the cluster be kept up to date with the current state of cluster configuration and status. This is achieved by use of the *gossip* protocol. Every second each member of the cluster will transmit information about its state and the state of any other nodes it is aware of to up to three other nodes in the cluster. In this way, cluster status is constantly being updated across all members of the cluster.

The gossip protocol is aptly named: when people gossip, they generally tend to gossip about other people! Likewise, in Cassandra, the nodes gossip about other nodes as well as about their own state.

Cluster configuration is persisted in the system *keyspace,* which is available to all members of the cluster. A keyspace is roughly analogous to a schema in a relational database—the system keyspace contains tables that record metadata about the cluster configuration.

This architecture eliminates any single point of failure within the cluster. Although distributed databases with master nodes have strategies to allow for rapid failover, the crash of a master node usually creates a temporary reduction in availability, such as momentarily falling back to read-only mode.

One of the main topics of gossip within a Cassandra cluster is node availability. The traditional mechanism for detecting node failure is to send heartbeats between nodes. However, in a widely distributed system, the heartbeats may be lost because of network issues rather than actual node failure. For this reason, Cassandra failure detection is more probabilistic: if you like, nodes in the cluster become increasingly "worried" about other nodes. If it seems likely that a node is down, then the operations will be directed to "known good" nodes.

Consistent Hashing

Cassandra and other dynamo-based databases distribute data throughout the cluster by using consistent hashing. The rowkey (analogous to a primary key in an RDBMS) is hashed. Each node is allocated a range of hash values, and the node that has the specific range for a hashed key value takes responsibility for the initial placement of that data.

In the default Cassandra partitioning scheme, the hash values range from -2^{63} to $2^{63}-1$. Therefore, if there were four nodes in the cluster and we wanted to assign equal numbers of hashes to each node, then the hash ranges for each would be approximately as follows:

Node	Low Hash	High Hash
Node A	-2^{63}	$-2^{63}/2$
Node B	$-2^{63}/2$	0
Node C	0	$2^{63}/2$
Node D	$2^{63}/2$	2^{63}

We usually visualize the cluster as a ring: the circumference of the ring represents all the possible hash values, and the location of the node on the ring represents its area of responsibility. Figure 8-10 illustrates simple consistent hashing: the value for a rowkey is hashed, which determines its position on "the ring." Nodes in the cluster take responsibility for ranges of values within the ring, and therefore take ownership of specific rowkey values.

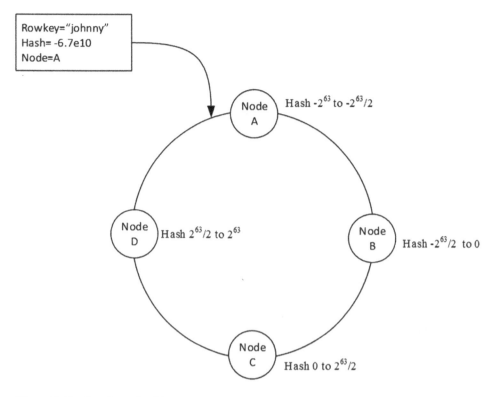

Figure 8-10. *Consistent hashing*

The four-node cluster in Figure 8-10 is well balanced because every node is responsible for hash ranges of similar magnitude. But we risk unbalancing the cluster as we add nodes. If we double the number of nodes in the cluster, then we can assign the new nodes at points on the ring between existing nodes and the cluster will remain balanced. However, doubling the cluster is usually impractical: it's more economical to grow the cluster incrementally.

Early versions of Cassandra had two options when adding a new node. We could either remap all the hash ranges, or we could map the new node within an existing range. In the first option we obtain a balanced cluster, but only after an expensive rebalancing process. In the second option the cluster becomes unbalanced; since each node is responsible for the region of the ring between itself and its predecessor, adding a new node without changing the ranges of other nodes essentially splits a region in half. Figure 8-11 shows how adding a node to the cluster can unbalance the distribution of hash key ranges.

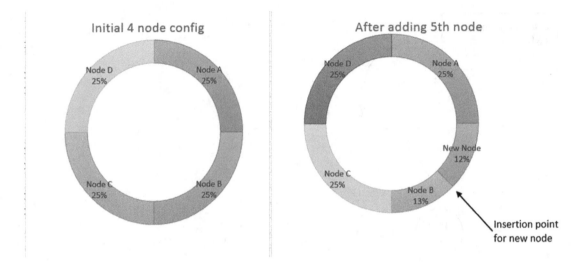

Figure 8-11. *Adding a node to a Cassandra cluster (without virtual nodes)*

Virtual nodes, implemented in Cassandra, Riak, and many other Dynamo-based systems, provide a solution to this issue. When using virtual nodes, the hash ranges are calculated for a relatively large number of virtual nodes—256 virtual nodes per physical node, typically—and these virtual nodes are assigned to physical nodes. Now when a new node is added, specific virtual nodes can be reallocated to the new node, resulting in a balanced configuration with minimal overhead. Figure 8-12 illustrates the relationship between virtual nodes and physical nodes.

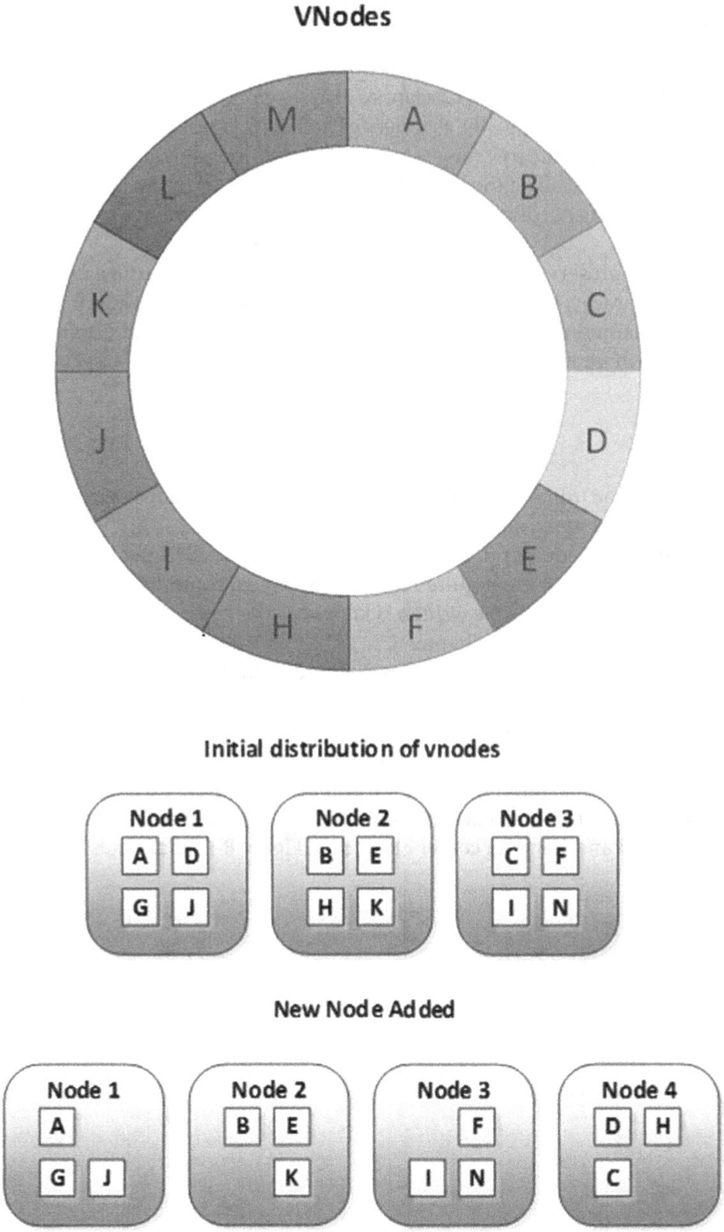

VNodes

Figure 8-12. *Using virtual nodes to partition data among physical nodes*

Virtual nodes have some other advantages. For instance, it is easier to balance a cluster made up of heterogeneous systems, since you can allocate more virtual nodes to more powerful new machines and fewer virtual nodes to underpowered older machines. Also, if a node dies it can be reconstituted from a larger number of physical machines, thus sharing the overhead of recovery more equitably across the cluster.

Order-Preserving Partitioning

The Cassandra *partitioner* determines how keys are distributed across nodes. The default partitioner uses consistent hashing, as described in the previous section. Cassandra also supports *order-preserving partitioners* that distribute data across the nodes of the cluster as ranges of actual (e.g., not hashed) rowkeys. This has the advantage of isolating requests for specific row ranges to specific machines, but it can lead to an unbalanced cluster and may create hotspots, especially if the key value is incrementing. For instance, if the key value is a timestamp and the order-preserving partitioner is implemented, then all new rows will tend to be created on a single node of the cluster.

In early versions of Cassandra, the order-preserving petitioner might be warranted to optimize range queries that could not be satisfied in any other way; however, following the introduction of secondary indexes, the order-preserving petitioner is maintained primarily for backward compatibility, and Cassandra documentation recommends against its use in new applications.

Replicas

So far, we have seen how Cassandra allocates the initial copy of a data item to a node. The consistent hashing algorithm also determines where replicas of data items are stored.

The node responsible for the hash range that equates to a specific rowkey value is called the *coordinator* node. The coordinator is responsible for ensuring that the required number of replica copies of the data are also written. The number of nodes to which the data must be written is known as the *replication factor*, and is the "N" in the NWR notation that we first encountered in Chapter 3.

By default, the coordinator will write copies of the data to the next N-1 nodes on the ring. So if the replication factor is 3, the coordinator will send replicas of the data item to the next two nodes on the ring. In this scenario, each node will be replicating data *from* the previous two nodes on the ring and replicating *to* the next two nodes on the ring. This simple scheme is referred to as the *simple replication strategy*.

Cassandra also allows you to configure a more complex and highly available scheme. The *Network Topology Aware replication strategy* ensures that copies will be written to nodes on other server racks within the same data center, or optionally to nodes in another data center altogether. Figure 8-13 illustrates these two replication strategies.

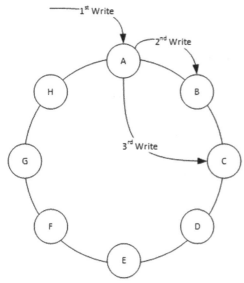

Simple replication strategy: Replicas written to next adjacent nodes on the ring

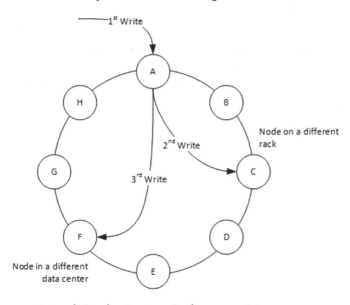

Network Topolgy Strategy: Replicas are written to nodes on another rack or optionally another data center

Figure 8-13. *Replication strategies in Cassandra*

Snitches

Cassandra uses *snitches* to help optimize read and write operations. A variety of snitches may be configured.

- The **simpleSnitch** returns only a list of nodes on the ring. This is sufficient for the simple replication strategy we discussed in the previous section.

- The **RackInferringSnitch** uses the IP addresses of hosts to infer their rack and data center location. This snitch supports the network aware replication strategy.

- The **PropertyFileSnitch** uses data in the configuration file rather than IP addresses to determine the data center and rack topology.

In addition, all snitches monitor the read latency for requests and use this to build a statistical model that can route requests to the best-performing nodes.

Specialized snitches exist that understand the networked topology inside various cloud platforms, such as Amazon EC2.

Summary

In this chapter we've reviewed distributed database patterns for traditional relational databases and for several nonrelational systems. Relational database architecture was developed in an era of large, monolithic database servers, and most relational databases still run as a single instance. However, shared-nothing clustering is commonplace in massively parallel data warehouses, and Oracle has a commercially successful shared-disk clustered RDBMS.

We looked in detail at three distributed nonrelational database systems. MongoDB uses a combination of sharding and replication to enable distributed processing. HBase leverages the distributed file system of the Hadoop Distributed File System together with a range-partitioning strategy to achieve a highly scalable solution. Cassandra uses the consistent hashing scheme pioneered in Amazon's Dynamo system to create a symmetrical clustering solution in which no master servers are required.

In a distributed database, multiple copies of data are typically maintained across the cluster. In the next chapter, we'll see how these databases manage data consistency within such a distributed system.

■ ■ ■

CHAPTER 9

Consistency Models

For changes to be of any true value, they've got to be lasting and consistent.

—Tony Robbins, motivational speaker

Consistency is contrary to nature, contrary to life. The only completely consistent people are dead.

—Aldous Huxley

One of the biggest factors powering the nonrelational database revolution is a desire to escape the restrictions of strict ACID consistency. It's widely believed that the new breed of nonrelational databases provide only weak or at best eventual consistency, and that the underlying consistency mechanisms are simplistic. This belief represents a fundamental misunderstanding of nonrelational database systems. Nonrelational systems offer a range of consistency guarantees, including strict consistency, albeit at the single-object level. And in fact, there are some complex architectures required to balance an acceptable degree of consistency when we lose the strict and predictable rules provided by the ACID transaction model.

In the absence of the ACID transaction model, a variety of approaches to consistency have emerged: these include relatively familiar concepts such as eventual consistency and various tunable consistency models. Many nonrelational databases are, in fact, strictly consistent with respect to individual objects, even if they don't support strict multi-object consistency. And although ACID transactions are absent, systems such as Cassandra support a simpler, lightweight transaction model.

Consistency models have a huge effect on database concurrency—the ability for multiple users to access data simultaneously—and on availability. Understanding how a database system treats consistency is essential in order to determine whether that database can meet the needs of an application.

Types of Consistency

Ironically, there is significant variation in how the term "consistency" is used in the database community. Consistency might mean any of the following:

- **Consistency with other users**: If two users query the database at the same time, will they see the same data? Traditional relational systems would generally try to ensure that they do, while nonrelational databases often take a more relaxed stance.

- **Consistency within a single session**: Does the data maintain some logical consistency within the context of a single database session? For instance, if we modify a row and then read it again, do we see our own update?

- **Consistency within a single request**: Does an individual request return data that is internally coherent? For instance, when we read all the rows in a relational table, we are generally guaranteed to see the state of the table as it was at a moment in time. Modifications to the table that occurred after we began our query are not included.

- **Consistency with reality**: Does the data correspond with the reality that the database is trying to reflect? For example, it's not enough for a banking transaction to simply be consistent at the end of the transaction; it also has to correctly represent the actual account balances. Consistency at the expense of accuracy is not usually acceptable.

ACID and MVCC

Relational databases responded to the requirements of consistency using two major architectural patterns: *ACID transactions* and *multi-version concurrency control (MVCC)*.

We've covered ACID transactions extensively already in this book. To recap, ACID transactions should be:

- **Atomic**: The transaction is indivisible—either all the statements in the transaction are applied to the database or none are applied.

- **Consistent**: The database remains in a consistent state before and after transaction execution.

- **Isolated**: While multiple transactions can be executed by one or more users simultaneously, one transaction should not see the effects of other in-progress transactions.

- **Durable**: Once a transaction is saved to the database (in SQL databases via the COMMIT command), its changes are expected to persist even if there is a failure of operating system or hardware.

■ **Note** Even relational databases such as Oracle don't implement the strict isolation between transactions that ACID demands by default. The overhead for completely isolating all transactions is usually too high.

The easiest way to implement ACID consistency is with *locks*. Using lock-based consistency, if a session is reading an item, no other session can modify it, and if a session is modifying an item, no other session can read it. However lock-based consistency leads to unacceptably high contention and low concurrency.

To provide ACID consistency without excessive locking, relational database systems almost universally adopted the *multi-version concurrency control (MVCC)* model. In this model, multiple copies of data are tagged with timestamps or change identifiers that allow the database to construct a *snapshot* of the database at a given point in time. In this way, MVCC provides for transaction isolation and consistency while maximizing concurrency.

For example, in MVCC, if a database table is subjected to modifications between the time a session starts reading the table and the time the session finishes, the database will use previous versions of table data to ensure that the session sees a consistent version. MVCC also means that until a transaction commits, other sessions do not see the transaction's modifications—other sessions look at older versions of the data. These older copies of the data are also used to roll back transactions that do not complete successfully.

Figure 9-1 illustrates the MVCC model. A database session initiates a transaction at time t1 (1). At time t2, the session updates data in a database table (2); this results in a new version of that data being created (3). At about the same time, a second database session queries the database table, but because the transaction from the first session has not yet been committed, they see the previous version of the data (4). After the first session commits the transaction (5), the second database session will read from the modified version of the data (6).

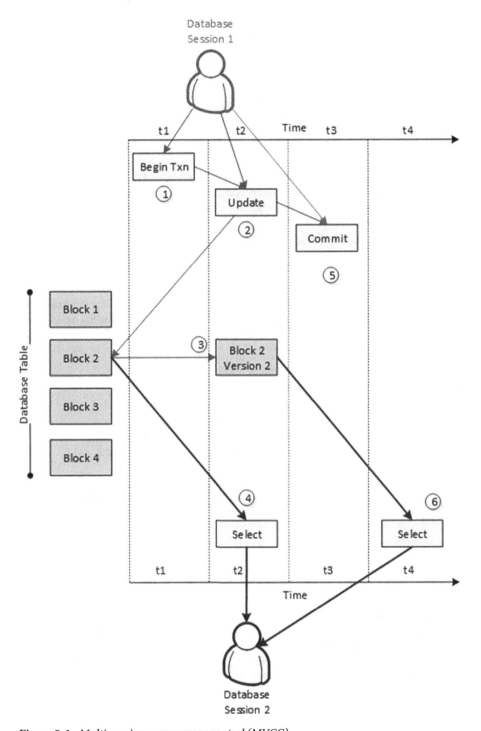

Figure 9-1. *Multi-version concurrency control (MVCC)*

The big advantage of MVCC is a reduction in lock overhead. In the example shown in Figure 9-1, without MVCC the update would have created a blocking lock that would have prevented the second session from reading the data until the transaction was completed.

Global Transaction Sequence Numbers

MVCC can use transaction timestamps to determine which versions of data should be made visible to specific queries. However, most databases use a global transaction ID rather than an explicit timestamp. This is called the *system change number* (*SCN*) in Oracle and the *transaction sequence number* in Microsoft SQL Server.

This sequence number is incremented whenever a transaction is initiated, and it is recorded in the structure of modified rows (or database blocks). When a query commences, it looks for rows that have a sequence number less than or equal to the value of the sequence number that was current when the query began. If the query encounters a row with a higher sequence number, it knows it must request an older version of that row.

Two-phase Commit

MVCC works in concert with the ACID transaction model to provide isolation between transactions running on a single system. Transactions that span databases in a distributed RDBMS are achieved using a *two-phase-commit* (*2PC*) protocol.

The two phases of 2PC are:

- **Commit-request phase**, in which the coordinator asks other nodes to prepare the transaction. Typically, the preparation phase involves locking the table rows concerned and applying changes without a commit.

- **Commit phase,** in which the coordinator signals all nodes to commit their transactions if the commit-request phase succeeded across all nodes. Alternatively, if any node experiences difficulties, a rollback request is sent to all nodes and the transaction fails.

It's possible for a problem to occur between the two phases, in which case the transaction may succeed on some nodes but not others; in this case, *in-doubt transactions* are created and need to be reconciled by the database administrator.

Other Levels of Consistency

The multi-table ACID transaction model is somewhat of a high-water mark in database consistency. While many next-generation databases continue to support ACID, none attempts to provide a higher level of transactional consistency, while many offer lower consistency guarantees.

The first and most significant reduction in consistency is to limit its scope to a single operation or object. In an RDBMS, we can maintain consistency across multiple statements; for instance, we can delete a row in one table and insert a row in another table as an atomic operation. In most relational databases we can require that a set of queries accessing multiple tables return a consistent view of the data from the moment the query commenced. Almost no nonrelational systems support this level of multi-object consistency.

Even within single-object operations, there are a variety of consistency levels that we can expect. In practice, the most significant levels of consistency are:

- **Strict consistency**: A read will always return the most recent data value.

- **Causal consistency**: Reads may not return the most recent value, but will not return values "out of sequence." This implies that if one session created updates A, B, and C, another session should never see update C without also being able to see update B.

- **Monotonic consistency**: In this mode, a session will never see data revert to an earlier point in time. Once we read a data item, we will never see an earlier version of that data item.

- **Read your own writes**: This is a form of eventual consistency in which you are at least guaranteed to see any operations you executed.

- **Eventual consistency**: The system may be inconsistent at any point in time, but all individual operations will eventually be consistently applied. If all updates stop, then the system will eventually reach a consistent state.

- **Weak consistency**: The system makes no guarantee that the system will ever become consistent—if, for instance, a server fails, an update might be lost.

In practice, nonrelational systems implement either strict or eventual consistency while RDBMS systems offer ACID consistency. Causal or monotonic consistency levels are not directly supported in most nonrelational systems.

Consistency in MongoDB

By default—in a single-server deployment—a MongoDB database provides strict single-document consistency. When a MongoDB document is being modified, it is locked against both reads and writes by other sessions.

However, when MongoDB replica sets are implemented, it is possible to configure something closer to eventual consistency by allowing reads to complete against secondary servers that may contain out-of-date data.

MongoDB Locking

Consistency for individual documents is achieved in MongoDB by the use of locks. Locks are used to ensure that two writes do not attempt to modfy a document simultaneously, and also that a reader will not see an inconsistent view of the data.

We saw earlier how a multi-version concurrency control (MVCC) algorithm can be used to allow readers to continue to read consistent versions of data concurrently with update activity. MVCC is widely used in relational databases because it avoids blocking readers—a reader will read a previous "version" of a data item, rather than being blocked by a lock when an update is occurring. MongoDB does not implement an MVCC system, and therefore readers are prevented from reading a document that is being updated.

The granularity of MongoDB locks has changed during its history. In versions prior to MongoDB 2.0, a single global lock serialized all write activity, blocking all concurrent readers and writers of any document across the server for the duration of any write.

Lock scope was increased to the database level in 2.2, and to the collection level in 2.8. In the MongoDB 3.0 release, locking is applied at the document level, providing the collection is stored using the WiredTiger storage engine. When document-level locking is in effect, an update to a document will only block readers or writers who wish to access the same document.

Locking is a controversial topic in MongoDB; the original "global" lock and lack of MVCC compared poorly with the mechanisms familiar in relational databases. Now that lock scope is limited to the document level, these concerns have been significantly reduced.

Replica Sets and Eventual Consistency

In a single-server MongoDB configuration—and in the default multi-server scenario—MongoDB provides strict consistency. All reads are directed to the primary server, which will always have the latest version of a document.

However, we saw in the previous chapter that we can configure the MongoDB *read preference* to allow reads from secondary servers, which might return stale data. Eventually all secondary servers should receive all updates, so this behavior can loosely be described as "eventually consistent."

HBase Consistency

HBase provides strong consistency for individual rows: HBase clients cannot simultaneously modify a row in a way that would cause it to become inconsistent. This behavior is similar to what we see in relational systems that generally use row-level locking to prevent any simultaneous updates to a single row. However, the implementation is more complex in HBase because rows may contain thousands of columns in multiple column families, which may have distinct disk storage. During an update to any column or column family within a row, the entire row will be locked by the RegionServer to prevent a conflicting update to any other column.

Read operations do not acquire locks and reads are not blocked by write operations. Instead, read operations use a form of multi-version concurrency control (MVCC), which we discussed earlier in this chapter. When read and write operations occur concurrently, the read will read a previous version of the row rather than the version being updated.

HBase uses a variation on the SCN pattern that we discussed earlier to achieve MVCC. When a write commences, it increments a write number that is stored in the cell (e.g., specific column value within the row) being modified. When the read commences, it is assigned a *read point number* that corresponds to the highest completed write point. The read can then examine data items to ensure it does not read a cell whose write number suggests it was updated since the read began.

Eventually Consistent Region Replicas

In earlier versions of HBase, strong consistency for all reads was guaranteed—you were always certain to read the most recently written version of a row. However, with the introduction of *region replicas,* introduced in Chapter 8, the possibility of a form of eventual consistency is presented.

Region replicas were introduced in order to improve HBase availability. A failure of a RegionServer would never result in data loss, but it could create a minor interruption in performance while a new RegionServer was instantiated. Region replicas allow immediate failover to a backup RegionServer, which maintains a copy of the region data.

By default, in HBase all reads are directed to the primary RegionServer, which results in strictly consistent behavior. However, if consistency for a read is configured for *timeline consistency,* then a read request will first be sent to the primary RegionServer, followed shortly by duplicate requests to the secondary RegionServer. The first server to return a result completes the request. Remember that the primary gets a head start in this contest, so if the primary is available it will usually be the first to return.

The scheme is called *timeline consistency* because the secondary RegionServer always receives region updates in the same sequence as the primary. However, this architecture does not guarantee that a secondary RegionServer will have up-to-date information; and if there are multiple secondary RegionServers, then it's possible that reads will return writes out of order, since there may be race conditions occurring among the multiple secondary servers and the primary.

Figure 9-2 illustrates RegionServer replica processing. An HBase client is issuing writes in sequential order to the master RegionServer (1). These are being replicated asynchronously to the secondary RegionServers (2); at any given moment in time some of these replications may not yet have completed (3). If a client is using timeline consistency, then it may read data from the master, but if the master is unresponsive, it may read data from one of the secondary RegionServers (4). Successive reads may return data from either of the secondaries or from the primary—so data can be returned in any sequence. The "timeline" nature of the consistency only applies to an individual secondary, not to the system as a whole.

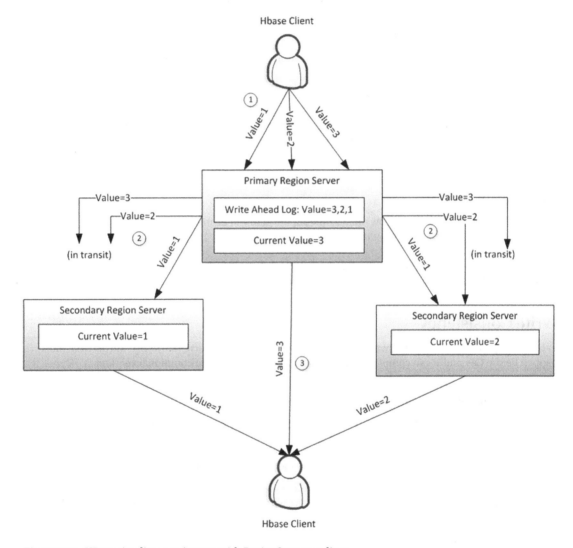

Figure 9-2. *HBase timeline consistency with RegionServer replicas*

■ **Note** Timeline consistency is not the default in HBase. By default, a client will read from the master RegionServer, in which case HBase will provide strong consistency.

Cassandra Consistency

Cassandra uses the Amazon Dynamo model of tunable consistency. This tunable consistency provides a variety of consistency levels, most of which can be specified at the level of individual requests.

We touched on the Dynamo consistency model in Chapter 3. At a high level, this model allows the following three variables to be configured independently to provide a variety of outcomes:

- **N** is the number of copies of each data item that the database will maintain.

- **W** is the number of copies of the data item that must be written before a write can return control to the application.

- **R** is the number of copies that the application will access when reading the data item.

As we saw in Chapter 3, these variables can be configured to allow for strong consistency, weak consistency, and to balance read and write performance.

Cassandra follows the Dynamo model pretty closely, but has its own unique implementation. So while the following discussion should be broadly applicable to other Dynamo systems such as Riak or DynamoDB, the details are specific to Cassandra.

Replication Factor

The replication factor determines how many copies of the data will be maintained across multiple nodes. This is specified at the keyspace (roughly equivalent to a schema) level and is equivalent to the "N" in Dynamo NRW notation.

As we saw in the previous chapter, various replication strategies can be established to ensure that replicas are distributed across multiple racks or data centers

Write Consistency

Each write operation can specify a write consistency level. The write consistency level controls what must happen before Cassandra can complete a write request. Some of the more common levels are:

- **ALL**: The write must be propagated to all nodes. This results in very strong consistency, but should a node be unavailable, the write cannot complete.

- **ONE|TWO|THREE**: The write must be propagated to the specified number of nodes. A level of ONE maximizes write performance but possibly at the expense of consistency. Depending on the read consistency settings and replication factor, TWO and THREE may or may not provide stronger consistency guarantees.

- **QUORUM**: The write must complete to a *quorum* of replica nodes. A quorum requires the majority of replicas accept the write before the write operation completes.

- **EACH_QUORUM**: The write must complete to a quorum of replica nodes in each data center. So if there are two data centers with three replicas each, at least two replicas from each data center must complete the write request before the operation can complete.

- **LOCAL_QUORUM**: Requires that a quorum of replicas be written in the current data center only.

- **ANY**: The write will succeed providing it is written to any node, even if that node is not responsible for storing that particular data item. If no node directly responsible for storing a replicas of the data item can be reached, then a *hinted handoff*—described in detail later in this chapter—on any node will be sufficient to complete the write. This is an extremely low reliability setting, since by default hinted handoffs are deleted after three hours; the best you could say about this setting is that data *might* be written.

Some additional write consistency levels are described in the section on lightweight transactions below.

Read Consistency

Read consistency levels are similar to write consistency levels. The key words are identical, though the semantics are of course somewhat different. A setting for write consistency does not imply any particular read consistency setting, though as we shall see it is the interaction between the two that determines the overall behavior of the database.

The most common consistency levels for reads are:

- **ALL**: All replicas are polled.

- **ONE|TWO|THREE**: Read requests will be propagated to the "closest" ONE, TWO, or THREE nodes. "Closeness" is determined by a snitch (see Chapter 8).

- **LOCAL_ONE**: The read request will be sent to the closest node in the current data center.

- **QUORUM**: The read completes after a quorum has returned data: a quorum involves a majority of replicas across all data centers.

- **EACH_QUORUM**: The read completes after a quorum of replicas in each data center have responded.

- **LOCAL_QUORUM**: The read completes after a quorum of replicas in the local data center respond.

Some additional read consistency levels are described in the section on lightweight transactions that follows.

Note that when requesting a read from multiple replicas, Cassandra does not need to see the entire data content from each node. Instead, the coordinator will often request a *digest* of the data. The digest is a hashed representation of the data that can be used to determine if two sets of returned data are identical. We'll discuss this further in the sections on read repair and hinted handoff.

Interaction between Consistency Levels

The settings of read and write consistency interact to create a variety of performance, consistency, and availability outcomes. Strong consistency and high availability can be configured at the cost of lower performance; high availability and performance can be configured at the cost of consistency; or consistency and performance can be achieved at the cost of availability. Some of these trade-offs were illustrated in Figure 3-6. Table 9-1 describes some of the combinations and their implications.

Table 9-1. *Interaction between Read and Write Consistency Levels in Cassandra*

Write \ Read	ONE	QUORUM	ALL
ONE	High performance and availability but no consistency		Fast and highly available for writes; consistent but slow and not highly available reads
QUORUM		Intermediate performance, good availability, strong consistency	
ALL	Slow and not highly available for writes; fast and consistent reads		Strictest consistency, but lowest availability and performance

Hinted Handoff and Read Repair

We spoke about *hinted handoff* and *read repair* in the context of Cassandra clustering in the previous chapter, but since they form an important part of Cassandra's consistency story, some further discussion is in order.

Unless the write consistency level is set to ALL, inconsistencies will collect within the Cassandra cluster. Network partitions or temporary node downtime (from reboots, for instance) will prevent some replica writes from completing. Over time these inconsistencies will build up, creating disorder and chaos—what is often referred to as *entropy* in thermodynamics. *Anti–entropy* mechanisms in Cassandra and other Dynamo-based databases seek to actively return the system to a consistent state.

Hinted handoffs allow a node to store an update that is intended for another node if that node is temporarily unavailable. If the node comes back online within a short interval (by default, three hours), the write will be transmitted. If the node does not come back online within that period, the hinted handoff is deleted. A hinted handoff can substitute for a successful write if the consistency level is set to ANY.

Read repair is a mechanism that Cassandra can use to repair inconsistencies that might arise, for instance, when a node is down longer than the hinted handoff limit. When Cassandra assembles a read from multiple nodes, it will detect any nodes that have out-of-date data. An update will be sent to the out-of-date replicas to correct the inconsistency.

As noted earlier, Cassandra does not request the entire data value from all replicas during a multi-node read. Instead, one node is issued a direct read request for the actual data, while other nodes are sent requests for hashed *digests* of the data. If the results are inconsistent, the most recent data is retrieved by a direct read, and a read repair instruction is issued to the out-of-date nodes.

Figure 9-3 provides an example of a read-repair operation. A coordinator node requests a direct read (e.g., the actual data) from one replica (1) and digests (e.g., hashes) from two other replicas (2). One of the replicas has out-of-date data (3). After returning the correct result to the client (4), the coordinator issues a read repair to the out-of-date replica (5).

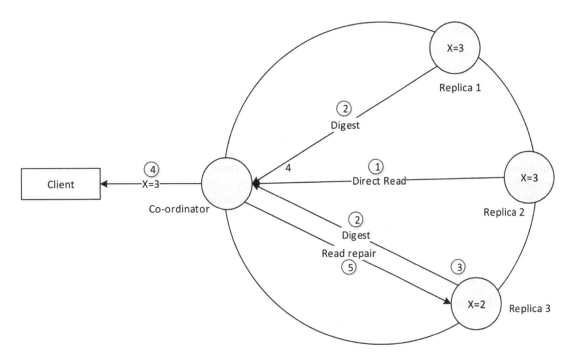

Figure 9-3. *Read repair in Cassandra*

As noted in the previous chapter, there is also the ability to schedule or manually invoke batch read-repair operations that find inconsistencies across entire keyspaces. This mechanism will be discussed further in Chapter 10, when we discuss compaction strategies.

Timestamps and Granularity

Cassandra uses timestamps to determine which replica is the most up to date. Other Dynamo systems such as Riak use a different algorithm, known as a *vector clock,* which we'll discuss in the next section.

The Cassandra approach involves comparing the timestamps of conflicting writes and choosing the one with the highest timestamp; this strategy is referred to as *last write wins*.

The *last write wins* approach has some potential drawbacks when applied to large, complex objects such as you would find in a document database or in a key-value store. One user might modify the user's email address while seconds later another user modifies the user's date of birth. We don't want the date-of-birth modification to obliterate the email address update. MongoDB and HBase lock the entire document or row during an update to avoid this potential problem.

The issue is addressed in Cassandra by making the unit of modification, concurrency, and conflict resolution the individual cell: the intersection of row and column. This means that two users can happily modify the same row simultaneously, providing they are not modifying the same column. If one user updates the date of birth and another user updates the email address for a row, neither update will conflict with the other.

Vector Clocks

Cassandra uses timestamps to work out which is the "latest" transaction. If there are two conflicting modifications to a column value, the one with the highest timestamp will be considered the most recent and the most correct.

Other Dynamo systems use a more complex mechanism known as a *vector clock*. The vector clock has the advantage of not requiring clock synchronization across all nodes, and helps us identify transactions that might be in conflict.

Despite its name, the vector clock does not include any timestamps. Rather, it is composed of a set of counters. These counters are incremented when operations complete, in a way that's similar to the traditional *system change number* pattern discussed earlier. The set contains one counter for each node in the cluster. Whenever an operation occurs on a node, that node will increment its own counter within its vector clock. Whenever a node transmits an operation to another node, it will include its vector clock within the request. The transmitted vector clock will include the highest counter for the transmitting node and the highest counters from other nodes that the transmitting node has ever seen.

When a node receives possibly conflicting updates from other nodes, it can compare the vector clocks to determine the relative sequencing of the requests. There is a defined set of vector clock operations that can tell if:

- The two vector clocks come from nodes that are completely in sync.

- One node is out of date with respect of the other node.

- The clocks are concurrent in that each node has some information that is more up to date than the other node. In this case, we can't choose which update is truly the more correct.

Vector clocks are notoriously difficult to understand, though the underlying algorithm is really quite simple. Figure 9-4 shows an example of three vector clocks incrementing across three nodes. The algorithm is somewhat simplified to improve clarity.

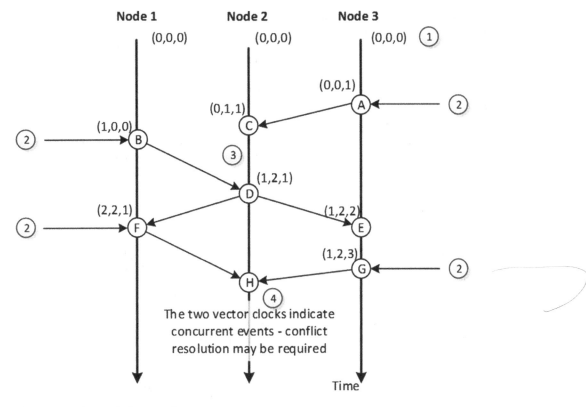

Figure 9-4. *Vector clock example*

In Figure 9-4, the vector clocks start out set to 0 for all nodes (1). Updates to nodes from external clients cause the nodes to increment their own element of the vector clock (2). When these changes are propagated to other nodes, the receiving node updates its vector clock and merges the vector clocks from the other nodes (3). Event (H) occurs when node 2 receives the vector clock (F) from node 1 and (G) from node 3 (4). Each of these vector clocks contains elements higher than the other; vector clock (F) has the higher value for node 1, while vector clock (G) has the higher value for node 3. There is no way for node 2 to be sure which of the two vector clocks represents the most up-to-date data—each of the sending nodes "knows" something that the other node does not, and consequently it's not clear which of the two nodes "knows" best.

The vector clock in Figure 9-4 tells us that version (G) and version (F) are conflicting—each contains information from unique updates that could both contain important information. What, then, is the system to do? Here are some of the options:

- **Revert to last write wins**: Two updates are unlikely to have occurred at the exact same nanosecond, so one will have a higher timestamp value. We could decide that the highest timestamp "wins."

- **Keep both copies**: This requires that the application or the user resolve the conflict.

- **Merge the data**: This is the approach taken by the original Dynamo, which managed Amazon's shopping cart. If there are two conflicting shopping carts, they are merged and the worst that can happen (from Amazon's point of view) is that you buy some things twice. Another merge can occur with things like counters; rather than having one counter increment overwrite another, we can deduce that both operations wanted to increment the counter and increment it twice. A special class of data types— *conflict-free replicated data type* (*CRDT*)—exists that allows these sorts of merges to be predefined.

There are advocates for the vector clock and advocates for the timestamp system used in Cassandra. Neither party disputes the concrete implications of the two approaches; they differ on the desirability of the consequences. Last write wins represents a simpler model for the application developer and administrator, while vector clocks allow for conflicts to be identified but that must then be resolved.

Lightweight Transactions

Cassandra is a lockless architecture, which uses conflict resolution rather than locking to allow high availability and performance. However, sometimes operations need to atomically combine a read operation and a write operation. For instance, consider the scenario shown in Figure 9-5: a familiar transactional operation modifying two account balances. Two Cassandra sessions issue *Cassandra Query Language* (*CQL*) statements to retrieve the current balance of an account (1). Based on this information, the first session applies an interest payment (2) and momentarily afterwards the second session increases the balance to process a deposit (3). The second update overwrites the first update and the interest payment is lost.

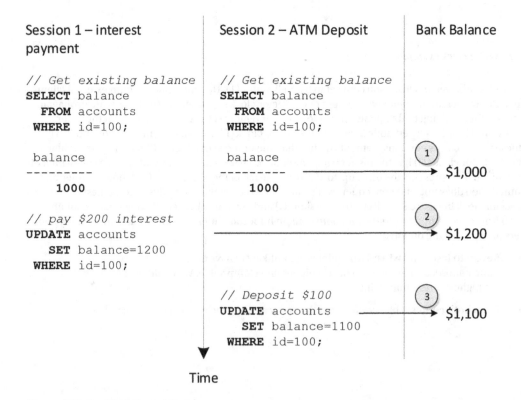

Figure 9-5. Lost update problem

Of course, the lack of ACID transactions is one of the reasons Cassandra might not be suitable for this sort of banking application. However, it is common in almost all applications for some form of atomic operation to be required, and Cassandra offers *lightweight transactions* (*LWT*) to support these requirements.

Cassandra transactions are called "lightweight" because they apply to only a single operation and support only a *compare-and-set* (*CAS*) pattern. A CAS operation is an atomic operation that checks a value, and if the value is as expected, sets another value.

In Cassandra, the lightweight transactions are expressed in the Cassandra Query Language using the IF clause. Figure 9-6 illustrates how this could solve the lost update scenario that we encountered in Figure 9-5.

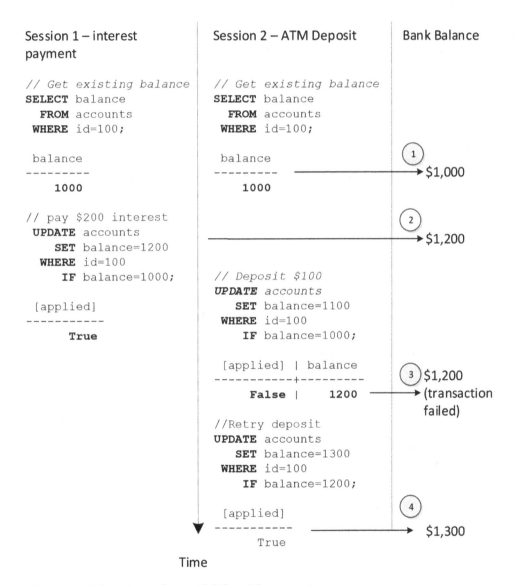

Figure 9-6. *Solving lost updates with lightweight transactions*

As before, each session queries the current balance (1). The first session applies the interest payment, which succeeds because the balance specified in the IF clause is correct (2). However, the second transaction that attempts to add a $100 deposit fails because the balance has changed since the time it was first read (3). The new balance is returned in the failure message, allowing the session to retry the transaction successfully (4).

Those familiar with relational database transactions will recognize the scenario in Figure 9-6 as the *optimistic locking* pattern.

Cassandra's lightweight transactions use a quorum-based transaction protocol called *Paxos*. The Paxos protocol is notoriously difficult to describe and is complicated in implementation, but it resembles a form of the *Two Phase Commit* (*2PC*) protocol discussed earlier in the context of distributed relational database transactions. The key difference with Paxos is that it uses a quorum—that is, a majority—to determine success or failure rather than requiring that every node successfully apply the change.

The modified Cassandra Paxos protocol works in four phases:

1. **Prepare/promise**. Any node may propose a modification; this node is referred to as the leader. The leader sends a proposal to all replica nodes. Nodes can respond in three ways:

    a. They may promise to accept this proposal and not to accept any subsequent proposals.

    b. If the node already is in possession of an earlier proposal, then the earlier proposal will be included with its promise. If the majority of nodes reply with an earlier proposal, then that earlier proposal will have to be applied before the new proposal can be processed.

    c. The node may decline the proposal because it has already promised to apply a later proposal.

2. **Read current value**. The current value of the data item will be requested from each node to confirm that the value conforms to the IF clause in the UPDATE or INSERT statement.

3. **Propose/accept.** The new value is proposed to all nodes and nodes reply if they are able to apply the new value.

4. **Commit/acknowledge.** If the propose/accept step succeeds, then the leader will indicate to all nodes that the transaction can be completed. The proposed value is applied to normal Cassandra storage and is visible to everyone.

Remember that Paxos is a quorum-based protocol, which means that each step succeeds providing a majority of replicas agree. Replicas that cannot be reached or can for other reasons not participate will be corrected at a later time through normal anti-entropy mechanisms.

The Cassandra lightweight transaction implementation involves a significantly larger number of round trips than the nontransactional alternatives—four times as many round trips are involved in a simple case, and could be potentially more should multiple conflicting proposals need to be reconciled.

Figure 9-7 shows a simplified sequence of events in a successful Cassandra lightweight transaction. In phase 1, the leader proposes a change to a data item and replicas promise not to accept any earlier proposals. In phase 2, the leader checks that the value of the data is what is expected and as specified in the CQL IF clause. In phase 3, the leader proposes the new value for the data item and replicas accept the proposal. In phase 4, the leader commits the proposal and each replica acknowledges that the commit succeeded.

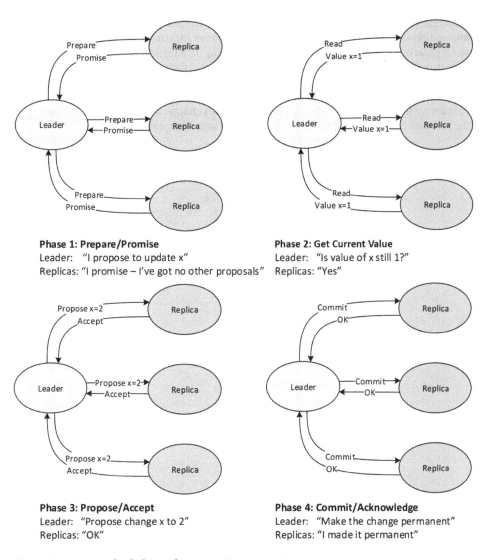

Phase 1: Prepare/Promise
Leader: "I propose to update x"
Replicas: "I promise – I've got no other proposals"

Phase 2: Get Current Value
Leader: "Is value of x still 1?"
Replicas: "Yes"

Phase 3: Propose/Accept
Leader: "Propose change x to 2"
Replicas: "OK"

Phase 4: Commit/Acknowledge
Leader: "Make the change permanent"
Replicas: "I made it permanent"

Figure 9-7. *Cassandra lightweight transaction processing*

Conclusion

Many next-generation systems—generally those described as NewSQL—employ the time-tested consistency models of the traditional RDBMS, most significantly ACID transactions and multi-version concurrency control (MVCC).

Next-generation databases of the NoSQL variety have an undeserved reputation for offering only simplistic consistency controls. In fact, as we have seen in this chapter, maintaining a predictable yet flexible consistency model while meeting availability and scalability requirements of a distributed database requires architectures at least as complicated as those we have come to know in the relational world.

We have concentrated in this chapter on three approaches employed in the NoSQL world. MongoDB employs a relatively traditional pessimistic locking model that preserves consistency by blocking conflicting operations. HBase employs only very short-lived locks, instead relying on a version of MVCC to allow high-frequency mutations to occur without creating row-level inconsistencies. Cassandra employs the Dynamo model of tunable consistency, which allows the application to choose among consistency, availability, and performance. Cassandra also adds a lightweight Paxos-based transaction.

In the next chapter, we'll see how the consistency concepts of this chapter and distributed database architectures of the previous chapter are supported by data models and storage systems.

CHAPTER 10

■ ■ ■

Data Models and Storage

A model's just an imitation of the real thing.

—Mae West

The ocean flows of online information are all streaming together, and the access tools are becoming absolutely critical. If you don't index it, it doesn't exist. It's out there but you can't find it, so it might as well not be there.

—Barbara Quint

The relational database model provided a strong theoretical foundation for the representation of data that eliminated redundancy and maximized flexibility of data access. Many next-generation database systems, particularly those of the NewSQL variety, continue to embrace the relational model: their innovations generally focus on the underlying physical storage of data.

However, databases of the NoSQL variety explicitly reject the fixed schema of the relational model. This rejection is not based on any theoretical disagreement with the principles of relational data modeling but, rather, from a practical desire to facilitate agility in application development by allowing schemas to evolve with the application. Additionally, NoSQL databases seek to avoid the overhead created by operations such as joins, which are a necessary consequence of relational normalization.

Underneath the data model, all databases adopt physical storage mechanisms designed to optimize typical access paths. Following our review of new and traditional data models in this chapter, we'll examine how storage is designed to support the models.

Data Models

Today's databases adopt a variety of data models:

- **Relational models** serve as the inspiration for the representation of data in the traditional RDBMS (Oracle, SQL Server, etc.), as well as for NewSQL databases such as Vertica and VoltDB.

- **Key-value** stores theoretically impose no structure or limitation on the "value" part of the key value. However, in practice, most key-value stores provide additional support for certain types of data structures to allow for indexing and conflict resolution.

- Databases based on Google's **BigTable** database implement the wide column store described in the BigTable specification. However, some significant innovations have been introduced in databases such as Cassandra.

145

- **Document databases** use JSON or XML documents, which generally impose no restriction on the data that can be represented, but which provide a self-describing and predictable data representation.

- **Graph databases** represent data as nodes, relationships, and properties. Graph databases were described in detail in Chapter 5.

Review of the Relational Model of Data

Before diving into nonrelational data models, let's quickly recapitulate the relational model, which dominated the last generation of database systems and which remains the most widely adopted data model today. The relational model forms the basis not just for the traditional RDBMS but also for databases of the NewSQL variety—databases such as Vertica and VoltDB, for instance. We provided an overview of the relational model back in Chapter 1, and of course the relational data model is supported by a vast body of literature. What follows is a brief summary.

The relational model organizes values into *tuples* (rows). Multiple tuples are used to construct *relations* (tables). Rows are identified by *key values* and—at least in third normal form—all values will be locatable by the entire primary key and nothing else. *Foreign keys* define relationships between tables by referencing the primary keys in another table.

The process of eliminating redundancy from a relational model is known as *normalization*. Figure 10-1 provides an example of un-normalized and normalized data.

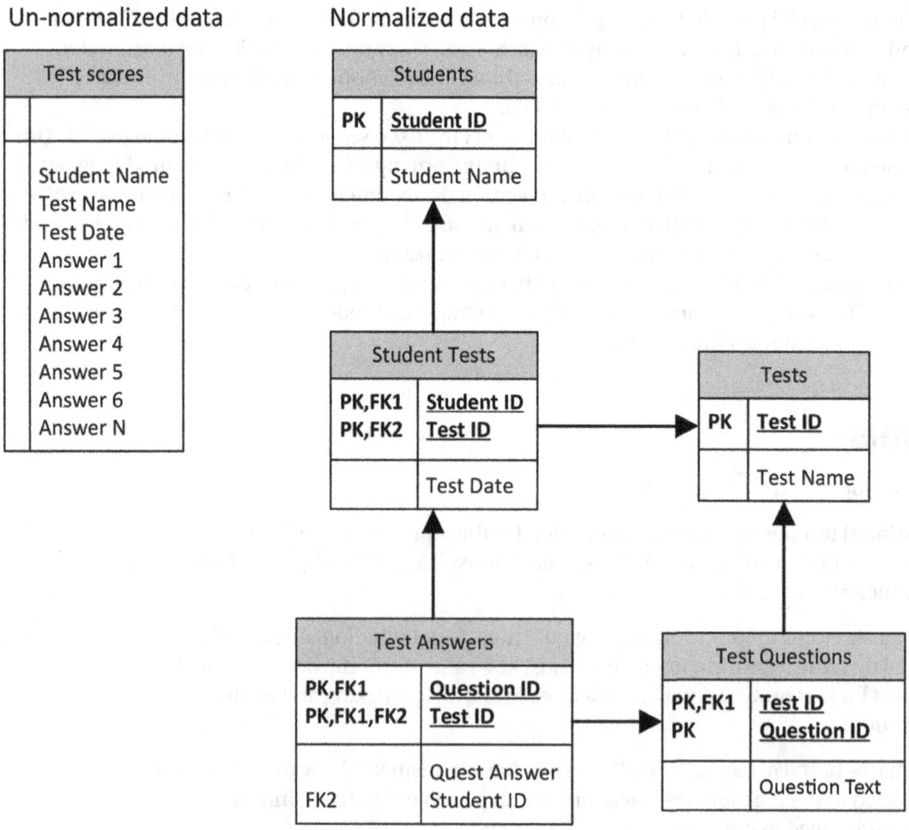

Figure 10-1. Normalized relational data model

The *star schema* represents a data modeling pattern commonly found—indeed, almost always found—in data warehouses. In a star schema, a large "fact" table contains detailed business data and contains foreign keys to smaller more static "dimension" tables that categorize the fact items in business terms, typically including time, product, customer, and so on.

Figure 10-2 shows an example of a star schema. The central SALES fact table contains sales totals that are aggregated across various time periods, products, and customers. The detail and explanation of each aggregation can be found by joining to the dimension tables TIMES, PRODUCTS, and CUSTOMERS.

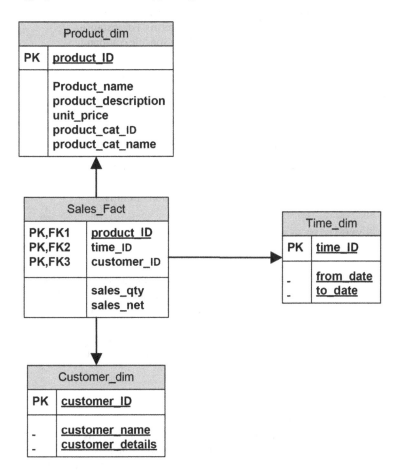

Figure 10-2. *Star schema*

Key-value Stores

Unlike the relational model, there is no formal definition for how data is represented in a key-value store. Typically a key-value store will accept any binary value within specific size limits as a key and is capable of storing any binary data as a value. In this respect, we might say that the key-value store is *data-type agnostic*. However, most key-value stores provide additional support for certain types of data. The support stems from the desire to provide one of the following features:

- **Secondary indexes**. In a pure key-value store, the only way to locate an object is via its key. However, most applications perform lookups on non-key terms. For instance, we may wish to locate all users within a geography, all orders for a specific company, and so on.

- **Conflict resolution**. Key-value stores that provide eventual consistency or Amazon Dynamostyle tunable consistency may implement special data types that facilitate conflict resolution.

Riak, a key-value store based on Amazon's Dynamo specification, illustrates both of these patterns. As well as binary objects, Riak allows for data to be defined as one of the following:

- A Riak **convergent replicated data type** (CRDT). These data types, described in more detail below, include maps, sets, and counters. Conflicting operations on these data types can be resolved by Riak without requiring application or human intervention.

- A **document type**, such as XML, JSON, or Text.

- A **custom data type**.

Riak includes *Solr*, an open-source text search engine. When a Riak value is defined as one of the built-in data types, or as a custom data type for which you have provided custom search code, then Solr will index the value and provide a variety of lookup features, including exact match, regular expression, and range searches.

In the case of JSON, XML, and Riak maps, searches can be restricted to specific fields within the document. So, for instance, you could search for documents that have a specific value for a specific JSON attribute.

Convergent Replicated Data Types

We touched on *convergent replicated data types* (*CRDT*) in Chapter 9. As we noted there, Riak users vector clocks to determine if two updates potentially conflict. By default, if after the examination of the vector clocks for two conflicting updates the system cannot determine which of the updates is most correct, then Riak will maintain both versions of the update by creating *sibling values*, which must be resolved by the user or application.

CRDTs allow two conflicting updates to be merged even if their vector clocks indicate that they are concurrent. A CRDT encapsulates deterministic rules that can be used either to merge the conflicting values or to determine which of two conflicting values should "win" and be propagated.

When a CRDT value is propagated between nodes, it includes not just the current value of the object but also a history of operations that have been applied to the object. This history is somewhat analogous to the vector clock data that accompanies each update in a Riak system, but unlike a vector clock, it contains information specifically pertaining to the history of a specific object.

The simplest example of CRDT merging involves the *g-counter* (*grow-only counter*) data type. This is a monotonically incrementing counter that cannot be decremented (e.g., you can increase the counter, but you cannot decrease its value).

You might think that you could merge g-counter updates simply by adding up all the increment operations that have occurred on every node to determine the total counter value. However, this approach ignores the possibility that some of these increment operations are replicas of other increment operations. To avoid such double counting, each node maintains an array of the counter values received from every node. Upon incrementing, the node increments its element in the array and then transmits the entire array to other nodes. Should a conflict between updates be detected (through the vector clock mechanism), we take the highest element for each node in each version and add them up.

That last sentence was quite a mouthful, but it's still simpler than the mathematical notation! Stepping through the example shown in Figure 10-3 will, we hope, illuminate the process.

- At time t0, each node has a value of 0 for the counter, and each element in the array of counters (one for each node) is also set to 0.

- Around time t1, node 1 receives an increment operation on the counter of +1, while node 2 receives an increment operation of +2. Nodes 1 and 2 transmit their counter values to node 3.

- Around time t2, node 1 receives an increment of +4 and an update from node 2, while node 3 receives an increment of +2. Each node now has a different value for the counter: 7 (5,0,2), 3 (1,0,2), or 4 (0,0,4).

- Around time t3, node 2 receives updates from node 1 and node 3. These updates are potentially conflicting, so node 2 has to merge the three counter arrays. By taking the highest element for each node from each array, node 2 concludes that the correct value for the counter is (5,0,4), which adds up to 9.

- At time t4, node 2 propagates the correct values of the counter to the other nodes and the cluster is now back in sync.

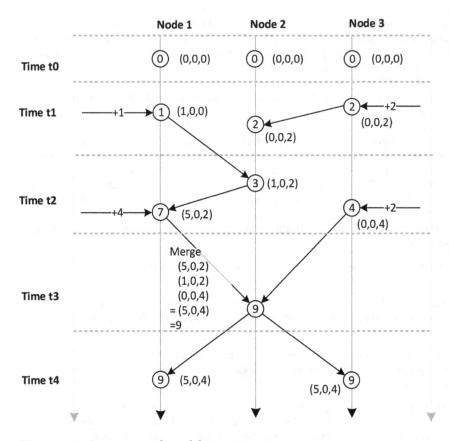

Figure 10-3. *Convergent replicated data type g-counter*

Other CRDTs are defined in academia and implemented in Riak or in other databases. For instance:

- The **PN-counter** type allows counters to increment and decrement safely. It is implemented as two g-counters, one which maintains increments and the other which maintains decrements.

- The **G-set** type implements a collection of objects to which you can add elements but never remove them.

- The **2P-set** provides a collection to which elements can be removed as well as inserted. However, an object can be removed only once.

- The **LWW-set a**llows multiple insertions and deletes, with a last-write-wins policy in the event of conflicting operations.

Other CRDT types provide further flexibility in the operations they support, but in a manner similar to the LWW-set type, specify winners and losers in the event of conflict. The winner might be determined by timestamps or by comparing the relative number of operations to which the element has been subjected, or by some other domain-specific logic.

Data Models in BigTable and HBase

Google's *BigTable* paper was published in 2006 and was the basis for the data model used in HBase, Cassandra, and several other databases. Google also makes BigTable storage available as a service in the *Google Cloud BigTable* product.

BigTable tables have the following characteristics:

- Data is organized as *tables* that—like relational tables—have columns and rows.

- Tables are indexed and sorted by a single *rowkey*.

- A table includes one or more *column families,* which are named and specified in the table definition.

- Column families are composed of *columns*. Column names are dynamic, and new columns can be created dynamically upon insertion of a new value. Use of the term "column" is somewhat misleading: BigTable column families are more accurately described as sorted multidimensional maps, in which values are identified by column name and timestamp.

- Data for a specific column family is stored together on disk.

- Tables are *sparse*: empty columns do not take up space.

- A *cell* (intersection of row and column) may contain multiple versions of a data element, indexed by timestamp.

Column Family Structure

Column families can be used to group related columns for convenience, to optimize disk IO by co-locating columns that are frequently accessed together on disk, or to create a multidimensional structure that can be used for more complex data.

Figure 10-4 illustrates a simple column family structure. Rows are grouped into three column families, but each row has identical column names. In this configuration, the table resembles a relational table that has been vertically partitioned on disk for performance reasons.

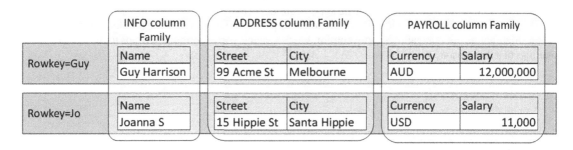

Figure 10-4. *Simple column family structure*

The uniqueness of the BigTable data model becomes more apparent when we create a "wide" column family. In this case, column names represent the name portion of a name:value pair. Any given row key may have any arbitrary collection of such columns, and there need be no commonality between rowkeys with respect of column names.

Figure 10-5 illustrates such a wide column family. In the FRIENDS column family, we have a variable number of columns, each corresponding to a specific friend. The name of the column corresponds to the name of the friend, while the value of the column is the friend's email. In this example, both Guy and Joanna have a common friend John, so each share that column. But other columns that represent friends who are not shared, and those columns appear only in the row required.

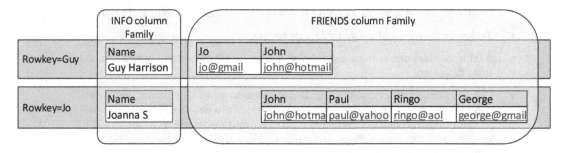

Figure 10-5. *Wide column family structure*

BigTable/HBase column families are described as sparse because no storage is consumed by columns that are absent in a given row. Indeed, a BigTable column family is essentially a "map" consisting of an arbitrary set of sorted name:value pairs.

Versions

Each cell in a BigTable column family can store multiple versions of a value, indexed by timestamp. Timestamps may be specified by the application or automatically assigned by the server. Values are stored within a cell in descending timestamp order, so by default a read will retrieve the most recent timestamp. A read operation can specify a timestamp range or specify the number of versions of data to return.

A column family configuration setting specifies the maximum number of versions that will be stored for each value. In HBase, the default number of versions is three. There is also a minimum version count, which is typically combined with a *time to live* (*TTL*) setting. The TTL setting instructs the server to delete values that are older than a certain number of seconds. The minimum version count overrides the TTL, so typically at least one or more copies of the data will be kept regardless of age.

Figure 10-6 illustrates multiple values with timestamps. For the row shown, the info:loc column has only a single value, but the readings:temp column has five values corresponding perhaps to the last five readings of a thermostat.

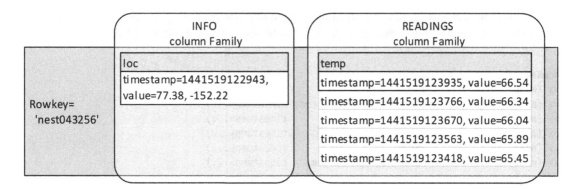

Figure 10-6. *Multiple versions of cell data in BigTable*

Deletes in a BigTable database are implemented by creating *tombstone* markers that indicate all versions of a column or column family less than a given timestamp have been removed. By default, a delete uses the current timestamp, thus eliminating all previous row values.

Deleted elements persist on disk until a *compaction* occurs. We'll discuss compaction later in this chapter.

Cassandra

Cassandra's data model is based on the BigTable design, but has evolved significantly since its initial release. Indeed, it can be hard to recognize the BigTable structure when working with Cassandra through the *Cassandra Query Language* (*CQL*).

The CQL CREATE TABLE statement allows us to define composite primary keys, which look like familiar multi-column keys in relational databases. For instance, in the CQL shown below, we create a table FRIENDS, which is keyed on columns NAME and FRIEND corresponding to the user's name and the name of each of his or her friends:

```
CREATE TABLE friends
 (user text,
  friend text,
  email text,
PRIMARY KEY (user,friend));
```

CQL queries on this table return results that imply one row exists for each combination of user and friend:

```
cqlsh:guy>   SELECT * FROM friends;

 user | friend | email
------+--------+------------------
   Jo | George | George@gmail.com
   Jo |    Guy |    Guy@gmail.com
   Jo |   John |   John@gmail.com
  Guy |     Jo |     Jo@gmail.com
```

But when we look at the column family using the (now depreciated) thrift client, we can see we have two rows, one with four columns and the other with six columns (the output here has been edited for clarity):

```
RowKey: Jo
=> (name=George:,       value=,                   timestamp=...)
=> (name=George:email,  value=George@gmail.com,    timestamp=...)
=> (name=Guy:,          value=,                   timestamp=...)
=> (name=Guy:email,     value=Guy@gmail.com,      timestamp=...)
=> (name=John:,         value=,                   timestamp=...)
=> (name=John:email,    value=John@gmail.com,     timestamp=...)
-------------------
RowKey: Guy
=> (name=Jo:,           value=,                   timestamp=...)
=> (name=Jo:email,      value=Jo@gmail.com,       timestamp=...)
=> (name=John:,         value=,                   timestamp=...)
=> (name=John:email,    value=John@gmail.com,     timestamp=...)

2 Rows Returned.
```

The first part of the CQL primary key (USER, in our example) is used to specify the rowkey for the table and is referred to as the *partition key*. The second parts of the primary key (FRIEND, in our example) are *clustering keys* and are used to create a wide column structure in which each distinct value of the CQL key column is used as part of the name of a BigTable-style column. So for instance, the column Guy:email is constructed from the value "Guy" within the CQL column "Friend" together with the name of the CQL column "email."

That's quite confusing! So it's no wonder that Cassandra tends to hide this complexity within a more familiar relational style SQL-like notation. Figure 10-7 compares the Cassandra CQL representation of the data with the underlying BigTable structure: the apparent five rows as shown in CQL are actually implemented as two BigTable-style rows in underlying storage.

```
cqlsh>    SELECT * FROM friends;
```

name	friend	email
Jo	George	George@gmail.com
Jo	Guy	Guy@gmail.com
Jo	John	John@gmail.com
Guy	Jo	Jo@gmail.com
Guy	John	John@gmail.com

```
CREATE TABLE friends
  (name    text,
   friend text,
   email  text,
   PRIMARY KEY (name,friend))
```

Cassandra CQL view of column family

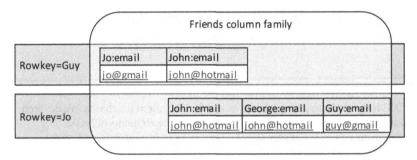

Actual column family structure

Figure 10-7. *Cassandra CQL represents wide column structure as narrow tables*

■ **Note**   Cassandra uses the term "column family" differently from HBase and BigTable. A Cassandra column family is equivalent to a table in HBase. For consistency's sake, we may refer to Cassandra "tables" when a Cassandra purist would say "column family."

The underlying physical implementation of Cassandra tables explains some of the specific behaviors within the Cassandra Query Language. For instance, CQL requires that an ORDER BY clause refer only to composite key columns. WHERE clauses in CQL also have restrictions that seem weird and arbitrary unless you understand the underlying storage model. The partition key accepts only equality clauses (IN and "="), which makes sense when you remember that rowkeys are hash-partitioned across the cluster, as we discussed in Chapter 8. Clustering key columns do support range operators such as ">" and "<", which again makes sense when you remember that in the BigTable model the column families are actually sorted hash maps.

Cassandra Collections

Cassandra's partitioning and clustering keys implement a highly scalable and efficient storage model. However, Cassandra also supports *collection data types* that allow repeating groups to be stored within column values.

For instance, we might have implemented our FRIENDS table using the MAP data type, which would have allowed us to store a hash map of friends and emails within a single Cassandra column:

```
CREATE TABLE friends2
 (person text,
  friends map<text,text>,
  PRIMARY KEY (person ));

  INSERT into friends2(person,friends)
  VALUES('Guy',
          {'Jo':'jo@gmail.com',
           'john':'john@gmail.com',
           'Chris':'chris@gmail.com'});
```

Cassandra also supports SET and LIST types, as well as the MAP type shown above.

JSON Data Models

JavaScript Object Notation (JSON) is the de facto standard data model for document databases. We devoted Chapter 4 to document databases; here, we will just formally look at some of the elements of JSON.

JSON documents are built up from a small set of very simple constructs: *values*, *objects,* and *arrays*.

- **Arrays** consist of lists of values enclosed by square brackets ("[" and "]") and separated by commas (",").

- **Objects** consist of one or more name value pairs in the format "name":"value" , enclosed by braces ("{" and "}") and separated by commas (",").

- **Values** can be Unicode strings, standard format numbers (possibly including scientific notation), Booleans, arrays, or objects.

The last few words in the definition are very important: because values may include objects *or* arrays, which themselves contain values, a JSON structure can represent an arbitrarily complex and nested set of information. In particular, arrays can be used to represent repeating groups of documents, which in a relational database would require a separate table.

Document databases such as CouchBase and MongoDB organize documents into buckets or collections, which would generally be expected to contain documents of a similar type. Figure 10-8 illustrates some of the essential JSON elements.

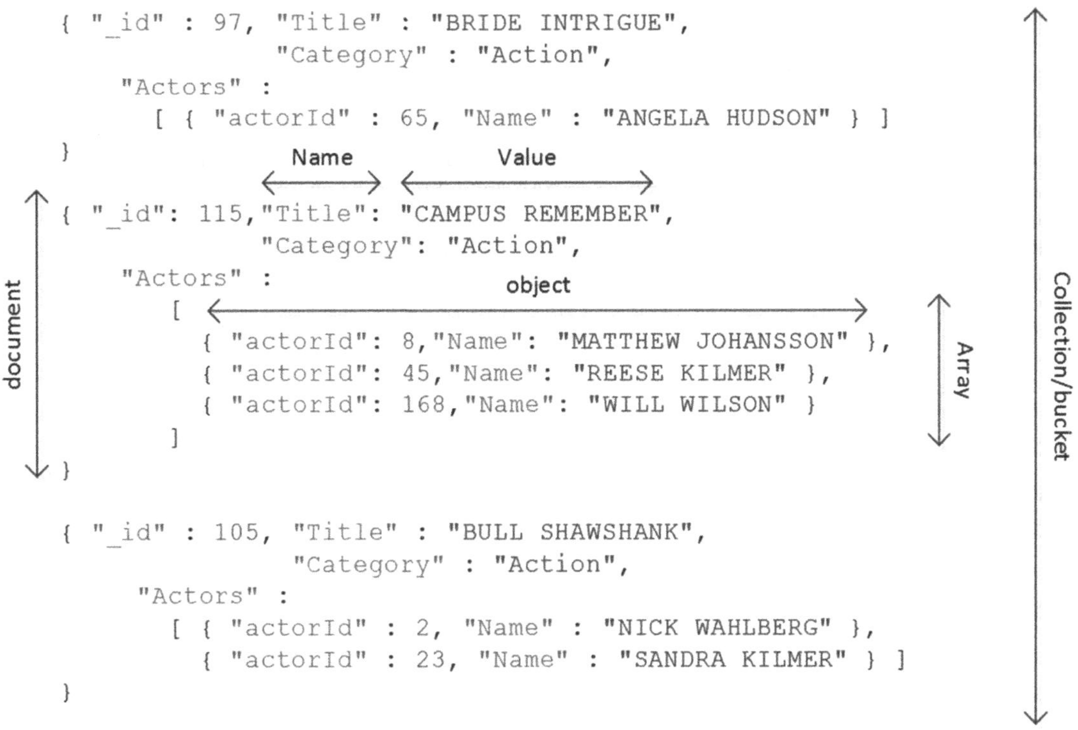

```
{ "_id" : 97, "Title" : "BRIDE INTRIGUE",
              "Category" : "Action",
     "Actors" :
       [ { "actorId" : 65, "Name" : "ANGELA HUDSON" } ]
}
```

```
{ "_id": 115,"Title": "CAMPUS REMEMBER",
             "Category": "Action",
     "Actors" :
       [
           { "actorId": 8,"Name": "MATTHEW JOHANSSON" },
           { "actorId": 45,"Name": "REESE KILMER" },
           { "actorId": 168,"Name": "WILL WILSON" }
       ]
}
```

```
{ "_id" : 105, "Title" : "BULL SHAWSHANK",
               "Category" : "Action",
      "Actors" :
        [ { "actorId" : 2, "Name" : "NICK WAHLBERG" },
          { "actorId" : 23, "Name" : "SANDRA KILMER" } ]
}
```

Figure 10-8. JSON documents

Binary JSON (BSON)

MongoDB stores JSON documents internally in the BSON format. BSON is designed to be a more compact and efficient representation of JSON data, and it uses more efficient encoding for numbers and other data types. In addition, BSON includes field length prefixes that allow scanning operations to "skip over" elements and hence improve efficiency.

Storage

One of the fundamental innovations in the relational database model was the separation of logical data representation from the physical storage model. Prior to the relational model it was necessary to understand the physical storage of data in order to navigate the database. That strict separation has allowed the relational representation of data to remain relatively static for a generation of computer scientists, while underlying storage mechanisms such as indexing have seen significant innovation. The most extreme example of this decoupling can be seen in the columnar database world. Columnar databases such as Vertica and Sybase IQ continue to support the row-oriented relational database model, even while they have tipped the data on its side by storing data in a columnar format.

We have looked at the underlying physical storage of columnar systems in Chapter 6, so we don't need to examine that particular innovation here. However, there has been a fundamental shift in the physical layout of modern nonrelational databases such as HBase and Cassandra. This is the shift away from B-tree storage structure optimized for random access to the log-structured Merge tree pattern, which is optimized instead for sequential write performance.

157

Typical Relational Storage Model

Most relational databases share a similar high-level storage architecture.

Figure 10-9 shows a simplified relational database architecture. Database clients interact with the database by sending SQL to database processes (1). The database processes retrieve data from database files on disk initially (2), and store the data in memory buffers to optimize subsequent accesses (3). If data is modified, it is changed within the in-memory copy (4). Upon transaction commit, the database process writes to a transaction log (5), which ensures that the transaction will not be lost in the event of a system failure. The modified data in memory is written out to database files asynchronously by a "lazy" database writer process (6).

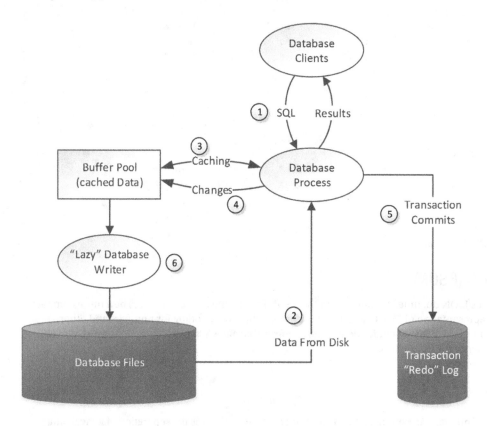

Figure 10-9. *Relational database storage architecture*

Much of the architecture shown in Figure 10-9 can be found in nonrelational systems as well. In particular, some equivalent of the transaction log is present in almost any transactional database system.

Another ubiquitous RDBMS architectural pattern—at least in the operational database world—is the B-tree index. The B-tree index is a structure that allows for random access to elements within a database system.

Figure 10-10 shows a B-tree index structure. The B-tree index has a hierarchical tree structure. At the top of the tree is the header block. This block contains pointers to the appropriate branch block for any given range of key values. The branch block will usually point to the appropriate leaf block for a more specific range or, for a larger index, point to another branch block. The leaf block contains a list of key values and the physical addresses of matching table data.

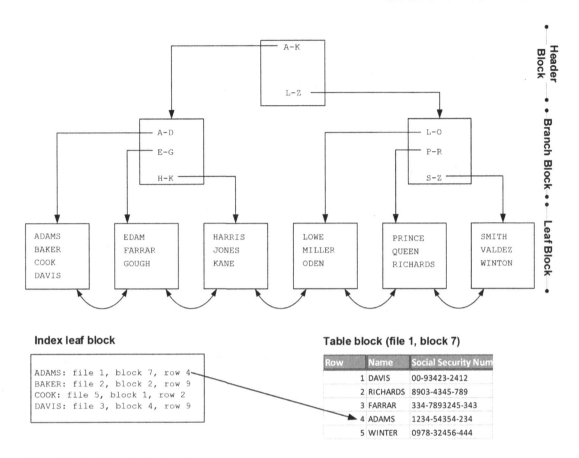

Figure 10-10. *B-tree index structure*

Leaf blocks contain links to both the previous and the next leaf block. This allows us to scan the index in either ascending or descending order, and allows range queries using the ">", "<" or "BETWEEN" operators to be satisfied using the index.

B-tree indexes offer predictable performance because every leaf node is at the same depth. Each additional layer in the index exponentially increases the number of keys that can be supported, and for almost all tables, three or four IOs will be sufficient to locate any row.

However, maintaining the B-tree when changing data can be expensive. For instance, consider inserting a row with the key value "NIVEN" into the table index diagrammed in Figure 10-10. To insert the row, we must add a new entry into the L-O block. If there is no free space within a leaf block for a new entry, then an index split is required. A new block must be allocated and half of the entries in the existing block have to be moved into the new block. As well as this, there is a requirement to add a new entry to the branch block (in order to point to the newly created leaf block). If there is no free space in the branch block, then the branch block must also be split.

These index splits are an expensive operation: new blocks must be allocated and index entries moved from one block to another, and during this split access times will suffer. So although the B-tree index is an efficient random read mechanism, it is not so great for write-intensive workloads.

The inherent limitations of the B-tree structure are somewhat mitigated by the ability to defer disk writes to the main database files: as long as a transaction log entry has been written on commit, data file modifications—including index blocks—can be performed in memory and written to disk later. However, during periods of heavy, intensive write activity, free memory will be exhausted and throughput will be limited by disk IO to the database blocks.

There have been some significant variations on the B-tree pattern to provide for better throughput for write-intensive workloads: Both Couchbase's *HB+-Trie* and Tokutek's *fractal tree index* claim to provide better write optimization.

However, an increasing number of databases implement a storage architecture that is optimized from the ground up to support write-intensive workloads: the *log-structured merge* (*LSM*) tree.

Log-structured Merge Trees

The *log-structured merge* (*LSM*) tree is a structure that seeks to optimize storage and support extremely high insert rates, while still supporting efficient random read access.

The simplest possible LSM tree consists of two indexed "trees":

- An **in-memory tree**, which is the recipient of all new record inserts. In Cassandra, this in-memory tree is referred to as the *MemTable* and in HBase as the *MemStore*.

- A number of **on-disk trees**, which represent copies of in-memory trees that have been flushed to disk. In Cassandra, this on-disk structure is referred to as the *SSTable* and in HBase as the *StoreTable*.

The on-disk tree files are initially point-in-time copies of the in-memory tree, but are merged periodically to create larger consolidated stores. This merging process is called *compaction*.

■ **Note**   The log-structured merge tree is a very widely adopted architecture and is fundamental to BigTable, HBase, Cassandra, and other databases. However, naming conventions vary among implementations. For convenience, we use the Cassandra terminology by default, in which the in-memory tree is called a *MemTable* and the on-disk trees are called *SSTables*.

The LSM architecture ensures that writes are always fast, since they operate at memory speed. The transfer to disk is also fast, since it occurs in append-only batches that allow for fast sequential writes. Reads occur either from the in-memory tree or from the disk tree; in either case, reads are facilitated by an index and are relatively swift.

Of course, if the server failed while data was in the in-memory store, then it could be lost. For this reason database implementations of the LSM pattern include some form of transaction logging so that the changes can be recovered in the event of failure. This log file is roughly equivalent to a relational database transaction (redo) log. In Cassandra, it is called the *CommitLog* and in HBase, the *Write-Ahead Log* (*WAL*). These log entries can be discarded once the in-memory tree is flushed to disk.

Figure 10-11 illustrates the log-structured merge tree architecture, using Cassandra terminology. Writes from database clients are first applied to the CommitLog (1) and then to the MemTable (2). Once the MemTable reaches a certain size, it is flushed to disk to create a new SSTable (3). Once the flush completes, CommitLog records may be purged (4). Periodically, multiple SSTables are merged (compacted) into larger SSTables (5).

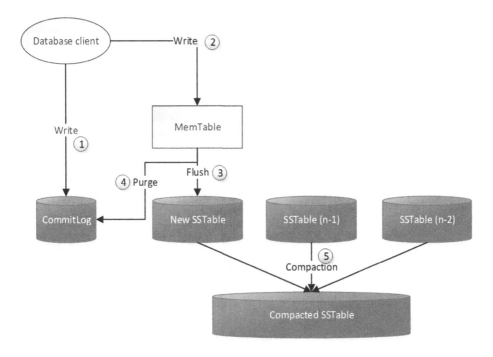

Figure 10-11. *LSM architecture (Cassandra terminology)*

SSTables and Bloom Filters

The on-disk portion of the LSM tree is an indexed structure. For instance, in Cassandra, each SSTable is associated with an index that contains all the rowkeys that exist in the SSTable and an offset to the location of the associated value within the file. However, there may be many SSTables on disk, and this creates a multiplier effect on index lookups, since we would theoretically have to examine every index for every SSTable in order to find our desired row.

To avoid these multiple-index lookups, *bloom filters* are used to reduce the number of lookups that must be performed.

Bloom filters are created by applying multiple hash functions to the key value. The outputs of the hash functions are used to set bits within the bloom filter structure. When looking up a key value within the bloom filter, we perform the same hash functions and see if the bits are set. If the bits are not set, then the search value must not be included within the table. However, if the bits are set, it may have been as a result of a value that happened to hash to the same values. The end result is an index that is typically reduced in size by 85 percent, but that provides false positives only 15 percent of the time.

Bloom filters are compact enough to fit into memory and are very quick to navigate. However, to achieve this compression, bloom filters are "fuzzy" in the sense that they may return false positives. If you get a positive result from a bloom filter, it means only that the file *may* contain the value. However, the bloom filter will never incorrectly advise you that a value is not present. So if a bloom filter tells us that a key is not included in a specific SSTable, then we can safely omit that SSTable from our lookup.

Figure 10-12 shows the read pattern for a log-structured merge tree using Cassandra terminology. A database request first reads from the MemTable (1). If the required value is not found, it will consult the bloom filters for the most recent SSTable (2). If the bloom filter indicates that no matching value is present, it will examine the next SSTable (3). If the bloom filter indicates a matching key value may be present in the SSTable, then the process will use the SSTable index (4) to search for the value within the SSTable (5). Once a matching value is found, no older SSTables need be examined.

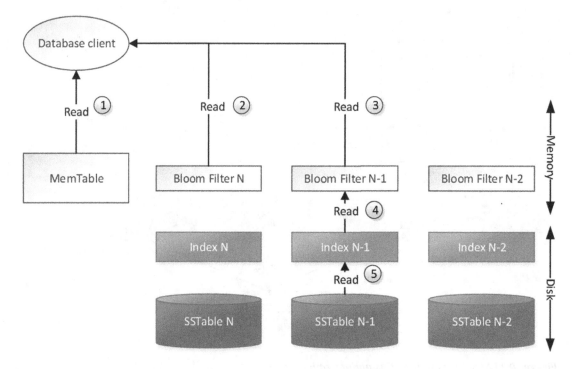

Figure 10-12. *Log-structured merge tree reads (Cassandra terminology)*

Updates and Tombstones

SSTables are *immutable*—that is, once the MemTable is flushed to disk and becomes an SSTable, no further modifications to the SSTable can be performed. If a value is modified repeatedly over a period of time, the modifications will build up across multiple SSTables. When retrieving a value, the system will read SSTables from the youngest to the oldest to find the most recent value of a column, or to build up a complete row. Therefore, to update a value we need only insert the new value, since the older values will not be examined when a newer version exists.

Deletions are implemented by writing *tombstone* markers into the MemTable, which eventually propagates to SSTables. Once a tombstone marker for a row is encountered, the system stops examining older entries and reports "row not found" to the application.

Compaction

As SSTables multiply, read performance and storage degrade as the numbers of bloom filters, indexes, and obsolete values increase. So periodically the system will *compact* multiple SSTables into a single file. During compaction, rows that are fragmented across multiple SSTables are consolidated and deleted rows are removed.

However, tombstones will remain in the system for a period of time to ensure that a delayed update to a row will not resurrect a row that should remain deleted. This can happen if a tombstone is removed while older updates to that row are still being propagated through the system. To avoid this possibility, default settings prevent tombstones from being deleted for over a week, while hinted handoffs (see Chapter 8) generally expire after only three hours. But in the event of these defaults being adjusted, or in the event of an unreasonably long network partition, it is conceivable that a row that has been deleted will be resurrected.

Secondary Indexing

A secondary index allows us to quickly find rows that meet some criteria other than their primary key or rowkey value.

Secondary indexes are ubiquitous in relational systems: it's a fundamental characteristic of a relational system that you be able to navigate primary key and foreign key relationships, and this would be impractical if only primary key indexes existed. In relational systems, primary key indexes and secondary indexes are usually implemented in the same way: most commonly with B-tree indexes, or sometimes with bitmap indexes.

We discussed in Chapter 6 how columnar databases often use projections as an alternative to indexes: this approach works in columnar systems because queries typically aggregate data across a large number of rows rather than seeking a small number of rows matching a specific criteria. We also discussed in Chapter 5 how graph databases use index-free adjacency to perform efficient graph traversal without requiring a separate index structure.

Neither of these solutions are suitable for nonrelational operational database systems. The underlying design of key-value stores, BigTable systems, and document databases assumes data retrieval by a specific key value, and indeed in many cases—especially in earlier key-value systems—lookup by rowkey value is the only way to find a row.

However, for most applications, fast access to data by primary key alone is not enough. So most nonrelational databases provide some form of secondary index support, or at least provide patterns for "do-it-yourself" secondary indexing.

DIY Secondary Indexing

Creating a secondary index for a key-value store is conceptually fairly simple. You create a table in which the key value is the column or attribute to be indexed, and that contains the rowkey for the primary table.

Figure 10-13 illustrates the technique. The table USERS contains a unique identifier (the rowkey) for each user, but we often want to retrieve users by email address. Therefore, we create a separate table in which the primary key is the user's email address and that contains the rowkey for the source table.

Index table on EMAIL

Rowkey	BaseTableKey
bamflux@gmail	100007
crilly1@aol	100006
dbman@gmail	100001
georgy@gmail	100002
jane@outlook	100003
kate@yahoo	100004
Mike@gmail	100005

Base Table USERS

Rowkey	UserName	Email	Country
100001	dbman	dbman@gmail	USA
100002	georgy	georgy@gmail	USA
100003	jane	jane@outlook	USA
100004	kate	kate@yahoo	Australia
100005	Mike	Mike@gmail	USA
100006	crilly1	crilly1@aol	USA
100007	bamflux	bamflux@gmail	Australia

Index table on COUNTRY

RowKey	100001	100002	100003	100005	100006
USA					

RowKey	100004	100007
Australia		

Figure 10-13. *Do-it-yourself secondary indexing*

Variations on the theme allow for indexing of non-unique values. For instance, in a wide column store such as HBase, an index entry might consist of multiple columns that point to the rows matching the common value as shown in the "COUNTRY" index in Figure 10-13.

However, there are some significant problems with the do-it-yourself approach outlined above:

- It's up to the application code to consistently maintain both the data in the base table and all of its indexes. Bugs in application code or ad hoc manipulation of data using alternative clients can lead to missing or incorrect data in the index.

- Ideally, the operations that modify the base table and the operation that modifies the index will be atomic: either both succeed or neither succeeds. However, in nonrelational databases, multi-object transactions are rarely available. If the index operation succeeds but not the base table modification (or vice versa), then the index will be incorrect.

- Eventual consistency raises a similar issue: an application may read from the index an entry that has not yet been propagated to every replica of the base table (or vice versa).

- The index table supports equality lookups, but generally not range operations, since unlike as in the B-tree structure, there is no pointer from one index entry to the next logical entry.

Do-it-yourself indexing is not completely impractical, but it places a heavy burden on the application and leads in practice to unreliable and fragile implementations. Most of these issues are mitigated when a database implements a native secondary indexing scheme. The secondary index implementation can be made independent of the application code, and the database engine can ensure that index entries and base table entries are maintained consistently.

Global and Local Indexes

Distributed databases raise additional issues for indexing schemes. If index entries are partitioned using normal mechanisms—either by consistent hashing of the key value or by using the key value as a shard key—then the index entry for a base table row is typically going to be located on a different node. As a result, most lookups will usually span two nodes and hence require two IO operations.

If the indexed value is unique, then the usual sharding or hashing mechanisms will distribute data evenly across the cluster. However, if the key value is non-unique, and especially if there is significant skew in the distribution of values, then index entries and hence index load may be unevenly distributed. For instance, the index on COUNTRY in Figure 10-13 would result in the index entries for the largest country (USA, in our example) being located on a single node.

To avoid these issues, secondary indexes in nonrelational databases are usually implemented as *local indexes*. Each node maintains its own index, which references data held only on the local node. Index-dependent queries are issued to each node, which returns any matching data via its local index to the query coordinator, which combines the results.

Figure 10-14 illustrates the local secondary indexing approach. A database client requests data for a specific non-key value (1). A query coordinator sends these requests to each node in the cluster (2). Each node examines its local index to determine if a matching value exists (3). If a matching value exists in the index, then the rowkey is retrieved from the index and used to retrieve data from the base table (4). Each node returns data to the query coordinator (5), which consolidates the results and returns them to the database client (6).

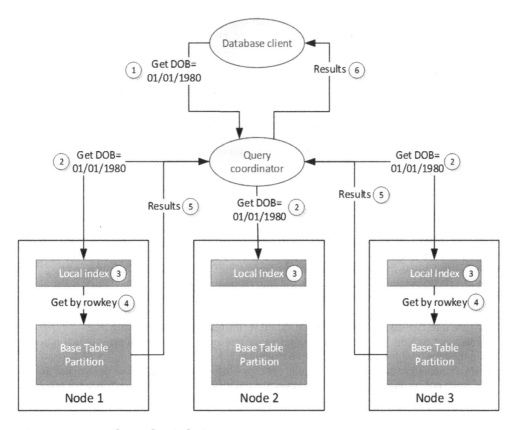

Figure 10-14. *Local secondary indexing*

Secondary Indexing Implementations in NoSQL Databases

Although most nonrelational databases implement local secondary indexes, the specific implementations vary significantly.

- **Cassandra** provides local secondary indexes. The implementation in Cassandra Query Language (CQL) uses syntax that is familiar to users of relational databases. However, internally the implementation involves column families on each node that associate indexed values with rowkeys in the base column family. Each index row is keyed on the indexed value and a wide column structure in the index row contains the rowkeys of matching base column family rows. The architecture is similar to the COUNTRY index example shown in Figure 10-13.

- **MongoDB** allows indexes to be created on nominated elements of documents within a collection. MongoDB indexes are traditional B-tree indexes similar to those found in relational systems and as illustrated in Figure 10-10.

- **Riak** is a pure key-value store. Since the values associated with keys in Riak are opaque to the database server, there is no schema element for Riak to index. However, Riak allows tags to be associated with specific objects, and local indexes on each node allow fast retrieval of matching tags. Riak architects now recommend using the built-in Solr integration discussed earlier in this chapter instead of this secondary indexing mechanism.

- **HBase** does not provide a native secondary index capability. If your HBase implementation requires secondary indexes, you are required to implement some form of DIY secondary indexing. However, HBase has a *coprocessor* feature that significantly improves the robustness of DIY indexes and reduces the overhead for the programmer. An HBase *observer coprocessor* acts like a database trigger in an RDBMS—it allows the programmer to specify code that will run when certain events occur in the database. Programmers can use observer coprocessors to maintain secondary indexes, thereby ensuring that the index is maintained automatically and without exception. Some third parties have provided libraries that further assist programmers who need to implement secondary indexes in HBase.

Conclusion

In this chapter we've reviewed some of the data model patterns implemented by nonrelational next-generation databases. NoSQL databases are often referred to as schema-less, but in reality schemas are more often flexible than nonexistent.

HBase and Cassandra data models are based on the Google BigTable design, which implements a sparse distributed multidimensional map structure. Column names in BigTable-oriented tables are in reality closer to the keys in a Java or .NET map structure than to the columns in relational systems. Although Cassandra uses BigTable-oriented data structures internally, the Cassandra engineers have implemented a more relational-style interface on top of the BigTable structure: the Cassandra Query Language.

Many nonrelational systems use the log-structured merge tree architecture, which can sustain higher write throughput than the traditional relational B-tree structures.

The initial implementation of many nonrelational systems—those based on BigTable or Dynamo in particular—supported only primary key access. However, the ability to retrieve data based on some other key is an almost universal requirement, so most nonrelational systems have implemented some form of secondary indexing.

■ ■ ■

CHAPTER 11

Languages and Programming Interfaces

Any fool can write code that a computer can understand. Good programmers write code that humans can understand.

—Martin Fowler

As far as the customer is concerned, the interface is the product.

—Jef Raskin

Crucial to the dominance of the relational database was the almost universal adoption of the SQL language as the mechanism for querying and modifying data. SQL is not a perfect language, but it has demonstrated sufficient flexibility to meet the needs of both non-programming database users and professional database programmers. Programmers embed SQL in programming languages, while non-programmers use SQL either explicitly within a query tool or implicitly when a BI tool uses SQL under the hood to talk to the database. Prior to the introduction of SQL, most IT departments labored with a backlog of requests for reports; SQL allowed the business user to "self-serve" these requests.

SQL remains the most significant database language. Not only does it remain the universal language for RDBMS, but it is also widely adopted in next-generation database systems of the NewSQL variety.

However, even though NoSQL has been retrospectively amended to mean "Not Only SQL" rather than "Hell No SQL!," SQL is not usually available for next-generation databases of the NoSQL variety. In this chapter, we look at how we can interact with these databases in the absence of SQL, and see how SQL is increasingly finding its way back into the world of nonrelational databases.

■ **Note** The code examples in this chapter are intended only to provide a flavor of database programming languages[1]—this chapter is not intended to serve as a tutorial or reference for any of the languages concerned.

SQL

SQL remains the most significant database programming language, even within the scope of next-generation database systems. Hundreds of books have been written on the topic of SQL (indeed, I've written a couple), and it would be superfluous to provide a full review of the language here. However, it is probably worth recapping the variations that exist within SQL implementations today, as well as key ingredients of the SQL language.

The SQL language consists of these major categories of statements:

- **Data query language (DQL)**, represented by the ubiquitous **SELECT** statement.

- **Data manipulation language (DML),** which includes statements that modify data in the database, such as UPDATE, DELETE, INSERT, and MERGE, together with transactional control statements (COMMIT, ROLLBACK, BEGIN TRANSACTION) and—for the purposes of this discussion—**data control language (DCL)** statements such as GRANT.

- **Data definition language (DDL),** which includes statements that create or alter tables and other structures (indexes, materialized views, etc.). DML also allows for the specification of stored procedures and triggers. These statements are usually highly vendor specific, since they incorporate support for proprietary programming languages (Oracle PL/SQL, for instance) or for storage clauses that are unique to the database in question.

The SQL language is the subject of several ANSI and ISO standard specifications. Some of these standards are:

- **SQL-89:** The first major standard to be widely adopted. This standard describes the core elements of the SQL language as we know it today.

- **SQL-92 (SQL2):** Added the modern join syntax, in which join conditions are fully qualified within the FROM clause, and added a standard metadata interface that provides descriptions of objects in the database and which is implemented by at least some vendors. SQL-92 introduced the concept of an "entry-level" subset of the specification (which was very similar to SQL-89).

- **SQL:1999 (SQL3):** An explosion on the moon propels the moon into interstellar space. Whoops, sorry, that was *Space: 1999*. SQL:1999 was somewhat less interesting, introducing object-oriented relational database features that almost nobody uses and a few minor language changes.

- **SQL:2003:** Introduced analytic "window" functions—an important innovation for analytics—and SQL/XML. It also finalized a specification for stored procedures.

- **SQL:2006, SQL:2008, SQL:2011:** Miscellaneous refinements, such as INSTEAD OF triggers, the MERGE statement, and temporal queries.

In my opinion, the various SQL standards have become increasingly disconnected from real-world SQL language implementations. It's common to hear vendors describe their SQL support as "entry-level SQL-92," effectively claiming credit for adhering to the minimum level of a 14-year-old specification.

In practice, you can expect an RDBMS to implement everything in SQL-92 at least with respect to the SELECT statement and DML. SQL:2003 windowing functions, which allow a calculation within a row to have visibility into a "window" of adjacent rows, are widely implemented and are probably the most significant single innovation introduced in the last 15 years of the SQL language standards.

DDL statements and stored procedure code will generally not be compatible across databases. DDL statements such as CREATE TABLE share a common syntax, but usually contain vendor-specific constructs such as custom data types or proprietary storage clauses. While the ANSI stored procedure syntax is implemented by DB2 and MySQL, Oracle and Microsoft SQL Server implement a completely incompatible stored program language.

NoSQL APIs

Databases that are described as NoSQL clearly have to provide a mechanism for inserting, modifying, and retrieving data. Since most of these databases were developed "by programmers for programmers," they usually primarily provide low-level APIs supported in a language such as Java.

Riak

Riak is an open-source implementation of the Amazon Dynamo model. It implements a pure key-value system: objects in Riak are located through the object's key and the object retrieved by the key is a binary object whose contents are opaque to the database engine.

Given the relatively simple interaction just described, we expect a fairly straightforward API, and that is what we get. Let's look at some Java code that inserts a value into a Riak bucket:

```
1. RiakClient myClient = RiakClient.newClient(myServer);
2. // Create the key, value and set the bucket
3. String myKey = Long.toString(System.currentTimeMillis());
4. String myValue = myKey + ":" + Thread.getAllStackTraces().toString();
5. Location myLocation = new Location(new Namespace("MyBucket"), myKey);
6. StoreValue sv = new StoreValue.Builder(myValue).withLocation(myLocation)
      .build();
7. StoreValue.Response svResponse = myClient.execute(sv);
8. System.out.println("response="+svResponse);
```

In lines 3 to 5, we define a key (set to the current time in milliseconds), a value (a string representation of the current stack trace), and the bucket ("MyBucket") that will receive the value. Line 6 prepares a StoreValue object—this object contains the key-value pair and the bucket name that it will be associated with. We execute the StoreValue in line 7, effectively adding the data to the database.

The StoreValue object takes options that can control optional behaviors such as quorums. In the example that follows, we specify that the write can complete as long as at least one node completes the write IO (see Chapter 9 for a discussion of quorums):

```
sv = new StoreValue.Builder(Thread.getAllStackTraces()).
      withLocation(myLocation).
      withOption(StoreValue.Option.W,Quorum.oneQuorum()).build();
```

This example also utilizes one of the cool features of the Riak API: if we pass a Java object as our value, Riak will automatically convert it to a JSON document.

Here, we retrieve the data we just inserted. Note that we use the same Location object (MyLocation) that we used for the insert:

```
FetchValue fv = new FetchValue.Builder(myLocation).build();
FetchValue.Response fvResp = myClient.execute(fv);
String myFetchedData = fvResp.getValue(String.class);
System.out.println("value=" + myFetchedData);
```

The value returned is a string containing a JSON representation of the stack trace object we inserted earlier:

```
value=
{"Thread[nioEventLoopGroup-2-8,10,main]":
   [{"methodName":"poll0","fileName":null,
     "lineNumber":-2,
     "className":"sun.nio.ch.WindowsSelectorImpl$SubSelector" ...
```

For some applications, this put/get programming model may be sufficient. However, there are significant nuances to Riak programming that arise from the Dynamo consistency model. You may remember from Chapters 8 and 9 that conflicting updates may result in *siblings* that need to be resolved by the application. Riak provides interfaces you can implement to automate the resolution of such conflicts.

Next is a simplistic conflict resolver class. This resolver will be invoked when siblings of type String are detected. The class is passed a list of strings and returns the "resolved" result. Any application code could be implemented here, but in my example I've just returned the first string in the list.

```
public class MyResolver implements ConflictResolver<String> {
    public String resolve(List<String> siblings) {
        return(siblings.get(0) );
    }
}
```

The conflict resolver needs to be registered in order to become active:

```
ConflictResolverFactory factory = ConflictResolverFactory.getInstance();
factory.registerConflictResolver(String.class, new MyResolver());
```

Now, if we fetch a string value that includes siblings, the conflict resolver will be invoked and will resolve them. In our case, we used almost the simplest object type—string—and used trivial resolution logic: in a production application, the object types would likely be an application-defined complex class, and the resolution might involve highly complex logic to merge the two objects.

As well as resolving siblings, the Riak API allows for modifications to complex data types to be handled. Application code need not provide a complete copy of the new object to be inserted, but instead specify only a change vector that is to be applied to an existing object. For instance, if an object were a list of friends, we could add a new friend simply by specifying the new friend's name, without having to retrieve and reinsert all existing friends.

By extending the UpdateValue super class, we can define how an update value is applied to a Riak object. In the example that follows, the apply method defines that the update will simply be appended (after a "\n" carriage return) to the Riak object.

```
public class MyRiakUpdater extends UpdateValue.Update<String> {
    private final String updatedString;
    public MyRiakUpdater(String updatedString) {
        this.updatedString = updatedString;
    }
    public String apply(String original) {
        return original + "\n" + updatedString;
    }
}
```

To invoke the updater, we create a new object instance from the updater class we created earlier and apply it to the original version using the withUpdate method.

```
MyRiakUpdater myUpdatedData = new MyRiakUpdater(newData);
UpdateValue myUpdate = new UpdateValue.Builder(myLocation)
      .withUpdate(myUpdatedData).build();
UpdateValue.Response updateResponse = myClient.execute(myUpdate);
```

This code will apply the update to the Riak object after first resolving siblings (providing we have registered an appropriate conflict resolver).

Hbase

The HBase API bears some resemblance to the put/get pattern we saw in the Riak API. However, because HBase tables have a wide column structure, some additional complexity is introduced.

HBase supports a simple shell that allows access to basic data definition and manipulation commands. Here, we launch the HBase shell and issue commands to create a table ourfriends with two column families: info and friends:

```
$ hbase shell
hbase(main):003:0* create 'ourfriends', {NAME => 'info'}, {NAME => 'friends'}
0 row(s) in 1.3400 seconds
```

Each put command populates one cell within a row, so these four commands populate columns in the row identified by rowkey 'guy':

```
hbase(main):005:0* put 'ourfriends', 'guy','info:email','guy@gmail.com'
0 row(s) in 0.0900 seconds
hbase(main):006:0> put 'ourfriends', 'guy','info:userid','9990'
0 row(s) in 0.0070 seconds
hbase(main):007:0> put 'ourfriends', 'guy','friends:Jo','jo@gmail.com'
0 row(s) in 0.0050 seconds
hbase(main):008:0> put 'ourfriends', 'guy','friends:John','john@gmail.com'
0 row(s) in 0.0040 seconds
```

The get command pulls the values for the specific rowkey, allowing us to see the cell values we just input:

```
hbase(main):018:0* get 'ourfriends','guy'
COLUMN                     CELL
 friends:Jo                timestamp=1444123707299, value=jo@gmail.com
 friends:John              timestamp=1444123707324, value=john@gmail.com
 info:email                timestamp=1444123707214, value=guy@gmail.com
 info:userid               timestamp=1444123707274, value=9990
4 row(s) in 0.0390 seconds
```

Note that this is a wide column structure, where the column names in the column family friends represent the names of friends. This is the data structure that was illustrated in Chapter 10, Figure 10-5.

The shell is suitable for simple experimentation and data validation, but most real work in HBase is done within Java programs. Here, we see simple code to connect to an HBase server from a Java program:

```
Configuration config = HBaseConfiguration.create();
config.set("hbase.zookeeper.quorum", myServer);
config.set("hbase.zookeeper.property.clientport", "2181");
HBaseAdmin.checkHBaseAvailable(config);
Connection connection = ConnectionFactory.createConnection(config);
```

For column families with a fixed column structure, such as info in our example, we can retrieve the data fairly simply:

```
1. Table myTable = connection.getTable(TableName.valueOf("ourfriends"));
2. byte[] myRowKey = Bytes.toBytes("guy");
3. byte[] myColFamily=Bytes.toBytes("info");
4. byte[] myColName=Bytes.toBytes("email");

5. Get myGet = new Get(myRowKey);
6. Result myResult = myTable.get(myGet);
7. byte[] myBytes = myResult.getValue(myColFamily, myColName);
8. String email = Bytes.toString(myBytes);
9. System.out.println("Email address="+email);
```

Lines 1 through 4 specify the table, rowkey, column family, and column name to be retrieved. Lines 5 and 6 retrieve the row for the specified rowkey, and line 7 extracts a cell value for the specified column family and column name. Line 8 converts the value from a byte array to a string. This is one of the less endearing features of the HBase API: you are constantly required to convert data to and from HBase native byte arrays.

For dynamic column names, we need to retrieve the names of the columns for each row before we can retrieve the data. The getFamilyMap method returns a map structure from a result object identifying the column names within a specific row:

```
NavigableMap<byte[], byte[]>
      myFamilyMap = myResult.getFamilyMap(myColFamily);
```

We can then iterate through the column names and use the standard getValue call to retrieve them:

```
for (byte[] colNameBytes : myFamilyMap.keySet()) {
      // Get the name of the column in the column family
      String colName = Bytes.toString(colNameBytes);
      byte[] colValueBytes = myResult.getValue(myColFamily, colNameBytes);
      System.out.println("Column " + colName + "=" + Bytes.toString(colValueBytes));
}
```

The HBase put method is similar in form to the get method and allows us to place a new column value into a cell. Remember as discussed in Chapter 10, Hbase cells may contain multiple versions of data, identified by timestamp. So the put method really adds a new value rather than overwriting the existing value.

Here, we add a new friend:

```
myColFamily=Bytes.toBytes("friends");
byte [] myNewColName=Bytes.toBytes("paul");
byte [] myNewColValue=Bytes.toBytes("paul@fmail.com");
Put myPut=new Put(myRowKey);
myPut.addColumn(myColFamily,myNewColName,myNewColValue);
myTable.put(myPut);
```

The HBase API does not need to include methods for sibling resolution as does Riak, since HBase uses locking and strict consistency to prevent such siblings from ever being created.

The HBase API includes additional methods for scanning rowkey ranges, which can be useful when the rowkey includes some kind of natural partitioning value, such as a customer ID, or where the rowkey indicates some kind of temporal order. Also, you may recall from our discussion in Chapter 10 that HBase supports a *coprocessor* architecture allowing code to be invoked when certain data manipulation operations occur. This architecture provides a database trigger-like capability that allows us to perform validation on input values, maintain secondary indexes, or maintain derived values.

MongoDB

The APIs we've seen in Riak and HBase are not overly complex when compared to popular development frameworks like Spring or J2EE. However, for the casual user—especially one not proficient in programming—they are virtually inaccessible. The languages require that you explicitly navigate to the desired values and do not provide any direct support for complex queries.

MongoDB goes some of the way toward addressing these restrictions by providing a rich query language implemented in JavaScript, and exposed through the MongoDB shell. Collection objects within MongoDB include a find() method that allows fairly complex queries to be constructed. Figure 11-1 provides a comparison of a MongoDB query with an equivalent SQL statement.

```
db.films.find({
    "Rating": "PG","Rental Duration": "7"}          SELECT title, length
                                                       FROM film
    ,                                                  WHERE rating = 'PG'
    {"Title": 1,"Length": 1})                          AND rental_duration=7
    .sort({"Length": -1})                        ORDER BY length DESC
    .limit(5)                                      LIMIT 5
```

Figure 11-1. *Comparison of MongoDB JavaScript query and SQL*

■ **Note**   The example data for MongoDB and Couchbase is based on a port of the MySQL "Sakila" sample schema, which describes a database for a DVD rental business. DVD rental businesses are largely gone now, but the sample database provides a schema familiar to MySQL users. The converted database is available at http://bit.ly/1LwY9xl.

Quite complicated queries can be constructed using the find() method, but for queries that want to aggregate across documents, we need to use the aggregate() method. The aggregate() method implements a logical equivalent of the SQL GROUP BY clause. Figure 11-2 compares a SQL GROUP BY statement with its MongoDB equivalent.

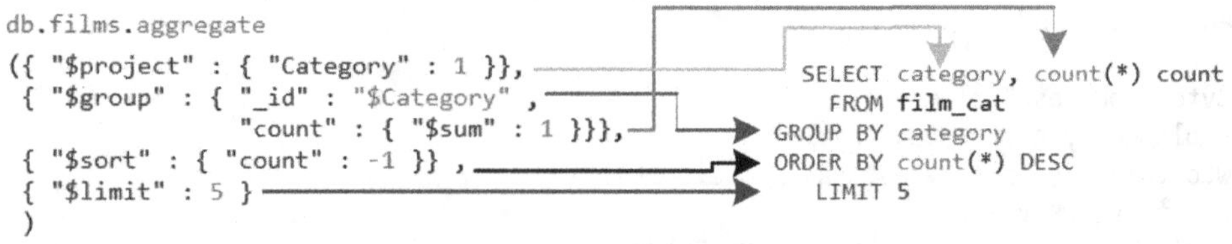

```
db.films.aggregate
({ "$project" : { "Category" : 1 }},
  { "$group" : { "_id" : "$Category" ,                    SELECT category, count(*) count
                 "count" : { "$sum" : 1 }}},                 FROM film_cat
  { "$sort" : { "count" : -1 }} ,                         GROUP BY category
  { "$limit" : 5 }                                        ORDER BY count(*) DESC
  )                                                         LIMIT 5
```

Figure 11-2. *MongoDB aggregation framework compared with SQL*

The JavaScript-based MongoDB shell language is not directly embeddable within other programming languages. Historically, MongoDB drivers for various languages implemented interfaces inspired by the JavaScript interface, but with significant divergence across languages. More recently, a cross-driver specification has been developed that improves consistency among the driver implementations for various programming languages.

Using Java as an example, here is some code that connects to a server and selects the "test" collection within the NGDBDemo database:

```
MongoClient mongoClient = new MongoClient(mongoServer);
MongoDatabase database = mongoClient.getDatabase("NGDBDemo");
MongoCollection<Document> collection = database.getCollection("test");
```

The following code creates and inserts a new document:

```
1.   Document people = new Document();              // A document for a person
2.   people.put("Name", "Guy");
3.   people.put("Email", "guy@gmail.com");
4.   BasicDBList friendList = new BasicDBList();    // List of friends

5.   BasicDBObject friendDoc = new BasicDBObject(); // A single friend

6.   friendDoc.put("Name", "Jo");
7.   friendDoc.put("Email", "Jo@gmail.com");
8.   friendList.add(friendDoc);                     // Add the friend
9.   friendDoc.clear();
10.  friendDoc.put("Name", "John");
11.  friendDoc.put("Email", "john@gmail.com");
12.  friendList.add(friendDoc);                     // Add another friend
13.  people.put("Friends", friendDoc);
14.  collection.insertOne(people);
```

Line 1 creates an empty document. Lines 2 and 3 add some values to the document. In lines 4 through 7, we create a List structure that represents an array of subdocuments and inserts the first document into that array. Lines 9 through 13 insert a second subdocument to the list. Line 14 inserts the new document (which includes two embedded friend documents) into MongoDB.

This programming pattern reflects the underlying structure of JSON documents as described in Chapter 10: JSON documents are composed of arbitrarily nested objects, values, and arrays. The MongoDB interface requires that we build these programmatically, although there are several utility classes available independently that allow Java objects to be converted to and from JSON documents.

Collection objects in the Java driver support a `find()` method that, although not syntactically identical with the JavaScript version, allows us to execute the same operations that we can perform in the JavaScript shell:

```
Document myDoc = collection.find(eq("Name", "Guy")).first();
System.out.println(myDoc.toJson());
```

The API provides scrollable cursors that allow us to navigate through a result set or an entire collection. This example iterates through all the documents in a collection:

```
MongoCursor<Document> cursor = collection.find().iterator();
try {
        while (cursor.hasNext()) {
                System.out.println(cursor.next().toJson());
        }
}
finally {
        cursor.close();
}
```

A more compact alternative fetch loop could be framed like this:

```
for (Document cur : collection.find()) {
        System.out.println(cur.toJson());
}
```

Cassandra Query Language (CQL)

Cassandra's underlying data structures are based on Google's BigTable model, which would lead us to expect an API syntactically similar to that of the HBase API. Indeed, the early thrift-based Cassandra APIs were easily as complex as the HBase programming API; arguably even more so since Cassandra had implemented a "SuperColumn" structure that extended the range of possible column family configurations, but which was hard to conceptualize and program against.

In version 0.8, the Cassandra team made a decisive shift from an API-centric interface to a language-based interface, inspired by SQL: the *Cassandra Query Language* (*CQL*). CQL uses familiar SQL idioms for data definition, manipulation, and query tasks, and is now the preferred method for interacting with Cassandra databases from query tools or within programs.

CQL provides Cassandra with an interactive ad hoc query capability through the `cqlsh` program. It also simplifies programming tasks by allowing for more succinct and comprehensible data manipulation code, which looks familiar to those who have coded in SQL-based interfaces such as JDBC.

But perhaps most significantly and most controversially, Cassandra CQL abstracts the underlying wide column BigTable-style data model in favor of a more relational-like tabular scheme. We discussed this in detail in in Chapter 10 and won't repeat that discussion here: see in particular, Figure 10-7 for a comparison of the Cassandra CQL representation of data compared with the underlying wide column structure.

The best—and maybe also the worst—thing about this CQL abstraction is that users can interact with Cassandra without understanding the nuances of the wide column data model. However, although you can write functional Cassandra CQL without understanding the underlying Cassandra data model, the best results will be attained if you do understand how the two relate.

Wide column structures in CQL are defined by using composite primary keys, where the first part of the key defines the partitioning (e.g., the rowkey), and the second part of the key defines the clustering columns. Clustering column values become the dynamic column names in the wide column family.

The CQL statements that follow—executed in the `cqlsh` shell—define and populate a Cassandra table roughly equivalent to the HBase table we created earlier in this chapter:

```
cqlsh:guy> CREATE TABLE friends
       ... (name text,
       ... friend_name text,
       ... friend_email text,
       ... PRIMARY KEY (name,friend_name));

cqlsh:guy>   INSERT INTO friends (name,friend_name,friend_email)
                 VALUES('Guy','Jo','Jo@gmail.com');
cqlsh:guy>   INSERT INTO friends (name,friend_name,friend_email)
                 VALUES('Guy','Chris','Chris@gmail.com');
cqlsh:guy>   INSERT INTO friends (name,friend_name,friend_email)
                 VALUES('Guy','John','John@gmail.com');
```

Familiar SQL-like constructs allow us to perform updates and deletes, create indexes, or issue queries.

However, the CQL SELECT statement has limited capabilities when compared to standard SQL: in particular, joins and aggregate (GROUP BY) operations are not supported. Furthermore, WHERE clauses and ORDER BY clauses are severely restricted. Ordering and range queries are limited to clustering columns within a specific partition key.

These limitations seem confusing if you think of CQL tables as relational structures. But if you remember that the first part of the key is actually a rowkey that is consistently hashed across the cluster, then the limitation seems more reasonable. Cassandra is unable to effectively perform a range scan across rowkey values that are hashed across the entire cluster. Nor is it possible to access the partition columns without accessing a specific row, since every row could have entirely distinct column values.

So this ORDER BY clause cannot be supported:

```
cqlsh:guy> SELECT * FROM friends ORDER BY name;
SInvalidRequest: code=2200 [Invalid query] message="ORDER BY is only supported when the
partition key is restricted by an EQ or an IN."
```

But this is legal:

```
cqlsh:guy> SELECT * FROM friends WHERE name = 'Guy'
           ORDER BY friend_name;

 name | friend_name | friend_email
------+-------------+------------------
 Guy  |       Chris | Chris@gmail.com
 Guy  |          Jo |    Jo@gmail.com
 Guy  |        John | John@gmail.com
```

A similar restriction prevents range operations on the partition key:

```
cqlsh:guy> SELECT * FROM friends WHERE name > 'Guy'  ;
InvalidRequest: code=2200 [Invalid query] message="Only EQ and IN relation are supported on
the partition key (unless you use the token() function)"
```

But allows a range query on the clustering key, provided the partition key is also specified:

```
cqlsh:guy> SELECT * FROM friends
            WHERE name='Guy' AND friend_name > 'Guy';
```

name	friend_name	friend_email
Guy	Jo	Jo@gmail.com
Guy	John	John@gmail.com

CQL is used within Java programs or other languages using a driver syntax that is similar to JDBC: CQL statements are passed as strings to methods that submit the CQL to the server and return result sets or return codes.

The following Java code connects to a Cassandra server and specifies a keyspace (lines 1-3), submits a CQL query (lines 5-6) and iterates through the results (lines 8-11):

```
1.  String myServer=args[0];
2.  Cluster cluster = Cluster.builder().addContactPoint(myServer).build();
3.  Session myKeySpace = cluster.connect("guy");
4.
5.  String cqlString = "SELECT * FROM friends where name='Guy'";
6.  ResultSet myResults = myKeySpace.execute(cqlString);
7.
8.  for (Row row : myResults.all()) {
9.      System.out.println(row.getString(0) +" "+
10. row.getString(1) + " " + row.getString(2));
11. }
```

If we don't know the structure of the result set in advance, then there is a metadata interface that allows us to extract column names and data types:

```
List<Definition> colDefs = myResults.getColumnDefinitions().asList();
System.out.println("Column count=" + colDefs.size());
System.out.println("Column Names:");
for (Definition colDef : colDefs) {
    System.out.println(colDef.getName());
}
```

MapReduce

The put and get methods provided by early NoSQL systems support only record-at-a-time processing and place a heavy programming burden on an application that needs to perform even simple analytics on the data. Google's MapReduce algorithm—first published in 2004—provided a solution for parallelizing computation across a distributed system, and it has been widely adopted not just by systems inspired by the Google stack, such as Hadoop and HBase, but also by many early NoSQL systems, such as CouchDB and MongoDB.

The canonical example of MapReduce is provided by the WordCount (https://wiki.apache.org/hadoop/WordCount) program, which represents almost the simplest possible MapReduce example. We showed a diagrammatic representation of WordCount way back in Figure 2-4.

In the WordCount example, the map phase uses a *tokenizer* to break up the input into words, then assigns a value of 1 to each word:

```java
public static class Map
                extends Mapper<LongWritable, Text, Text, IntWritable> {
    private final static IntWritable one = new IntWritable(1);
    private Text word = new Text();

    public void map(LongWritable key, Text value, Context context)
                    throws IOException, InterruptedException {
        String line = value.toString();
        StringTokenizer tokenizer = new StringTokenizer(line);
        while (tokenizer.hasMoreTokens()) {
            word.set(tokenizer.nextToken());
            context.write(word, one);
        }
    }
}
```

The reducer class takes these name:value pairs (where the value is always 1) and calculates the sum of counts for each word:

```java
public static class Reduce
                extends Reducer<Text, IntWritable, Text, IntWritable> {

    public void reduce(Text key, Iterable<IntWritable> values,
                    Context context)
                    throws IOException, InterruptedException {
        int sum = 0;
        for (IntWritable val : values) {
            sum += val.get();
        }
        context.write(key, new IntWritable(sum));
    }
}
```

The MapReduce job is invoked by mainline code that defines input and output types and files, specifies the map and reducer classes, and invokes the job:

```java
Job job  = Job .getInstance(conf, "wordcount");

job.setOutputKeyClass(Text.class);
job.setOutputValueClass(IntWritable.class);

job.setMapperClass(Map.class);
job.setReducerClass(Reduce.class);

job.setInputFormatClass(TextInputFormat.class);
job.setOutputFormatClass(TextOutputFormat.class);
```

```
FileInputFormat.addInputPath(job, new Path(args[0]));
FileOutputFormat.setOutputPath(job, new Path(args[1]));

job.waitForCompletion(true);
```

MapReduce coding in Java is somewhat cumbersome and involves a lot of boilerplate coding. Many alternative implementations are much simpler. For instance, here is the WordCount algorithm implemented in MongoDB's JavaScript MapReduce framework:

```
db.films.mapReduce(
  /* Map     */ function() {emit (this.Category,1);},
  /* Reduce */ function(key,values) {return Array.sum(values)} ,

  { out: "MovieRatings"  }
)
```

This JavaScript reads from the films collection, and does a word count on the categories of each film, which is output to the collection "MovieRatings":

```
> db.MovieRatings.find();
{ "_id" : "Action", "value" : 64 }
{ "_id" : "Animation", "value" : 66 }
{ "_id" : "Children", "value" : 60 }
{ "_id" : "Classics", "value" : 57 }
{ "_id" : "Comedy", "value" : 58 }
```

MapReduce is a flexible programming paradigm capable of being adapted to a wide range of data processing algorithms. However, it is rarely the most efficient algorithm for a given problem and is usually not the most programmer-efficient approach. Consequently, there have been many frameworks that provide alternative programming and processing paradigms.

Pig

It was early realized that the full potential of Hadoop could not be unlocked if commonplace operations required highly skilled Java programmers with experience in complex MapReduce programming. As we will see later in this chapter, at Facebook the development of Hive—the original SQL on Hadoop—was an important step toward finding a solution for this problem. At Yahoo! the Hadoop team felt that the SQL paradigm could not address a sufficiently broad category of MapReduce programming tasks. Yahoo! therefore set out to create a language that maximized productivity but still allowed for complex procedural data flows. The result was *Pig*.

Pig superficially resembles scripting languages such as Perl or Python in that it offers flexible syntax and dynamically typed variables. But Pig actually implements a fairly unique programming paradigm; it is best described as a *data flow language*. Pig statements typically represent data operations roughly analogous to individual operators in SQL—load, sort, join, group, aggregate, and so on. Typically, each Pig statement accepts one or more datasets as inputs and returns a single dataset as an output. For instance, a Pig statement might accept two datasets as inputs and return the joined set as an output. Users can add their own operations through a Java-based *user-defined function* (*UDF*) facility.

For those familiar with SQL programming, programming in Pig turns the programming model upside down. SQL is a nonprocedural language: you specify the data you want rather than outline the sequence of events to be executed. In contrast, Pig is explicitly procedural: the exact sequence of data operations is specified within your Pig code. For SQL gurus, it resembles more the execution plan of a SQL statement rather than the SQL statement itself.

SQL compilers and Hive's HQL compiler include optimizers that attempt to determine the most efficient way to resolve a SQL request. Pig is not heavily reliant on such an optimizer, since the execution plan is explicit. As the Pig gurus are fond of saying "Pig uses the optimizer between your ears."

Here is the ubiquitous word count implemented in Pig:

```
file= load 'some file';
b = foreach file generate flatten(TOKENIZE((chararray)$0)) as word;
c = group b by word;
d = foreach c generate COUNT(b), group;
store d into 'pig_wordcount';
```

Pig can be used to perform complex workflows and provide an ad hoc query capability similar to SQL. For instance, the example shown in Figure 11-3 performs joins, filters, and aggregations to provide a summary of customers in the Asian region. Figure 11-3 also includes a comparable SQL statement.

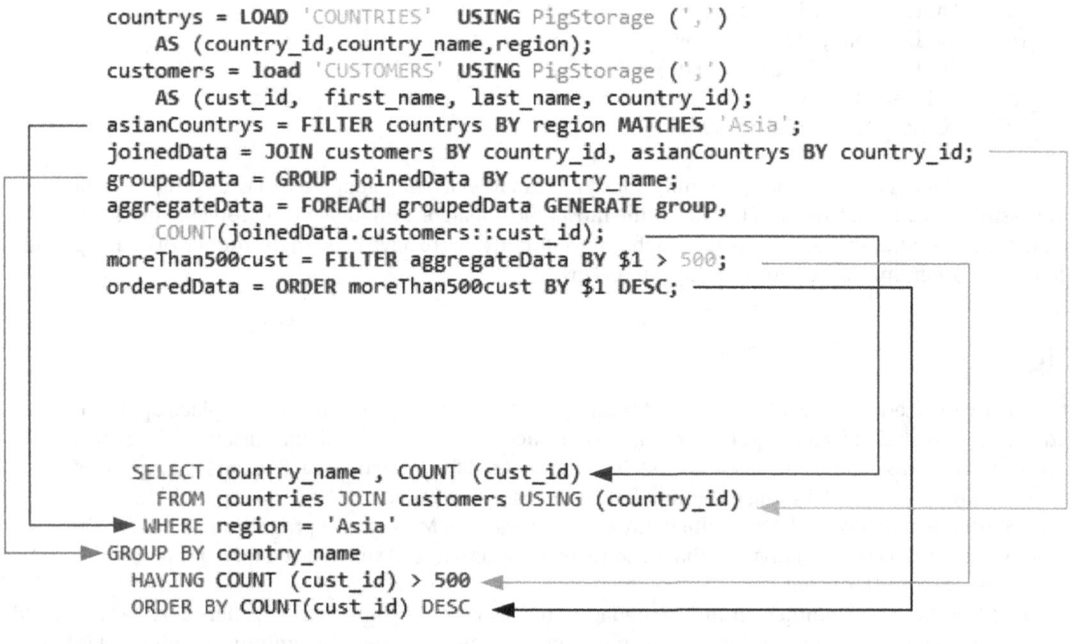

```
countrys = LOAD 'COUNTRIES' USING PigStorage (',')
    AS (country_id,country_name,region);
customers = load 'CUSTOMERS' USING PigStorage (',')
    AS (cust_id,  first_name, last_name, country_id);
asianCountrys = FILTER countrys BY region MATCHES 'Asia';
joinedData = JOIN customers BY country_id, asianCountrys BY country_id;
groupedData = GROUP joinedData BY country_name;
aggregateData = FOREACH groupedData GENERATE group,
    COUNT(joinedData.customers::cust_id);
moreThan500cust = FILTER aggregateData BY $1 > 500;
orderedData = ORDER moreThan500cust BY $1 DESC;




    SELECT country_name , COUNT (cust_id)
        FROM countries JOIN customers USING (country_id)
    WHERE region = 'Asia'
GROUP BY country_name
    HAVING COUNT (cust_id) > 500
    ORDER BY COUNT(cust_id) DESC
```

Figure 11-3. *Pig compared to SQL*

Although Pig is capable of expressing virtually any data query that can be expressed in SQL syntax, it is also capable of performing more complex data flows that would require multiple SQL statements chained together with procedural code in an RDBMS.

Nevertheless, while Pig is more flexible than SQL, it is not a Turing complete programming language: it lacks the control structures required for a complete general-purpose programming solution. However, Pig can be embedded in Python and other languages.

Directed Acyclic Graphs

Hadoop 1.0 was based on the MapReduce pattern. Complex programs could link multiple MapReduce steps to achieve their end result.

It's long been acknowledged that while MapReduce is a broadly applicable model that can support a wide range of job types, it is not the best model for all workloads. In particular, MapReduce has a very large startup cost, which means that even the simplest "Hello World" MapReduce job typically takes minutes rather than seconds; this alone makes MapReduce a poor choice for interactive workloads and low-latency operations.

Hadoop 2.0 introduced the YARN framework, which allows Hadoop to run workloads based on other processing patterns—of which MapReduce is just one.

The *Apache Tez* project (*Tez* is Hindi for "speed") is one of a number of YARN-based initiatives that provide Hadoop with a processing framework supporting both the massive batch processing that characterizes traditional Hadoop workloads and low-latency operations that allow Hadoop to support a wider variety of solutions.

Tez is based on a flexible processing paradigm known as *directed acyclic graph* (*DAG*). This intimidating term actually describes a familiar processing model. Anyone who has examined a SQL execution plan will have encountered a DAG. These graphs describe how a complex request is decomposed into multiple operations that are executed in a specific order and that can arbitrarily feed into each other. MapReduce itself is a DAG, but the MapReduce paradigm severely limits the types of graphs that can be constructed. Furthermore, MapReduce requires that each step in the graph be executed by a distinct set of processes, while Tez allows multiple steps in the graph to be executed by a single process, potentially on a specific node of the Hadoop cluster.

Cascading

Cascading is a popular open-source Java framework that abstracts Hadoop MapReduce or YARN-based processing primitives. In some respects, it resembles Pig in that it works with high-level data flows and transformations and spares the programmer the labor involved in constructing low-level parallelization classes. However, unlike Pig, Cascading is integrated within the Java language and is capable of creating solutions that are more modular and sophisticated.

The Cascading programming model is based on sources, sinks, and pipes assembled in data flows. The programmer assembles these pipes to construct programs that are more sophisticated than MapReduce. These workflows represent the DAG discussed in the previous section.

Spark

We looked at the origins and architecture of the *Spark* project in Chapter 7. Spark can be thought of as "memory-based Hadoop," but in truth it offers more than just an in-memory speed boost. The Spark API operates at a higher level of abstraction than native YARN or MapReduce code, offering improvements in programmer productivity and execution speed.

Sparks supports APIs in Python, Java, and other languages, but it is native to the Scala language, so our examples here will use the Scala API.

Here, we load text files (in this case, from HDFS) into Spark *Resilient Distributed Datasets* (RDDs)

```
val countries=sc.textFile("COUNTRIES")
val customers=sc.textFile("CUSTOMERS")
```

Spark RDDs are immutable: we can't alter the contents of an RDD; rather, we perform operations that create new RDDs.

The HDFS inputs are CSV files, so in our initial RDDs each line in the input file is represented as a single string. Here's the first element in the countries RDD:

```
scala> countries.first()
res9: String = "52790,United States of America,Americas"
```

In the next example, we use a map function to extract the key value from each of the CSV strings and create key-value pair RDDs.

```
val countryRegions=countries.map(x=>(x.split(",")(0),x.split(",")(2)))
val AsianCountries=countryRegions.filter(x=> x._2.contains("Asia") )
// Country codes and country names
val countryNames=countries.map(x=>(x.split(",")(0),x.split(",")(1)))
```

The first RDD countryRegions contains all country codes and their associated regions. The second (AsianCountries) uses the filter() method to create a RDD containing only Asian countries. The third (countryNames) creates an RDD with country names keyed by country ID. Here's the first element in the countryNames RDD:

```
scala> countryNames.first()
res12: (String, String) = (52790,United States of America)
```

Aggregations can be created by performing map and reduce operations. The first line that follows uses map to emit a country name and the numeral 1 for each customer. The second line invokes a reducer that emits an RDD containing the counts of customers in each country:

```
val custByCountry=customers.map(x=>(x.split(",")(3),1))
val custByCountryCount=custByCountry.reduceByKey((x,y)=> x+y)
```

In the next statement, we join the RDD containing customer counts by country ID with the list of Asian country IDs that we created earlier. Because we are using the default inner join method, this returns only customer counts for Asian regions.

```
val AsiaCustCount=AsianCountries.join(custByCountryCount)
```

The next join operation joins our RDD containing country names keyed by country code to the previous RDD. We now have an RDD that contains counts of customers by country name in the Asian region:

```
val AsiaCustCountryNames=AsiaCustCount.join(countryNames)
```

This Spark workflow is roughly equivalent to the Pig workflow shown in Figure 11-3. However, for massive datasets, the Spark job could be expected to complete in a fraction of the time, since every operation following the initial load from HDFS would complete in memory.

The Return of SQL

I don't know about you, but as I created the examples in this chapter I was struck by the "Tower of Babel" impression created by the new generation of database languages. Say what you will about SQL, but for more than two decades database programmers have all been speaking the same language. As a result of the explosion of nonrelational systems, we've all been forced to speak different languages. And while some of these languages offer definite advantages for working with unstructured data or for parallelization of programming tasks, in many cases the level of abstraction has been reduced and the work for the programmer increased.

So it's not surprising that within just a few years after the initial enthusiasm for NoSQL, we've seen SQL return to almost every new database niche. SQL just has too many advantages: it's a high-level abstraction that simplifies data access and manipulation, it's a language in which literally millions of database users are conversant, and there are hundreds of popular business intelligence and analytic tools that use it under the hood as the means for getting at data.

Hive

Hive is the original SQL on Hadoop. We discussed the origins and architecture of Hive in Chapter 2. From the very early days of Hadoop, Hive represented the most accessible face of Hadoop for many users.

Hive Query Language (*HQL*) is a SQL-based language that comes close to SQL-92 entry-level compliance, particularly within its SELECT statement. DML statements—such as INSERT, DELETE, and UPDATE—are supported in recent versions, though the real purpose of Hive is to provide query access to Hadoop data usually ingested via other means. Some SQL-2003 analytic window functions are also supported.

As discussed in Chapter 2, HQL is compiled to MapReduce or—in later releases—more sophisticated YARN-based DAG algorithms.

The following is a simple Hive query that performs the same analysis as our earlier Pig and Spark examples:

```
0: jdbc:Hive2://>   SELECT country_name, COUNT (cust_id)
0: jdbc:Hive2://>     FROM countries co JOIN customers cu
0: jdbc:Hive2://>       ON(cu.country_id=co.country_id)
0: jdbc:Hive2://>    WHERE region = 'Asia'
0: jdbc:Hive2://> GROUP BY country_name
0: jdbc:Hive2://>   HAVING COUNT (cust_id) > 500;

2015-10-10 11:38:55    Starting to launch local task to process map join;    maximum
memory = 932184064
<<Bunch of Hadoop JobTracker output deleted>>
2015-10-10 11:39:05,928 Stage-2 map = 0%,  reduce = 0%
2015-10-10 11:39:12,246 Stage-2 map = 100%,  reduce = 0%, Cumulative CPU 2.28 sec
2015-10-10 11:39:20,582 Stage-2 map = 100%,  reduce = 100%, Cumulative CPU 4.4 sec
+---------------+------+--+
| country_name  | _c1  |
+---------------+------+--+
| China         | 712  |
| Japan         | 624  |
| Singapore     | 597  |
+---------------+------+--+
3 rows selected (29.014 seconds)
```

HQL statements look and operate like SQL statements. There are a few notable differences between HQL and commonly used standard SQL, however:

- HQL supports a number of *table generating functions* which can be used to return multiple rows from an embedded field that may contain an array of values or a map of name:value pairs. The Explode() function returns one row for each element in an array or map, while json_tuple() explodes an embedded JSON document.

- Hive provides a SORT BY clause that requests output be sorted only within each reducer within the MapReduce pipeline. Compared to ORDER BY, this avoids a large sort in the final reducer stage, but may not return results in sorted order.

- DISTRIBUTE BY controls how mappers distribute output to reducers. Rather than distributing values to reducers based on hashing of key values, we can insist that each reducer receive contiguous ranges of a specific column. DISTRIBUTE BY can be used in conjunction with SORT BY to achieve an overall ordering of results without requiring an expensive final sort operation. CLUSTER BY combines the semantics of DISTRIBUTE BY and SORT BY operations that specify the same column list.

Hive can query data in HBase tables and data held in HDFS. Support for Spark is available, though still under active development.

Impala

It's difficult to overstate the significance of Hive to the early adoption of Hadoop. Hive allowed non-Java programmers a familiar mechanism for accessing data held in Hadoop, and allowed third-party analytic solutions to more easily integrate with Hadoop.

However, the similarity between Hive and RDBMS SQL led inevitably to unrealistic expectations. RDBMS users had become used to SQL as a real-time query tool, whereas even the simplest Hive queries would typically take minutes to complete, since even the simplest query had to undertake the overhead of initiating a MapReduce job. Furthermore, caching of data in memory typically reduces overall SQL response time by 90 percent or more, while Hive queries were totally I/O bound. Initial releases of Hive also employed fairly primitive query optimization.

Disappointment with Hive performance led to a fairly intensive effort to improve Hive, and modern versions of Hive outperform the initial releases by several orders of magnitude.

Cloudera's *Impala* project aims to provide low-latency ANSI-compliant SQL on Hadoop. The key difference between Impala's approach and that of Hive is that while Hive programs are translated to native Hadoop processing—initially MapReduce but today including Tez— Impala includes its own processing architecture that reads directly from native HDFS or HBase storage. Although Impala bypasses the Hadoop processing layer, it can access Hive and Pig metadata through the *HCatalog* interface, which means it knows the structure of Hive and Pig tables.

Impala architecture is heavily influenced by traditional massively parallel processing (MPP) data warehouse database architectures, which we discussed in Chapter 8. Impala deploys daemon processes— typically on each Hadoop data node—and distributes work to these daemons using algorithms similar to those used by RDBMS systems, such as Teradata or Oracle. These daemon processes are always ready for action, so there is no initial latency involved in job creation as there is in Hive.

There's no doubt that the Impala architecture offers a better performance experience for short-duration queries than Hive. However, given improvements in recent releases of Hive, there are those who claim that Hive still offers superior performance at greater scale. Some of this debate is driven by marketing groups within commercial Hadoop companies, so careful evaluation of competing claims is warranted.

Spark SQL

As noted earlier, there is some support for Spark within recent releases of Hive. However, Spark includes its own SQL dialect, called—not surprisingly—*Spark SQL.*

You may recall from Chapter 7 that Spark SQL works with data frames rather than RDDs. Data frames can be thought of as a more tabular and schematized relation to the RDD. A data frame can be created from an RDD, or from a Hive table.

SQL-92 compliance is a work in progress within Spark SQL.

Couchbase N1QL

So far we've seen SQL used within the context of analytic systems such as Hadoop and Spark. Operational databases of the NoSQL variety have not been so quick to implement SQL; however, in 2015, Couchbase announced *Non-first Normal Form Query Language (N1QL)*, pronounced "Nickel," a virtually complete SQL language implementation for use with document databases and implemented within the Couchbase server 4.0.

For example, consider the sample data shown in Figure 11-4 (this is the same sample data we used for MongoDB earlier).

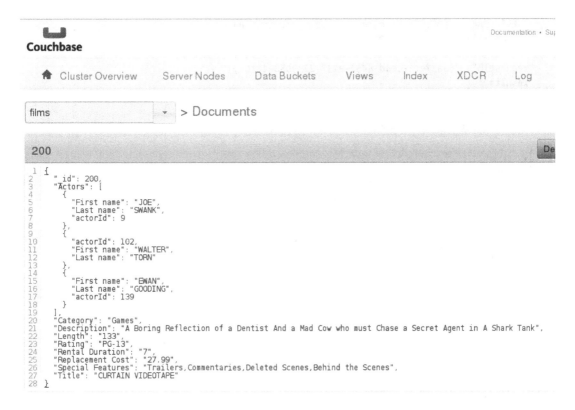

Figure 11-4. Couchbase sample document

N1QL allows us to perform basic queries to retrieve selected documents or attributes of selected documents:

```
cbq> SELECT `Title` FROM films WHERE _id=200;
{
    "requestID": "0d5cff15-f5e7-434d-9dc4-d950ef5e21f8",
    "signature": {
        "Title": "json"
    },
    "results": [
        {
            "Title": "CURTAIN VIDEOTAPE"
        }
    ],
    "status": "success",
```

N1QL allows us to access nested documents within the JSON structure using array notation. So, for instance, in the example that follows, Actors[0] refers to the first nested document within the actors array:

```
cbq> SELECT Actors[0].`First name` , Actors[0].`Last name`
    > FROM films where _id=200;
{
    "requestID": "5aa27ec1-ce4d-4452-a137-2239b88e47fe",
    "results": [
        {
            "First name": "JOE",
            "Last name": "SWANK"
        }
    ],
    "status": "success",
```

We can query for subdocuments that match a search criteria using WHERE ANY syntax:

```
cbq> SELECT `Title` FROM films
    > WHERE ANY Actor IN films.Actors SATISFIES
    > ( Actor.`First name`="JOE" AND Actor.`Last name`="SWANK" )END;
{
    "requestID": "f3d6dd05-912d-437b-984f-214770f87076",
    "results": [
        {
            "Title": "CHOCOLAT HARRY"
        },
        {
            "Title": "CHOCOLATE DUCK"
        },
... ...
```

The UNNEST command allows embedded documents to be "joined" back up to the parent document. So here we get one result for each actor who starred in film 200, with the film title included in the results:

```
cbq> SELECT f.`Title` ,a.`First name` ,a.`Last name`
  >   FROM films f
  >   UNNEST f.Actors a
  >   WHERE f._id=200;
{
    "requestID": "f8227647-3506-4bfd-a538-3f8a0d038198",

    "results": [
        {
            "First name": "JOE",
            "Last name": "SWANK",
            "Title": "CURTAIN VIDEOTAPE"
        },
        {
            "First name": "WALTER",
            "Last name": "TORN",
            "Title": "CURTAIN VIDEOTAPE"
        },
... ...
    ],
    "status": "success",
}
```

The UNNEST command allows us to perform the equivalent of joins between parent and child documents when the child documents are nested within the parent. N1QL also allows us to join between independent documents, providing that one of the documents contains a reference to the primary key in the other.

So, for instance, if we had a bucket of documents that contained the primary keys of "overdue" films in our imaginary (and by now definitely struggling) DVD store, then we can join that to the films collection to return-just those films using the ON KEYS join syntax:

```
cbq> SELECT  f.`Title` FROM overdues
  >   JOIN films f ON KEYS overdues.filmId ;
{
    "requestID": "6f0f505e-72f6-404d-9e20-953850dc9524",
    "results": [
        {
            "Title": "CURTAIN VIDEOTAPE"
        },
        {
            "Title": "HARPER DYING"
        }
    ],
    "status": "success",
```

N1QL also includes DML statements allowing us to manipulate the contents of documents and DDL statements allowing creation and modification of indexes.

N1QL is an ambitious attempt to bring SQL into the world of document databases. It's interesting to consider that at the same time as companies like CouchBase are introducing SQL support into their database, companies like Oracle are introducing strong JSON support into their SQL-based database. It would seem that the two worlds are coming together.

Apache Drill

So far we have looked at SQL variants that are tightly coupled with their underlying technology. It's true that technologies such as Hive can access data in HBase and Spark, as well as HDFS, but this speaks more to the integration of HDFS, HBase, and Spark than it does to some inherent heterogeneity of the Hive system.

The *Apache Drill* framework aims to provide a SQL engine that can operate across multiple distributed data stores such as HDFS or Amazon S3, as well as NoSQL systems such as MongoDB and HBase. Drill's architecture is based on Google's *Dremel* system, which provides the foundation for the Google *BigQuery* product.

Drill incorporates a distributed heterogeneous cost-based optimizer that can intelligently distribute data-access algorithms across multiple, disparate systems. This allows a SQL query to span Hadoop, MongoDB, Oracle, or other databases and—at least in theory—to do so in an efficient and optimal manner.

Currently, Drill can query data from relational systems that have a JDBC or ODBC connector, from systems that are supported by Hive, from a variety of cloud-based distributed file systems (Amazon S3, Google Cloud Drive), and from MongoDB.

Let's look at the MongoDB support, since it allows us to see how Drill deals with nontabular data. Here, we use Drill to query our sample MongoDB collections.

Simple queries are, of course, simple:

```
0: jdbc:drill:zk=local> SELECT Title FROM films WHERE Rating='G' LIMIT 5;
+--------------------+
|       Title        |
+--------------------+
| ACE GOLDFINGER     |
| AFFAIR PREJUDICE   |
| AFRICAN EGG        |
| ALAMO VIDEOTAPE    |
| AMISTAD MIDSUMMER  |
+--------------------+
5 rows selected (1.365 seconds)
```

We can drill into subdocuments using a notation that is similar to the N1QL array notation. So, here we retrieve data from the second document in the embedded actors array for the film *West Lion* using the array notation Actors[2]:

```
0: jdbc:drill:zk=local> SELECT Actors[2].`First name`, Actors[2].`Last name`
. . . . . . . . . . . >     FROM films WHERE Title='WEST LION';
+---------+-----------+
| EXPR$0  | EXPR$1    |
+---------+-----------+
| SEAN    | WILLIAMS  |
+---------+-----------+
```

The FLATTEN function returns one row for every document in an embedded array. It's somewhat similar to the Hive EXPLODE function or the N1QL UNNEST clause. Note that each document is returned in JSON format; there doesn't seem to be a way currently to schematize these results:

```
0: jdbc:drill:zk=local> SELECT Title, FLATTEN(Actors)
. . . . . . . . . . . >       FROM films WHERE Rating='G' LIMIT 5;
+-----------------+-----------------------------------------------------------
|      Title      |                           EXPR$1
+-----------------+-----------------------------------------------------------
| ACE GOLDFINGER  | {"First name":"BOB","Last name":"FAWCETT","actorId":19}
| ACE GOLDFINGER  | {"First name":"MINNIE","Last name":"ZELLWEGER",
| ACE GOLDFINGER  | {"First name":"SEAN","Last name":"GUINESS", "actorId":9
| ACE GOLDFINGER  | {"First name":"CHRIS","Last name":"DEPP","actorId":160}
| AFFAIR PREJUDICE| {"First name":"JODIE","Last name":"DEGENERES",
+-----------------+-----------------------------------------------------------
5 rows selected (0.589 seconds)
```

We can see that Drill has a basic ability to navigate complex JSON documents, and we can expect this capability to improve over time.

Drill can also navigate wide column store structures in HBase. Let's look at the data that we inserted into HBase earlier in this chapter, this time using Drill:

```
0: jdbc:drill:zk=local> SELECT * FROM friends;
+---------+---------+------+
| row_key | friends | info |
+---------+---------+------+
| [B@6fe2da0c | {"Jo":"am9AZ21haWwuY29t","John":"am9obkBnbWFpbC5jb20="} |
{"email":"Z3V5QGdtYWlsLmNvbQ==","userid":"OTk5MA=="} |
| [B@43be5d62 | {"John":"am9obkBnbWFpbC5jb20=","Guy":"Z3V5QGdtYWlsLmNvbQ==",
"Paul":"cGF1bEBnbWFpbC5jb20=","Ringo":"cmluZ29AZ21haWwuY29t"} | {"email":"am9AZ21haWwuY29t",
"userid":"OTk5MQ=="} |
+---------+---------+------+
2 rows selected (1.532 seconds)
```

Not very friendly output! Initially, Drill returns HBase data without decoding the internal byte array structure and without flattening any of the maps that define our wide column family.

However, we can use the FLATTEN function to extract one row for each column in our wide column family "friends", KVGEN function to convert the map to columns, and the CONVERT FROM function to cast the byte arrays into Unicode characters:

```
0: jdbc:drill:zk=local>
WITH friend_details AS
    (SELECT info, FLATTEN(KVGEN(friends)) AS friend_info FROM friends)
  SELECT CONVERT_FROM(friend_details.info.email,'UTF8') AS email,
        CONVERT_FROM(friend_details.friend_info.`value`,'UTF8')
            AS friend_email
    FROM friend_details;
```

189

```
+----------------+------------------+
|     email      |   friend_email   |
+----------------+------------------+
| guy@gmail.com  | jo@gmail.com     |
| guy@gmail.com  | john@gmail.com   |
| jo@gmail.com   | john@gmail.com   |
| jo@gmail.com   | guy@gmail.com    |
| jo@gmail.com   | paul@gmail.com   |
| jo@gmail.com   | ringo@gmail.com  |
+----------------+------------------+
```

Drill shows an enormous amount of promise. A single SQL framework capable of navigating the variety of data structures presented by relational and nonrelational systems is just what we need to resolve the Tower of Babel problem presented by the vast array of languages and interfaces characterizing the next generation databases of today and the future.

Other SQL on NoSQL

There are a number of other notable SQL-on-NoSQL systems:

- **Presto** is an open-source SQL engine similar in many respects to Drill that can query data in JDBC, Cassandra, Hive, Kafka, and other systems.

- Many relational database vendors provide connectors that allow their SQL language to retrieve data from Hadoop or other systems. Examples include **Oracle Big Data SQL**, **IBM BigSQL,** and **Terradata QueryGrid**.

- **Apache Phoenix** provides a SQL layer for HBase.

- Dell **Toad Data Point** provides SQL access to a variety of nonrelational systems, including MongoDB, Cassandra, HBase, and DynamoDB. (Disclaimer: I lead the team at Dell that develops Toad.)

Conclusion

This chapter tried to give you a feel for the languages and APIs provided by next-generation database systems. In many cases, low-level programming APIs are all that is provided. However, the trend for the future seems clear: SQL is reasserting itself as the lingua franca of the database world. Virtually all new databases are becoming accessible by SQL, and many systems are adopting SQL-like interfaces even for low-level programming.

It's unlikely that SQL will again become the sole interface to databases of the future: the unique requirements of wide column systems and document databases suggest that non-SQL idioms will be required, although Cassandra CQL and CouchBase N1QL do show how a SQL-like language remains a useful abstraction for dealing with data that might not be in relational format. Nevertheless, it seems increasingly likely that most next-generation databases will eventually support some form of SQL access, even if only through an independent layer such as Drill.

Note

1. Code examples can be found at https://github.com/gharriso/ NextGenDBSamples.

CHAPTER 12

■ ■ ■

Databases of the Future

The human brain had a vast memory storage. It made us curious and very creative.... And that brain did something very special. It invented an idea called "the future."

—David Suzuki

Every revolution has its counterrevolution—that is a sign the revolution is for real.

—C. Wright Mills

This book is the story of how a revolution in database technology saw the "one size fits all" traditional relational SQL database give way to a multitude of special-purpose database technologies. In the past 11 chapters, we have reviewed the major categories of next-generation database systems and have taken a deep dive into some of the internal architectures of those systems.

Most of the technologies we have reviewed are still evolving rapidly, and few would argue that we've reached an end state in the evolution of database systems. Can we extrapolate from the trends that we have reviewed in this book and the technology challenges we've observed to speculate on the next steps in database technology? Furthermore, is there any reason to think that any of the revolutionary changes we've reviewed here are moving along on the wrong track? Should we start a counterrevolution?

In this chapter I argue that the current state of play—in which one must choose between multiple overlapping compromise architectures—should and will pass away. I believe that we will see an increasing convergence of today's disparate technologies. The database of the future, in my opinion, will be one that can be configured to support all or most of the workloads that today require unique and separate database technologies.

The Revolution Revisited

As we discussed in Chapter 1, the three major eras of database technology correspond to the three major eras of computer applications: mainframe, client-server, and modern web. It's not surprising, therefore, that the story of the evolution of modern databases parallels the story of the development of the World Wide Web. The predominant drivers for the latest generation of database systems are the drivers that arose from the demands of Web 2.0, global e-commerce, Big Data, social networks, cloud computing, and—increasingly—the Internet of Things (IoT). These buzzwords represent more than simple marketing claims: they each demand and reflect significant changes in application architectures to which database technologies must respond. Today's application architectures and database technologies are continuously challenged to meet the needs of applications that demand an unparalleled level of scale, availability, and throughput.

The imperative represented by these challenges is irresistible: for most enterprises, Dig Data, social networks, mobile devices, and cloud computing represent key competitive challenges. The ability to leverage data to create competitive advantage is key to the survival of the modern business organization, as is the ability to deploy applications with global scope and with mobile and social context. It's hard to imagine a successful modern business that did not have a strategy to exploit data or to engage with users via social networks and mobile channels. For some industries, the IoT represents a similar threat and opportunity: Internet-enabled devices stand to revolutionize manufacturing, health care, transportation, home automation, and many other industries.

The shift in application architectures that has emerged from these demands has been conveniently summarized by the market-research company IDC and others as "the third platform."

Many of the key database variations we have reviewed in this book are optimized to satisfy one or more of the challenges presented by this third platform:

- **Hadoop and Spark** exist to provide a platform within which masses of semi-structured and unstructured data can be stored and analyzed.

- **Nonrelational operational databases** such as Cassandra and MongoDB exist to provide a platform for web applications that can support global scale and continuous availability, and which can rapidly evolve new features. Some, like Cassandra, appeal because of their ability to provide scalability and economies across a potentially global deployment. Others, like MongoDB, appeal because they allow more rapid iteration of application design.

- **Graph databases** such as Neo4j and Graph Compute Engines allow for the management of network data such as is found in social networks.

However, within each of these domains we see continual demand for the key advantages provided by traditional RDBMS systems. In particular:

- **SQL** provides an interface for data query that has stood the test of time and that is familiar to millions of human beings and involves thousands of analytic tools.

- **The relational model** of data represents a theoretically sound foundation for unambiguous and accessible data models. The relational model continues to be the correct representation for most computer datasets, even if the physical implementation takes a different form.

- **Transactions**, potentially multi-object and ACID, continue to be mandatory in many circumstances for systems that strive to correctly represent all interactions with the system.

Counterrevolutionaries

It would be hard for anyone to argue that some sort of seismic shift in the database landscape has not occurred. Hadoop, Spark, MongoDB, Cassandra, and many other nonrelational systems today form an important and growing part of the enterprise data architecture of many, if not most, Fortune 500 companies. It is, of course, possible to argue that all these new technologies are a mistake, that the relational model and the transactional SQL relational database represent a better solution and that eventually the market will "come to its senses" and return to the relational fold.

While it seems unlikely to me that we would make a complete return to a database architecture that largely matured in the client-server era, it is I think fairly clear that most next-generation databases represent significant compromises. Next-generation databases of today do not represent a "unified field theory" of databases; quite the contrary. We still have a long way to go.

A critic of nonrelational systems might fairly claim that the latest breed of databases suffer from the following weaknesses:

- **A return of the navigational model.** Many of the new breed of databases have reinstated the situation that existed in pre-relational systems, in which logical and physical representations of data are tightly coupled in an undesirable way. One of the great successes of the relational model was the separation of logical representation from physical implementation.

- **Inconsistent to a fault.** The inability in most nonrelational systems to perform a multi-object transaction, and the possibility of inconsistency and unpredictability in even single-object transactions, can lead to a variety of undesirable outcomes that were largely solved by the ACID transaction and multi-version consistency control (MVCC) patterns. Phantom reads, lost updates, and nondeterministic behaviors can all occur in systems in which the consistency model is relaxed.

- **Unsuited to business intelligence.** Systems like HBase, Cassandra, and MongoDB provide more capabilities to the programmer than to the business owner. Data in these systems is relatively isolated from normal business intelligence (BI) practices. The absence of a complete SQL layer that can access these systems isolates them from the broader enterprise.

- **Too many compromises.** There are a wide variety of specialized database solutions, and in some cases these specialized solutions will be an exact fit for an application's requirements. But in too many cases the application will have to choose between two or more NQR (not quite right) database architectures.

Have We Come Full Circle?

It's not unusual for relational advocates to claim that the nonrelational systems are a return to pre-relational architectures that were discarded decades ago. This is inaccurate in many respects, but in particular because pre-relational systems were nondistributed, whereas today's nonrelational databases generally adopt a distributed database architecture. That alone makes today's nonrelational systems fundamentally different from the pre-relational systems of the 1960s and '70s.

However, there is one respect in which many newer nonrelational systems resemble pre-relational databases: they entangle logical and physical representations of data. One of Edgar Codd's key critiques of pre-relational systems such as IDMS and IMS was that they required the user to be aware of the underlying physical representation of data. The relational model decoupled these logical and physical representations and allowed users to see the data in a logically consistent representation, regardless of the underlying storage model. The normalized relational representation of data avoids any bias toward a particular access pattern or storage layout: it decouples logical representation of data from underlying physical representation.

Many advocates of modern nonrelational systems explicitly reject this decoupling. They argue that by making all access patterns equal, normalization makes them all equally bad. But this assertion is dubious: it ignores the possibility of de-normalization as an optimization applied atop a relational model. It's clear that the structure presented to the end user does not have to be the same as the structure on disk.

Indeed, the motivation for abandoning the relational model was driven less by these access pattern concerns and more by a desire to align the databases' representation of data with the object-oriented representation in application code. An additional motivation was to allow for rapidly mutating schemas: to avoid the usually lengthy process involved in making a change to a logical data model and propagating that change through to a production system.

Was Codd wrong in 1970 to propose that the physical and logical representations of data should be separate? Almost certainly not. The ability to have a logical data model that represents an unambiguous and nonredundant view of the data remains desirable. Indeed, most nonrelational modeling courses encourage the user to start with some form of "logical" model.

I argue, therefore, that the need for a high-level logical model of the data is still desirable and that to allow users to interact with the database using that model remains as valid a requirement as it was when the relational model was first proposed. However, modern applications need the ability to propagate at least minor changes to the data model without necessitating an unwieldy database change control process.

An Embarrassment of Choice

Ten years ago, choosing the correct database system for an application was fairly straightforward: choose the relational database vendor with which one had an existing relationship or which offered the best licensing deals. Technical considerations or price might lead to a choice of Oracle over SQL Server, or vice versa, but that the database would be an RDBMS was virtually a given. Today, choosing the best database system is a much more daunting task, often made more difficult by the contradictory claims of various venders and advocates. Most of the time, some form of relational technology will be the best choice. But for applications that may seek to break outside the RDBMS comfort zone and seek competitive advantage from unique features of new database technologies, the choice of database can be decisive.

"Which is the best database to choose?" Often, there is no right answer to the question because each choice implies some form of compromise. An RDBMS may be superior in terms of query access and transactional capability, but fails to deliver the network partition tolerance required if the application grows. Cassandra may deliver the best cross-data-center availability, but may fail to integrate with BI systems. And so on …

Figure 12-1 illustrates some of the decision points that confront someone trying to decide upon a database today.

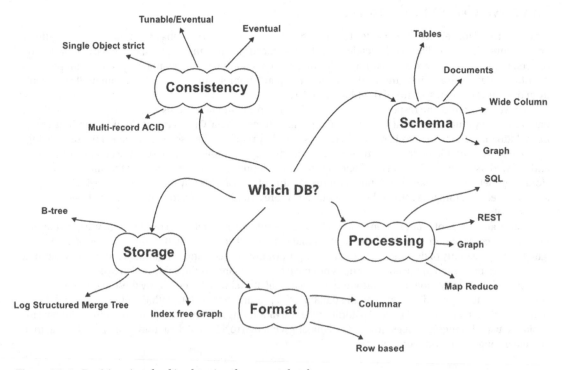

Figure 12-1. *Decisions involved in choosing the correct database*

Can We have it All?

I've become convinced that we can "have it all" within a single database offering. For instance, there is no architectural reason why a database system should not be able to offer a tunable consistency model that includes at one end strict multi-record ACID transactions and at the other end an eventual consistency style model. In a similar fashion, I believe we could combine the features of a relational model and the document store, initially by following the existing trend toward allowing JSON data types within relational tables.

The resistance to this sort of convergence will likely be driven as much by market and competitive considerations as by technological obstacles. It may not be in the interests of the RDBMS incumbents nor the nonrelational upstarts to concede that a mixed model should prevail. And supporting such a mixed model may involve technical complexity that will be harder for the smaller and more recent market entrants.

Nevertheless, this is what I believe would be the best outcome for the database industry as a whole. Rather than offering dozens of incompatible technologies that involve significant compromises, it would be better to offer a coherent database architecture that offers as configurable behaviors the features best meet application requirements. Let's look at each area of convergence and consider what would be required to combine technologies into a single system.

Consistency Models

Databases like Cassandra that are built on the Dynamo model already provide a tunable consistency model that allows the administrator or developer to choose a level of consistency or performance trade-off. Dynamo-based systems are well known for providing eventual consistency, but they are equally capable of delivering strict consistency—at least within a single-object transaction. RDBMS systems also provide control over isolation levels—providing levels that guarantee repeatable reads, for instance.

However, systems like Cassandra that are based on Dynamo cannot currently provide multi-object transactions. Meanwhile, RDBMS consistency in existing implementations is influenced by ACID transactional principles, which require that the database always present a consistent view to all users.

As we discussed in Chapter 3, the ultimate motivation for eventual consistency-type systems is the ability to survive network partitions. If a distributed database is split in two by a network partition—the "split brain" scenario—the database can only maintain availability if it sacrifices some level of strict consistency.

Implementing multi-row transactions within an eventually consistent, network partition-tolerant database would undoubtedly be a significant engineering challenge, but it is not obviously impossible. Such a database would allow the developer or the administrator to choose between strictly consistent ACID and eventually consistent transactions that involve multiple objects (as shown in Figure 12-2).

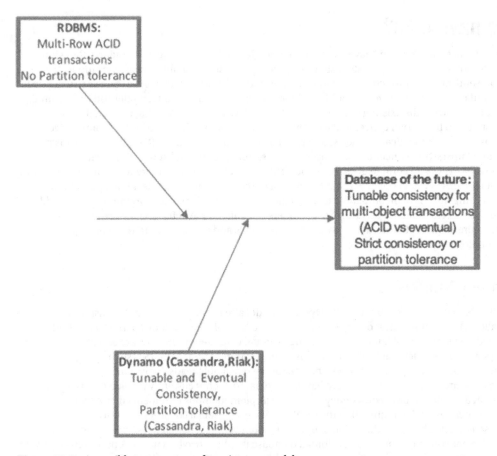

Figure 12-2. *A possible convergence of consistency models*

Schema

While relational fundamentalists may claim that commercial RDBMS systems have not implemented a pure version of the relational model, the traditional RDBMS has at least established a well-defined discipline on the data modeling process. Data "normalization" eliminates redundancy and ambiguity from the logical representation. By and large, the relational representation of data has proved invaluable in providing non-programmers with a comprehensible view of data and—together with the adoption of SQL as a common language for data access—has offered a predictable and accessible interface to business intelligence and query tools.

Dissent with the relational model arose for at least two reasons:

- Programmers desired a data store that could accept object-oriented data without the overhead and complexity involved in deconstructing and reconstructing from normal form.

- The lifecycle of a relational model represented somewhat of a waterfall process, requiring that the model be comprehensively defined at the beginning of a project and was difficult to change once deployed to production. Modern agile application development practices reject this waterfall approach in favor of an iterative development in which change to design is expected. Furthermore, modern web applications need to iterate new features fast in order to adapt to intense competitive environments. While modern RDBMS systems can perform online schema modifications, the coordination of code and schema change creates risk of application failure and generally requires careful and time-consuming change control procedures.

In short, modern applications require flexible schemas that can be modified if necessary on the fly by changed application code.

However, the need for a comprehensible and unambiguous data model that can be used for business intelligence is even more important in this world of Big Data than it was in the early relational era. Nonrelational databases are unable to easily integrate into an organization's business intelligence (BI) capability; in the worst case, the data they contain are completely opaque to BI frameworks.

Providing a best-of-both-worlds solution seems within the capabilities of some existing databases. A database that allows data to be represented at a high level in a relatively stable normal form, but which also allows for the storage of dynamically mutating data, only requires that columns in a relational table be able to store arbitrarily complex structures—JSON, for instance—and that these complex structures be supported by efficient query mechanisms integrated into SQL.

As we will see, such hybrid capabilities already exist. Virtually all databases—relational and nonrelational—are introducing support for JSON. For instance, Riak, Cassandra, PostgresSQL, and Oracle all provide specific mechanisms for indexing, storing, and retrieving JSON structures. It will soon be meaningless to describe a database as a "document" database, since all databases will provide strong support for JSON.

I'm sure that relational purists will argue such a hybrid solution is, in fact, the work of the devil in that it compromises the theoretical basis of the relational model. Perhaps so, and a relational implementation that allowed prototyping and rapid iteration of data models while preserving relational purity would be welcome. But for now I believe the short-term direction is set: we're going to embed JSON in relational tables to balance flexibility with the advantages of the relational model. Figure 12-3 illustrates a vision for the convergence of schema elements in a database of the future.

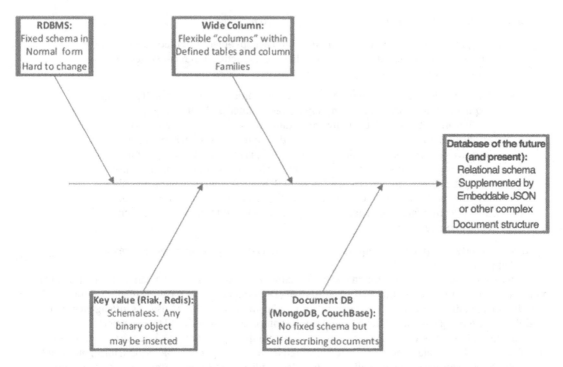

Figure 12-3. *A possible convergence of schema models*

Database Languages

Codd's definition of the relational database did not specify the SQL language, and it is perfectly possible for a formally relational database to use some other language. However over time the advantages of a single cross platform data access language became obvious and the industry united behind SQL.

The term "NoSQL" is unfortunate in that it implies a rejection of the SQL language rather than the more fundamental issues that were at the core of the changes in database technology. However, it is true that in many cases SQL was incompatible or inappropriate for these new systems that often supported record-at-a-time processing using low-level APIs described in Chapter 11.

Today, SQL has regained its status as the lingua franca of the database world, and it seems clear that most databases will allow for SQL queries, whether natively as in Couchbase's N1QL or via a SQL processing framework such as Apache Drill. Even for databases that cannot natively support the full range of SQL operations, we can see that a reduced SQL syntax enhances usability and programmer efficiency: compare, for instance, the API presented by HBase with the SQL-like interface provided by Apache Cassandra CQL (both are described in Chapter 11).

The emerging challenge to unify databases is not so much to provide SQL access to nonrelational systems as to allow non-SQL access to relational systems. While the SQL language can satisfy a broad variety of data queries, it is not always the most suitable language. In particular, there are data science problems that may call for a lower-level API such as MapReduce or a more complex directed acyclic graph (DAG) algorithm. We've also seen how graph traversal operations cannot easily be specified in SQL, and can be more easily expressed in an alternative syntax such as Gremlin or Cypher.

It's a formal principle of the relational model that one ought not to be able to bypass the set-based query language (e.g., SQL). This is specified in Codd's 13th rule (nonsubversion). However, if the relational database is going to maintain relevance across all realms, it may be necessary to either relax this rule or provide alternative processing APIs on top of a SQL foundation.

Additionally, when hybrid databases are storing data primarily within embedded JSON structures rather than in relational tables, requiring a SQL syntax to navigate these JSON documents may be unwieldy. An API closer to that native to MongoDB may be more appropriate. Expressing queries as JSON documents pushed to the database via a REST interface (as in existing JSON document databases) might be desirable.

In fact, some of the relational database vendors have already provided much of what is outlined above. We will see later in this chapter how Oracle has provided support for JSON REST queries and the Cypher graph language. Figure 12-4 illustrates the vision for integration of database languages and APIs.

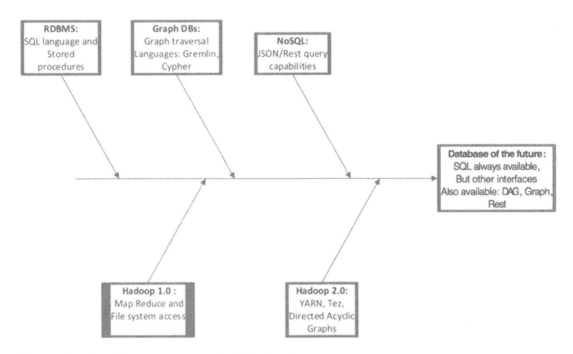

Figure 12-4. *A possible convergence path for database languages*

Storage

The structure of data on disk or other persistent media has an enormous effect on performance and the economics of the database. Chapter 7 discussed the need to be able to tier data in multiple storage layers (memory, SSD, disk, HDFS). We've also seen in Chapter 6 how the columnar representation of data can lead to significant improvements for analytical databases. Finally, we saw in Chapter 10 how the B-tree indexing structures that dominated in the traditional RDBMS can be inferior for write-intensive workloads to the log-structured merge tree architectures of Cassandra and HBase.

So, as with the other forks in our technology decision tree, there is no one correct storage layout that suits all workloads. Today, we generally have to pick the database that natively supports the storage layout that best suits our application.

Of course, the underlying storage mechanism for a database is hidden from an application: the access methods to retrieve data must reflect the schematic representation of data, but the structure on disk is generally opaque to the application. Furthermore, we have already seen databases that can maintain multiple storage engines: MySQL has had a pluggable storage engine interface for over 10 years, and MongoDB has recently announced a pluggable storage architecture supporting a handful of alternative storage engines.

We can also see in systems like Hana the ability to choose row-based or columnar storage for specific tables based on anticipated workload requirements.

This pluggable—or at least "choose-able"—storage engine architecture seems to be the right direction for databases of the future. I believe these databases should allow tables or collections to be managed as columnar or row-based, supported by B-trees or log-structured merge trees, resident in memory or stored on disk. In some cases we may even wish to store data in a native graph format to support real-time graph traversal (although in most cases it will be sufficient to layer a graph compute engine over a less restrictive structure). Figure 12-5 illustrates a vision for pluggable storage engines.

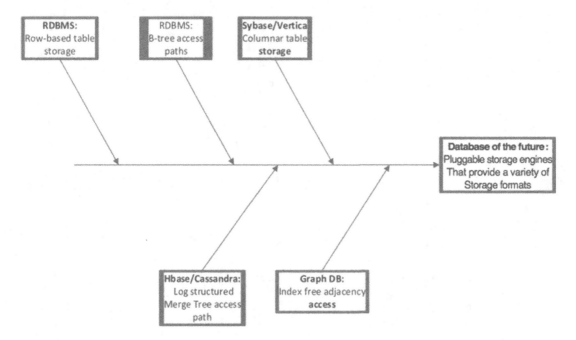

Figure 12-5. *Convergence options for database storage*

A Vision for a Converged Database

By consolidating the convergence visions for individual aspects of database technology, We are in a position to outline the characteristics of an ideal database management system. The key requirement can be summarized as follows:

■ **An ideal database architecture** would support multiple data models, languages, processing paradigms, and storage formats within the one system. Application requirements that dictate a specific database feature should be resolved as configuration options or pluggable features within a single database management system, not as choices from disparate database architectures.

Specifically, an ideal database architecture would:

- Support a **tunable consistency model** that allows for strict RDBMS-style ACID transactions, Dynamo-style eventual consistency, or any point in between.

- Provide support for an **extensible but relational compatible schema** by allowing data to be represented broadly by a relational model, but also allowing for application-extensible schemas, possibly by supporting embedded JSON data types.

- **Support multiple languages** and APIs. SQL appears destined to remain the primary database access language, but should be supplemented by graph languages such as Cypher, document-style queries based on REST, and the ability to express processing in MapReduce or other DAG algorithms.

- Support an underlying **pluggable data storage** model allowing the physical storage of data to be based on row-oriented or columnar storage is appropriate and on disk as B-trees, log-structured merge trees, or other optimal storage structures.

- Support a range of **distributed availability and consistency** characteristics. In particular, the application should be able to determine the level of availability and consistency that is supported in the event of a network partition and be able to fine-tune the replication of data across a potentially globally distributed system.

Meanwhile, Back at Oracle HQ …

Oracle was, of course, the company that first commercialized relational database technology, and as such might be expected to have the most vested interest in maintaining the RDBMS status quo. To some extent this is true: Oracle continues to dominate the RDBMS market, and actively evangelizes SQL and the relational model.

However, behind the scenes, Oracle has arguably come as close as any other vendor to pursuing the vision for the converged database of the future that I outlined earlier. In particular, Oracle has:

- Provided its own engineered system based on Hadoop: the **Oracle Big Data Appliance**. The Big Data appliance includes the Cloudera distribution of Hadoop (including Spark). It also incorporates significant innovations in performance by pushing predicate filtering down to data nodes, using technology originally created for the Oracle Exadata RDBMS appliance. Oracle also provides connectors that facilitate data movement between the Big Data appliance and Oracle RDBMS and **Oracle Big Data SQL**, which allows SQL from the Oracle RDBMS to target data held in the Oracle Big Data Appliance.

- Provided very strong support for **JSON embedded in the RDBMS**. JSON documents may be stored in LOB (see following section) or character columns, and may be retrieved using extensions to SQL. JSON in the database may also be accessed directly by a REST-based JSON query API **Simple Oracle Document Access** (**SODA**). This API strongly resembles the MongoDB query API.

- Offers **Oracle REST Data Services** (**ORDS**), which also provides a REST-based interface to data in relational tables. This provides a non-SQL based API for retrieving table data using embedded JSON query documents in REST calls that are similar to the JSON-based query language supported by SODA.

- Enhanced its **graph compute engine**. The new Oracle graph will allow graph analytics using OpenCypher (the graph language originated by Neo4j) to be performed on any data stored in the RDBMS or Big Data Appliance.

- Supports a shared-nothing **sharded distributed database**, which provides an alternative distributed database model that can support a more linearly scalable OLTP solution compared to the shared-disk RAC clustered database architecture.

Let's look at some of these offerings in more detail.

Oracle JSON Support

Oracle allows JSON documents to be stored in Oracle LOB (Long OBject) or character columns. Oracle provides a check constraint that can be used to ensure the data in those columns is a valid JSON document:

```
CREATE TABLE ofilms
(
   id                INTEGER PRIMARY KEY,
   json_document     BLOB
   CONSTRAINT ensure_json CHECK (json_document IS JSON)
)
```

Oracle supports functions within its SQL dialect that allow for JSON documents to be queried. Specifically:

- **JSON_QUERY** returns a portion of a JSON document; it uses JSON path expressions that are similar to XPATH for XML.

- **JSON_VALUE** is similar to JSON_QUERY, but returns a single element from a JSON document.

- **JSON_EXISTS** determines if a specific element exists in the JSON document.

- **JSON_TABLE** projects a portion of JSON as a relational table. For instance, JSON_TABLE can be used to project each subelement of a JSON document as a distinct virtual row.

The example that follows uses the "films" JSON document collection that appeared in Chapter 11 to illustrate MongoDB and Couchbase queries. To refresh your memory, these documents look something like this:

```
{
  "Title": "ACE GOLDFINGER",
  "Category": "Horror",
  "Description": "A Astounding Epistle of a Database Administrator And a Explorer who must
  Find a Car in Ancient China",
  "Length": "48",
  "Rating": "G",
  "Actors": [
    {
      "First name": "BOB",
      "Last name": "FAWCETT",
      "actorId": 19
    },
```

```
... ...
  {
    "First name": "CHRIS",
    "Last name": "DEPP",
    "actorId": 160
  }
 ]
}
```

Simple dot notation can be used to expand the JSON structures (o.json_document.Title, in the example that follows), while JSON_QUERY can return a complete JSON structure for a selected path within the document. In this example, JSON_QUERY returns the actors nested document.

```
SQL> SELECT o.json_document.Title,
  2         JSON_QUERY (json_document, '$.Actors') actors
  3    FROM "ofilms" o
  4   WHERE id = 4
  5  /

TITLE
------------------------------------------------------------
ACTORS
------------------------------------------------------------
AFFAIR PREJUDICE
[{"First name":"JODIE","Last name":"DEGENERES","actorId":41}
,{"First name":"SCARLETT","Last name":"DAMON","actorId":81} ...
```

Returning a nested JSON document as a string isn't helpful in a relational context, so this is where we could use JSON_TABLE to return a single row for each actor. Here is a query that returns the film title and the names of all the actors in the film:

```
SQL> SELECT f.json_document.Title,a.*
  2    FROM "ofilms" f,
  3         JSON_TABLE(json_document,'$.Actors[*]'
  4                    COLUMNS("First" PATH '$."First name"',
  5                            "Last" PATH '$."Last name"')) a
  6   WHERE id=4;

TITLE                First           Last
-------------------- --------------- ---------------
AFFAIR PREJUDICE     JODIE           DEGENERES
AFFAIR PREJUDICE     SCARLETT        DAMON
AFFAIR PREJUDICE     KENNETH         PESCI
AFFAIR PREJUDICE     FAY             WINSLET
AFFAIR PREJUDICE     OPRAH           KILMER
```

The query returns five rows from the single film document because there are five actors within the actors array in that document. JSON_TABLE is roughly equivalent to the UNNEST clause in N1QL or the FLATTEN clause within Apache Drill (both discussed in Chapter 11).

Accessing JSON via Oracle REST

Jason documents and collections can be created, manipulated, and retrieved entirely without SQL, using the REST-based *Simple Oracle Data Access* (*SODA*) protocol.

Although the collections can be created without any SQL-based data definition language statements, under the hood the implementation is as we discussed in the last section—a database table is created containing a LOB that stores the JSON documents.

Regardless of whether the collection was created by the REST API or through SQL, the documents may be interrogated using REST calls. For instance, Figure 12-6 shows a REST command retrieving a document with an ID of 4:

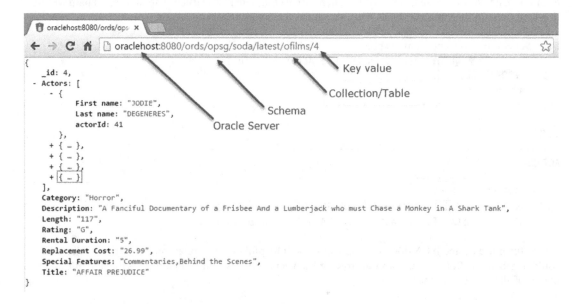

Figure 12-6. *Oracle REST JSON query fetching a row by ID*

The REST SODA interface can be used to perform CRUD (Create, Read, Update, Delete) operations. Adding a "document" to a "collection" creates a new row in the table.

The interface also supports a query mechanism that can be used to retrieve documents matching arbitrary filter criteria. Figure 12-7 illustrates a simple REST query using this interface (using the Google Chrome "Postman" extension that can be employed to prototype REST calls).

Figure 12-7. *Simple SODA REST query*

The JSON document filter syntax is extremely similar to that provided by MongoDB. Indeed, the Oracle developers intentionally set out to provide a familiar experience for users of MongoDB and other document databases.

Figure 12-8 illustrates a more complex query in which we search for movies longer than 60 minutes with a G rating, sorted by descending length.

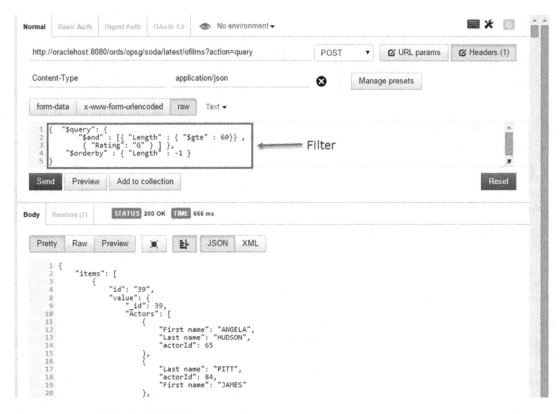

Figure 12-8. *Complex Oracle REST query*

REST Access to Oracle Tables

The Oracle REST data services API provides a REST interface for relational tables as well. The mechanism is virtually identical to the JSON SODA interface we examined earlier.

In Figure 12-9, we see a REST query retrieving data from the Oracle CUSTOMERS table, providing a simple query filter in the HTTP string.

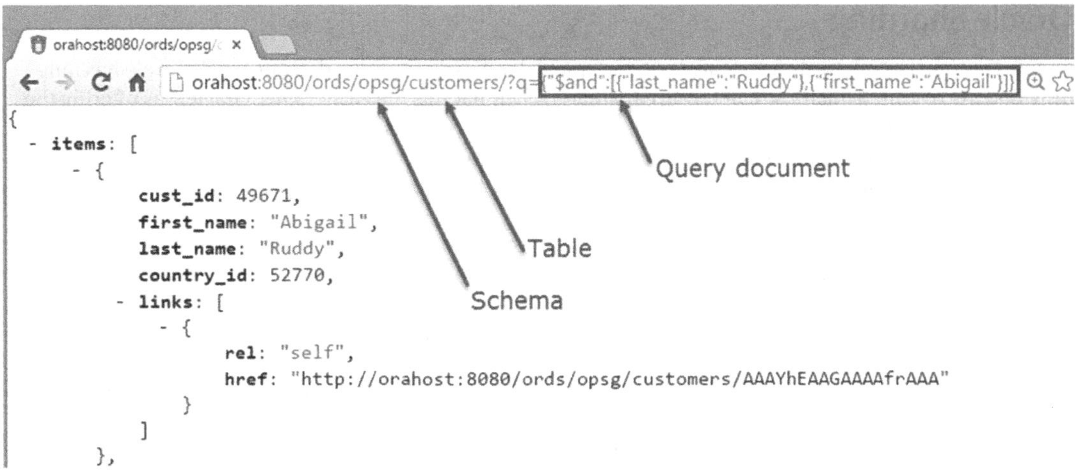

Figure 12-9. Oracle REST interface for table queries

Oracle Graph

Oracle has long supported an RDF-based graph capability within its *Oracle Spatial and Graph* option. This option was based on the RDF WC3 standard outlined in Chapter 6. However, while this capability provided some significant graph capabilities, it fell short of the capabilities offered in popular property graph databases such as Neo4J.

As you may recall from Chapter 6, an RDF system is an example of a *triple store,* which represents relatively simple relationships between nodes. In contrast, a *property store* represents the relationship between nodes but also allows the model to store significant information (properties) within the nodes and the relationships. While RDF graphs provide strong support for the development of ontologies and support distributed data sources, property graphs are often more attractive for custom application development because they provide a richer data model.

Oracle has recently integrated a property graph compute engine that can perform graph analytics on any data held in the Oracle RDBMS, the Oracle Big Data Hadoop system, or Oracle's own NoSQL system. The compute engine supports the openCypher graph language. Cypher is the language implemented within Neo4J, the most popular dedicated graph database engine, and openCypher has been made available as an open-source version of that language.

Oracle's implementation does not represent a native graph database storage engine. As you may recall from Chapter 6, a native graph database must implement *index free adjacency*, effectively implementing the graph structure in base storage. Rather, Oracle implements a *graph compute engine* capable of loading data from a variety of formats into memory, where it can be subjected to graph analytics. The advantage of this approach is that graph analytics can be applied to data held in any existing format, provided that format can be navigated as a graph. Many existing relational schemas do in fact implement graph relationships. For example, a typical organization schema will have foreign keys from employees to their managers, which can be represented as a graph.

Oracle Sharding

Oracle sharding is a relatively new feature of the Oracle database, announced in late 2015. Oracle has long provided a distributed database clustering capability. As far back as the early 1990s, Oracle was offering the *Oracle Parallel Server*—a shared-disk clustered database. This database clustering technology eventually evolved into *Oracle Real Application Clusters* (RAC), which was widely adopted and which represents the most significant implementation of the shared-disk database clustering model. We discussed shared-disk database clusters in more detail in Chapter 8.

However, the clustered architecture of RAC was more suited to data warehousing workloads than to massively scalable OLTP. Massive scaling of RAC becomes problematic with write-intensive workloads, as the overhead of maintaining a coherent view of data in memory leads to excessive "chatter" across the private database network. For this reason, typical RAC clusters have only a small number of nodes—the vast majority have fewer than 10.

The Oracle sharding option allows an OLTP workload to be deployed across as many as 1,000 separate Oracle instances, using an architecture that is similar to the do-it-yourself sharding of MySQL, which was reviewed in Chapter 3, and also quite similar to the MongoDB sharding architecture that was examined in Chapter 8.

Figure 12-10 shows a representation of the Oracle sharding architecture. The coordinator database (1) contains the catalog that describes how keys are distributed across shards. Each shard is implemented by a distinct Oracle database instance. Queries that include the shard key can be sent directly to the relevant database instance (3); the shard director is aware of the shard mappings and can provide the appropriate connection details to the application (4). Queries that do not specify the shard key or that are aggregating across multiple shards (5) are mediated by the coordinator database which acts as a proxy. The coordinator database sends queries to various shards to retrieve the necessary data (6) and then aggregates or merges the data to return the appropriate result set.

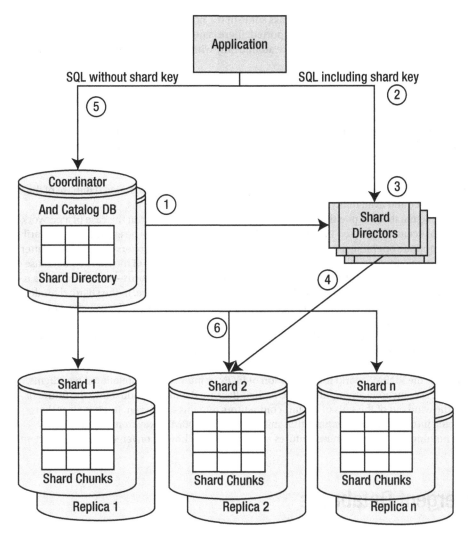

Figure 12-10. *Oracle sharding*

Oracle sharding supports distribution schemes similar to those supported by Oracle's existing table partitioning offerings. Data may be partitioned across shards by a hash, shard key ranges, or lists of shard key values. There is also a composite scheme in which data is partitioned primarily by list or range, and then hashed against a second shard key. When hash partitioning is used, Oracle can determine the load balancing automatically by redistributing shard chunks as data volumes change or as nodes are added or removed from the sharded system. Range or list partitioning requires user balancing of shards.

Each shard may be replicated using Oracle replication technologies (*DataGuard* or *Goldengate*). Replicas can be used to satisfy read requests, though this may require that the application explicitly request data from a replica rather than from the master.

Tables that don't conform to the shard key or that are relatively small can be duplicated on each shard rather than being sharded across the entire cluster. For instance, a products table might be duplicated across all shards, while other data is sharded by customer ID.

As with all sharding schemes, Oracle sharding breaks some of the normal guarantees provided by a traditional RDBMS. While joins across shards are supported, there is no guarantee of point-in-time consistency in results. Transactions that span shards are atomic only within a shard—there is no two-phase commit for distributed transactions.

Oracle as a Hybrid Database

It's surprising, and maybe even a little amusing, to see Oracle adopt a JSON interface that is clearly designed to be familiar to MongoDB users, and to finally adopt a distributed database strategy that admits the superiority of the shared-nothing architecture for certain workloads. But I for one find it encouraging to see the leading RDBMS vendor learn from alternative approaches.

However, Oracle is yet to attempt to address one of the key challenges for an integrated database of the future: balancing consistency and availability in the face of possible network partitions.

Oracle's RAC clustered database explicitly chooses consistency over availability in the case of a network partition: in a "split brain" scenario, isolated instances in the Oracle RAC cluster will be evicted or voluntarily shut down rather than continue operating in an inconsistent state. Oracle sharding offers a potentially better solution for an online system—theoretically, during a network partition some parts of the sharded database may continue to be available in each partition. However, only a subset—selected shards—will be available to each partition, and there is no mechanism to reconcile inconsistencies. Furthermore, in the sharded model, transactional integrity—even when the entire database is available—is not guaranteed. Transactions or queries that span shards may exhibit inconsistent behavior, for instance.

A mode in which a transactional relational database might maintain availability in the face of a network partition would require some sort of merger between the transactional behavior implemented in ACID RDBMS systems and Dynamo-style eventual consistency.

Oracle is not alone in the RDBMS world in its adoption of JSON or interest in nonrelational paradigms. Whether the Oracle folks are sincerely attempting to move their flagship database product into the future or simply trying to take the wind out of the sails of upstart competitors remains to be seen. But it is clear that significant effort is going into engineering features that shift the Oracle RDBMS away from its traditional RDBMS roots. And if nothing else, some of these features are suggestive of how a converged database system might behave.

Other Convergent Databases

There are several other attempts to converge the relational and nonrelational models that are worth mentioning here:

- **NuoDB** is a SQL-based relational system that uses optimistic asynchronous propagation of transactions to achieve near-ACID consistency in a distributed context. Slight deviations from strict ACID consistency might result from this approach: not all replicas will be updated simultaneously across the cluster. In a manner somewhat similar to that of Dynamo systems, the user can tune the consistency levels required. NuoDB also separates the storage layer from the transactional layer, allowing for a pluggable storage engine architecture.

- **Splice Machine** layers a relationally compatible SQL layer over an HBase-managed storage system. Although its key objective is to leverage HBase scalability to provide a more economically scalable SQL engine, it does allow for hybrid data access because the data may be retrieved directly from HBase using MapReduce or YARN, as well as via SQL from the relational layer.

- **Cassandra** has added strong support for JSON in its current release and is also integrating a graph compute engine into its enterprise edition. The Dynamo tunable consistency model, together with the Cassandra lightweight transaction feature, covers a broader range of transactional scenarios than other nonrelational competitors. However, there is no roadmap for full SQL or multi-object ACID transactions.

- **Apache Kudu** is an attempt to build a nonrelational system that equally supports full-scan and record-based access patterns. The technological approach involves combining in-memory row-based storage and disk-based columnar storage. The stated intent is to bridge the gap between HDFS performance for complete "table" scans and HBase row-level access. Of itself, this doesn't provide a truly hybrid solution, but coupled with Apache Impala, it could provide a SQL-enabled database that also provides key-value style access and Hadoop compatibility. However, there is no plan as yet for multi-row transactions.

Disruptive Database Technologies

So far, I've described a future in which the recent divergence of database technologies is followed by a period of convergence toward some sort of "unified model" of databases.

Extrapolating existing technologies is a useful pastime, and is often the only predictive technique available. However, history teaches us that technologies don't always continue along an existing trajectory. Disruptive technologies emerge that create discontinuities that cannot be extrapolated and cannot always be fully anticipated.

It's possible that a disruptive new database technology is imminent, but it's just as likely that the big changes in database technology that have occurred within the last decade represent as much change as we can immediately absorb.

That said, there are a few computing technology trends that extend beyond database architecture and that may impinge heavily on the databases of the future.

Storage Technologies

Since the dawn of digital databases, there has been a strong conflict between the economies of speed and the economies of storage. The media that offer the greatest economies for storing large amounts of data (magnetic disk, tape) come with the slowest times and therefore the worst economies for throughput and latency. Conversely, the media that offer the lowest latencies and the highest throughput (memory, SSD) are the most expensive per unit of storage.

As was pointed out in Chapter 7, although the price per terabyte of SSDs is dropping steadily, so is the price per terabyte for magnetic disk. Extrapolation does not suggest that SSDs will be significantly cheaper than magnetic disk for bulk storage anytime soon. And even if SSDs matched magnetic disk prices, the price/performance difference between memory and SSD would still be decisive: memory remains many orders of magnitude faster than SSD, but also many orders of magnitude more expensive per terabyte.

As long as these economic disparities continue, we will be encouraged to adopt database architectures that use different storage technologies to optimize the economies of Big Data and the economies of "fast" data. Systems like Hadoop will continue to optimize cost per terabyte, while systems like HANA will attempt to minimize the cost of providing high throughput or low latency.

However, should a technology arise that simultaneously provides acceptable economies for mass storage and latency, then we might see an almost immediate shift in database architectures. Such a *universal memory* would provide access speeds equivalent to RAM, together with the durability, persistence, and storage economies of disk.

Most technologists believe that it will be some years before such a disruptive storage technology arises, though given the heavy and continuing investment, it seems likely that we will eventually create a persistent fast and economic storage medium that can meet the needs of all database workloads. When this happens, many of the database architectures we see today will have lost a key part of their rationale for existence. For instance, the difference between Spark and Hadoop would become minimal if persistent storage (a.k.a. disk) was as fast as memory.

There are a number of significant new storage technologies on the horizon, including *Memristors* and *Phase-change* memory. However, none of these new technologies seems likely to imminently realize the ambitions of universal memory.

Blockchain

You would have to have been living under a rock for the past few years not to have heard of bitcoin. The bitcoin is an electronic *cryptocurrency* that can be used like cash in many web transactions. At the time of this writing, there are about 15 million bitcoins in circulation, trading at approximately $US 360 each, for a total value of about $US 5.3 billion.

The bitcoin combines peer-to-peer technology and public key cryptography. The owner of a bitcoin can use a private key to assert ownership and authorize transactions; others can use the public key to validate the transaction. As in other peer-to-peer systems, such as Bittorrent, there is no central server that maintains bitcoin transactions; rather, there is a distributed public ledger called the *blockchain*.

The implications of cryptocurrencies are way beyond our scope here, but there are definite repercussions for database technologies in the blockchain concept. Blockchain replaces the trusted third party that must normally mediate any transfer of funds. Rather than there being a centralized database that records transactions and authenticates each party, blockchain allows transactions and identities to be validated by consensus with the blockchain network; that is, each transaction is confirmed by public-key-based authentication from multiple nodes before being concluded.

The blockchain underlying the bitcoin is public, but there can be private (or *permissioned*) blockchains that are "invitation only." Whether private or public, blockchains arguably represent a new sort of shared distributed database. Like systems based on the Dynamo model, the data in the blockchain is distributed redundantly across a large number of hosts. However, the blockchain represents a complete paradigm shift in how permissions are managed within the database. In an existing database system, the database owner has absolute control over the data held in the database. However, in a blockchain system, ownership is maintained by the creator of the data.

Consider a database that maintains a social network like Facebook: although the application is programmed to allow only you to modify your own posts or personal details, the reality is that the Facebook company actually has total control over your online data. The staff there can— if they wish—remove your posts, censor your posts, or even modify your posts if they really want to. In a blockchain-based database, you would retain total ownership of your posts and it would be impossible for any other entity to modify them.

Applications based on blockchain have the potential to disrupt a wide range of social and economic activities. Transfers of money, property, management of global identity (passports, birth certificates), voting, permits, wills, health data, and a multitude of other transactional data could be regulated in the future by blockchains. The databases that currently maintain records of these types of transactions may become obsolete.

Most database owners will probably want to maintain control of the data in the database, and therefore it's unlikely that blockchain will completely transform database technology in the short term. However, it does seem likely that database systems will implement blockchain-based authentication and authorization protocols for specific application scenarios. Furthermore, it seems likely that formal database systems built on a blockchain foundation will soon emerge.

Quantum Computing

The origins of quantum physics date back over 100 years, with the recognition that energy consists of discrete packets, or *quanta*.

By the 1930s, most of the mindboggling theories of quantum physics had been fully articulated. Individual photons of light appear to pass simultaneously through multiple slits in the famous twin-slit experiment, providing they are not observed. The photons are *superimposed* across multiple states. Attempts to measure the path of the photons causes them to collapse into a single state. Photons can be *entangled*, in which case the state of one photon may be inextricably linked with the state of an otherwise disconnected particle—what Albert Einstein called "spooky action at a distance."

As Niels Bohr famously said, "If quantum mechanics hasn't profoundly shocked you, you haven't understood it yet." The conventional view of quantum physics is that multiple simultaneous probabilities do not resolve until perceived by a conscious observer. This Copenhagen interpretation serves as the basis for the famous Schrödinger's Cat thought experiment, in which a cat is simultaneously dead and alive when unobserved in an elaborate quantum contraption. Some have conjectured that Schrödinger's dog actually proposed this experiment.[1]

The undeniably mindboggling weirdness of various quantum interpretations does have significant implications for real-world technology: most modern electronics are enabled directly or indirectly by quantum phenomena, and this is especially true in computing, where the increasing density of silicon circuitry takes us ever closer to the "realm of the very small" where quantum effects dominate.

Using quantum effects to create a new type of computer was popularized by physicist Richard Feynman back in the 1980s. The essential concept is to use subatomic particle behavior as the building blocks of computing. In essence, the logic gates and silicon-based building blocks of today's physical computers would be replaced by mechanisms involving superimposition and entanglement at the subatomic level.

Quantum computers promise to provide a mechanism for leapfrogging the limitations of silicon-based technology and raise the possibility of completely revolutionizing cryptography. The promise that quantum computers could break existing private/public key encryption schemes seems increasingly likely, while quantum key transmission already provides a tamper-proof mechanism for transmitting certificates over distances within a few hundreds of kilometers.

If quantum computing realizes its theoretical potential, it would have enormous impact on all areas of computing—databases included. There are also some database-specific quantum computing proposals:

- **Quantum transactions**: Inspired by the concept of superimposition, it's proposed that data in a database could be kept in a "quantum" state, effectively representing multiple possible outcomes. The multiple states collapse into an outcome when "observed." For example, seat allocations in an aircraft could be represented as the sum of all possible seating arrangements, which "collapse" when final seat assignments are made; the collapse could be mediated by various seating preferences: requests to sit together or for aisle or window seats. This approach leverages quantum concepts but does not require a quantum computing infrastructure, though a quantum computer could enable such operations on a potentially massive scale.[2]

- **Quantum search**: A quantum computer could potentially provide an acceleration of search performance over a traditional database. A quantum computer could more rapidly execute a full-table scan and find matching rows for a complex non-indexed search term.[3] The improvement is unlikely to be decisive when traditional disk access is the limiting factor, but for in-memory databases, it's possible that quantum database search may become a practical innovation.

- **A quantum query language**: The fundamental unit of processing in a classical (e.g., non-quantum) computer is the *bit*, which represents one of two binary states. In a quantum computer, the fundamental unit of processing is the *qubit*, which represents the superimposition of all possible states of a bit. To persistently store the information from a quantum computer would require a truly quantum-enabled database capable of executing logical operations using qubit logic rather than Boolean bit logic. Operations on such a database would require a new language that could represent quantum operations instead of the relational predicates of SQL. Such a language has been proposed: *Quantum Query Language* (*QQL*).[4]

Promises of practical quantum computing have been made for several decades now, but to date concrete applications have been notably absent. It's quite possible that true quantum computing will turn out to be unobtainable or will prove to be impractical for mainstream applications. But if quantum computing achieves even some of its ambitions it will change the computing landscape dramatically, and databases will not be immune from the repercussions.

Conclusion

In this book I've tried to outline the market and technology forces that "broke" the decades-old dominance of the RDBMS. In Chapter 1, I argued that there was no one-size-fits-all architecture that could meet all the needs of diverse modern applications. I still believe that to be true.

I'd also like to reiterate that I believe the modern RDBMS—essentially a combination of relational model, ACID transactions, and the SQL language—represents an absolute triumph of software engineering. The RDBMS revolutionized computing, database management, and application development. I believe it is apparent that the RDBMS remains the best single choice for the widest variety of application workloads, and that it has and will continue to stand the test of time.

That having been said, it is also clear that the RDBMS architecture that was established in the 1990s does not form a universal solution for the complete variety of applications being built today. Even if it could, it is clear that in the world we live in, developers, application architects, CTOs, and CIOs are increasingly looking to nonrelational alternatives. It behooves us as database professionals to understand the driving forces behind these nonrelational alternatives, to understand their architectures, and to be in a position to advise on, manage, and exploit these systems.

As I have learned more about the technologies underpinning modern next-generation database architectures, I have come to believe that the Cambrian explosion of database diversity we've seen in the last 10 years would—or at least should—be followed by a period of convergence. There are too many choices confronting database users, and too many compromises required when selecting the best database for a given application workload. We shouldn't have to sacrifice multi-row transactions in order to achieve network partition tolerance, nor should we have to throw out the relational baby with the bathwater when we want to allow an application to dynamically evolve schema elements. Thus, I hope for a future in which these choices become a matter of configuration within a single database architecture rather than a Hobson's choice between multiple, not quite right systems.

Clear signs of convergence are around us: the universal acceptance of JSON into relational systems, the widespread readoption of SQL as the standard language for database access, and the introduction of lightweight transactions into otherwise nontransactional systems.

In this chapter I've tried to outline some of the options that an ideal database system should provide in order to reach this Nirvana. We are clearly many years away from being able to deliver such a converged system. But that doesn't stop a database veteran from dreaming!

I feel cautiously confident that convergence will be the dominant force shaping databases over the next few years. However, there are technologies on the horizon that could force paradigm shifts: quantum computing, blockchain, and universal memory, to mention a few.

Despite the compromises, and the bewildering array of often incompatible or inconsistent technology models, it remains an exciting time to be a database professional. The period of relational dominance allowed us to hone our skills and master a coherent technology stack. Today's challenge for the database professional is to understand the diversity of technologies that are available, to pick the best and most durable technologies for the job, and to optimize those technologies to the task at hand. Choosing and optimizing the right database enhances the capabilities and economies of the modern applications that— when put to the right purposes—help us build a more prosperous, benevolent, and integrated global community.

Notes

1. `http://bit.ly/1jowDoC`

2. `http://www.cs.cornell.edu/~sudip/quantumdb.pdf`

3. `http://arxiv.org/pdf/quant-ph/0301079v1.pdf`

4. `http://arxiv.org/pdf/0705.4303v1.pdf`

APPENDIX A

■ ■ ■

Database Survey

In this appendix I've provided a short description for the major database systems covered in this book.

There are currently a huge number of database managements systems in use: The DB-Engines site (http://db-engines.com/en/ranking) ranks database systems according to their popularity using website references, search frequency, job postings, social network and Stack Overflow mentions. They track more than 250 systems, of which more than 100 achieve a non-trivial score (a score greater than 1.0 using their ranking scheme). Obviously I can't include all of them here, and the choice of databases in this appendix— and within the book—represents nothing more than my subjective degree of interest in, and familiarity with, the various systems. Omission or inclusion shouldn't be interpreted as representing endorsement or otherwise of the architecture or suitability for purpose of the system. Of the traditional relational vendors, I've included only Oracle; the coverage of their non-relational features in Chapter 12 argued for inclusion. However, many other relational vendors are implementing similar features (JSON integration, for instance).

Although I've argued that the era of database proliferation is coming to an end, to be followed by an era of consolidation, nevertheless new database systems are being launched fairly frequently. Some of these might represent major innovations and prove to be game-changing. However, generally I have concentrated only on databases that have been in active use for at least a few years: experience suggests that many of the latest "revolutionary" new databases will fail to gain traction.

The db-engines.com site provides an invaluable resource for tracking the relative popularity of databases. Their ranking system reflects more on Internet "chatter" than on revenues or enterprise adoption, but it does represent the single best resource for judging the relative level of mindshare for database systems.

Aerospike

Database Name: Aerospike

License/Company: AGPL commercially distributed by Aerospike Corp.

Wikipedia description:

Aerospike is a flash-optimized in-memory open-source NoSQL database and the name of the company that produces it.

Vendor's description:

High-performance NoSQL database delivering speed at scale.

My take:

Aerospike uses an architecture that assumes fast flash SSD as the persistence layer and uses memory to cache indexes only.

Data model:

Key-value

Transactional model:

Strictly consistent single-server transactions and eventually consistent across a cluster

Clustering:

Sharding and replication

APIs:

Aerospike query language (AQL) - a subset of the SQL language-and drivers for most common languages.

Cassandra

Database Name: Apache Cassandra

License/Company: Open-source under Apache license

Datastax provides an Enterprise edition

Wikipedia description:

Apache Cassandra is an open-source distributed database management system designed to handle large amounts of data across many commodity servers, providing high availability with no single point of failure.

Vendor's description:

Cassandra's masterless, shared-nothing architecture provides organizations with constant uptime for their transactional/operational database applications, as well as a flexible data model capable of storing today's modern datatypes and operational simplicity for easy database management.

My take:

Cassandra was envisioned as a database system that could merge the best features from Google's BigTable and Amazon's Dynamo. Cassandra has achieved some of the most high-scale NoSQL implementations at sites like Netflix. Cassandra has implemented significant innovations beyond its BigTable and Dynamo influences and clearly stands as a leader in the NoSQL category.

Data model:

Based on the BigTable wide column model, but with a narrow column abstraction provided through the Cassandra Query Language (CQL) interface

Transactional model:

Dynamo-style tunable consistency together with a Paxos-based lightweight transaction capability

Clustering:

Consistent hashing

APIs:

Cassandra Query Language (CQL) is a SQL-like language that provides a data query and manipulation interface. CQL abstracts the underlying wide column data model, presenting a more relational-like tabular interface.

CouchBase

Database Name: Couchbase

License/Company: Apache licensed, commercial support from Couchbase, Inc.

Wikipedia description:

Couchbase Server, originally known as Membase, is an open-source, distributed (shared-nothing architecture) NoSQL document-oriented database that is optimized for interactive applications.

Vendor's description:

Couchbase Server is a distributed NoSQL database engineered for performance, scalability, and availability. It enables developers to build applications easier and faster by leveraging the power of SQL with the flexibility of JSON.

My take:

Today's CouchBase Server is derived both from the Memcached compatible Membase and the pioneering JSON database CouchDB. The CouchBase Server still supports both the key-value and document paradigms. The introduction of N1QL—a SQL language for documents—helps CouchBase differentiate from the other leading document database, MongoDB.

Data model:

Key-value and JSON

Transactional model:

Strict consistency for single-document transactions

Clustering:

Sharding and replication

APIs:

REST-based API with drivers for Java and other languages, and N1QL—a SQL language for working with documents

DynamoDB

Database Name: DynamoDB

License/Company: Amazon

Wikipedia description:

Amazon DynamoDB is a fully managed proprietary NoSQL database service that is offered by Amazon.com as part of the Amazon Web Services portfolio.

Vendor's description:

Amazon DynamoDB is a fast and flexible NoSQL database service for all applications that need consistent, single-digit millisecond latency at any scale. It is a fully managed cloud database and supports both document and key-value store models.

My take:

Amazon invented the Dynamo model and provides the dominant public cloud platform, so it's natural that it provides a cloud-based database based on the Dynamo model. DynamoDB offers high performance, almost limitless scalability, and very low administrative overhead. However, the lock-in to Amazon and the relatively high price probably limit its current market adoption.

Data model:

Key-value store with support for lists and maps and JSON documents. Secondary index support.

Transactional model:

Eventually consistent by default, but applications can request consistent reads

Clustering:

Consistent hashing

APIs:

REST-based API with drivers for Java, .NET, and PHP

HBase

Database Name: Apache HBase

License/Company: Apache license, commercially provided by Cloudera, MapR, Hortonworks, and others

Wikipedia description:

HBase is an open-source, nonrelational, distributed database modeled after Google's BigTable and written in Java. It is developed as part of Apache Software Foundation's Apache Hadoop project, and runs on top of HDFS (Hadoop Distributed Filesystem), providing BigTable-like capabilities for Hadoop.

Vendor's description:

HBase is the high-performance, distributed data store built for Apache Hadoop.

My take:

HBase achieved early market penetration and technical acceleration through its association with the Hadoop platform, and has been proven at scale at many sites. The tight integration with Hadoop HDFS helps it achieve very high availability and provides a built-in synergy for Big Data analytics.

Data model:

BigTable wide column families

Transactional model:

Strictly consistent single-row transactions

Clustering:

Range keys are partitioned into regions and a master server keeps track of this partitioning. At the disk level, HBase uses HDFS for distribution and replication.

APIs:

REST and Thrift interfaces with Java driver

MarkLogic

Database Name: MarkLogic

License/Company: Proprietary, MarkLogic Corp.

Wikipedia description:

MarkLogic is considered a multi-model NoSQL database for its ability to store, manage, and search JSON and XML documents and graph data (RDF triples).

Vendor's description:

MarkLogic is a new-generation database that is built with a flexible data model to store, manage, and search today's data without sacrificing any of the data resiliency and consistency features of last-generation relational databases.

My take:

MarkLogic had built a powerful and widely adopted XML database prior to the emergence of what we now call NoSQL databases. MarkLogic has recently added support for JSON and now positions as an enterprise NoSQL database.

Data model:

XML, RDF, JSON

Transactional model:

Strictly consistent

Clustering:

Sharding

APIs:

XQuery, XSTL, SPARQL, REST

MongoDB

Database Name: MongoDB

License/Company: GNU AGPL, Apache licensed drivers. Commercially supported by MongoDB, Inc.

Wikipedia description:

MongoDB (from hu*mongo*us) is a cross-platform document-oriented database. Classified as a NoSQL database, MongoDB eschews the traditional table-based relational database structure in favor of JSON-like documents with dynamic schemas (MongoDB calls the format BSON), making the integration of data in certain types of applications easier and faster.

Vendor's description:

MongoDB is an open-source, document database designed for ease of development and scaling. MongoDB provides high performance, high availability, and automatic scaling.

My take:

MongoDB has established a strong lead in NoSQL adoption, driven by its popularity with web developers, where the database has displaced MySQL as the default choice for websites built on modern open-source frameworks.

Data model:

JSON documents

Transactional model:

Strictly consistent by default for single-document transactions

Clustering:

Hash or range sharding with master nodes

APIs:

JavaScript query API and drivers for Java, .NET, Python, and other languages

Neo4J

Database Name: Neo4J

License/Company: GPL/AGPL, commercially provided by Neo Technology

Wikipedia description:

Neo4j is an open-source graph database implemented in Java and accessible from software written in other languages using the Cypher query language through a transactional HTTP endpoint.

Vendor's description:

Neo4j is the World's Leading Graph Database.

My take:

Neo4J represents the most widely used property graph database. The open-source version of Neo4J's Cypher programming language may become a standard.

Data model:

Property graph

Transactional model:

Strictly consistent

Clustering:

Master-slave replication

APIs:

Cypher graph programming language with drivers for most programming languages

NuoDB

Database Name: NuoDB

License/Company: Proprietary, provided by NuoDB Corp.

Wikipedia description:

NuoDB is a NewSQL database that works in the cloud. It can work both for single-vendor and multi-vendor cloud setup.

Vendor's description:

NuoDB's revolutionary durable distributed cache (DDC) architecture combines the strengths of traditional RDBMSs—rich ANSI SQL support, full ACID transactions, organization-class tooling for security, backup, and administration—with support for elastic scalability and continuous availability across multiple data centers.

My take:

NuoDB is a significant attempt at building an ACID-compliant distributed SQL database. It includes a tunable consistency model and a pluggable storage engine architecture.

Data model:

Relational model layered on top of a pluggable storage layer that may include nonrelational engines

Transactional model:

ACID with tunable consistency levels that may result in eventually consistent behavior

Clustering:

Proprietary clustering model

APIs:

SQL, with non-SQL access possible to underlying storage engines

Oracle RDBMS

Database Name: Oracle database 12c

License/Company: Oracle

Wikipedia description:

Oracle Database (commonly referred to as Oracle RDBMS or simply as Oracle) is an object-relational database management system produced and marketed by Oracle Corp.

Vendor's description:

Oracle Database 12c introduces a new multi-tenant architecture that makes it easy to consolidate many databases quickly and manage them as a cloud service. Oracle Database 12c also includes in-memory data processing capabilities delivering breakthrough analytical performance.

My take:

Oracle can claim to be the first successful commercial database based on the relational model and for roughly 30 years has dominated the database market.

From a technology position, Oracle has generally led the market as well, pioneering many core RDBMS architectures including row-level locking, MVCC, and shared-disk clustering.

Oracle provides a Hadoop appliance and a NoSQL key-value store. Within the core RDBMS it has implemented many document-oriented database features, including a JSON store with a REST interface.

Data model:

Relational with extensions for object types (varrays, nested tables, etc.) and embedded XML and JSON

Transactional model:

ACID with MVCC

Clustering:

Shared disk cluster database (RAC) or sharding

APIs:

SQL with a proprietary PL/SQL stored procedure language

Redis

Database Name: Redis

License/Company: BSD license, commercially supported by Redis Labs

Wikipedia description:

Redis is a data structure server. It is open-source, networked, in-memory; it stores keys with optional durability.

Vendor's description:

Redis is an open-source (BSD licensed), in-memory data structure store, used as database, cache, and message broker.

My take:

Redis is a popular lightweight in-memory key-value store.

Data model:

Key-value

Transactional model:

Strictly consistent within a single server

Clustering:

Master-slave replication

APIs:

API with drivers for most commonly used languages

Riak

Database Name: Apache Riak

License/Company: Apache open-source project, commercialized by Basho Technologies

Wikipedia description:

Riak is a distributed NoSQL key-value data store that offers high availability, fault tolerance, operational simplicity, and scalability. Riak implements the principles from Amazon's Dynamo paper with heavy influence from the CAP theorem.

Vendor's description:

Riak is a distributed NoSQL database that is highly available, scalable, and easy to operate. It automatically distributes data across the cluster to ensure fast performance and fault tolerance.

My take:

Riak is a fairly pure implementation of the Dynamo key-value store concept together with Solr integration, time series extensions, and an object cloud storage product. Riak has significant adoption and is technically sophisticated.

Data model:

Key-value

Transactional model:

Dynamo tunable consistency

Clustering:

Consistent hashing

APIs:

REST API with drivers for Java, Ruby, Python, etc.

SAP HANA

Database Name: Hana

License/Company: Proprietary, produced by SAP SE

Wikipedia description:

SAP HANA is an in-memory, column-oriented, relational database management system developed and marketed by SAP SE.

Vendor's description:

Accelerate the pace of innovation with SAP HANA—an in-memory platform that combines an ACID-compliant database with advanced data processing, application services, and flexible data integration services.

My take:

Hana combines columnar or row-oriented storage formats and in-memory technology on a certified hardware specification to provide low latencies for OLTP or OLAP workloads.

Data model:

Relational

Transactional model:

ACID

Clustering:

Shared-nothing partitioning

APIs:

SQL

TimesTen

Database Name: TimesTen

License/Company: Proprietary to Oracle

Wikipedia description:

TimesTen is an in-memory, relational database management system with persistence and recoverability.

Vendor's description:

Oracle TimesTen In-Memory Database (TimesTen) is a full-featured, memory-optimized, relational database with persistence and recoverability.

My take:

An early entrant to the in-memory database category and a good example of an in-memory transactional relational architecture. Mainly significant today as part of Oracle's broader software stack.

Data model:

Relational

Transactional model:

ACID

Clustering:

None

APIs:

SQL

Vertica

Database Name: Vertica

License/Company: Proprietary, provided by HP

Wikipedia description:

The cluster-based, column-oriented Vertica Analytics Platform is designed to manage large, fast-growing volumes of data and provide very fast query performance when used for data warehouses and other query-intensive applications.

Vendor's description:

HP Vertica is the most advanced SQL database analytics portfolio built from the very first line of code to address the most demanding Big Data analytics initiatives.

My take:

Vertica is a fairly faithful implementation of the concepts outlined in Stonebraker et al.'s seminal papers, which partially launched the NewSQL category. Together with SAP Sybase IQ, it represents an example of a database system based primarily on the columnar concepts.

Data model:

Relational

Transactional model:

ACID

Clustering:

Shared-nothing

APIs:

SQL

VoltDB

Database Name: VoltDB

License/Company: Proprietary, VoltDB Corp.

Wikipedia description:

VoltDB is an in-memory database designed by several well-known database system researchers, including A. M. Turing Award winner Michael Stonebraker. It is an ACID-compliant RDBMS that uses a shared-nothing architecture.

Vendor's description:

In-memory performance, never loses data. Streaming analytics with millisecond latency. OLTP in a scale-out architecture. SQL and JSON with ACID guarantees.

My take:

VoltDB implements a purer in-memory architecture than other databases that describe themselves as in-memory, but perform disk IOs during commit operations. The architecture is also notable for avoiding latching and locking within a single partition.

Data model:

Relational, but partitioning works best when data is hierarchical

Transactional model:

ACID

Clustering:

Shared-nothing

APIs:

SQL and Java stored procedures

Index

Get the eBook for only $5!

Why limit yourself?

Now you can take the weightless companion with you wherever you go and access your content on your PC, phone, tablet, or reader.

Since you've purchased this print book, we're happy to offer you the eBook in all 3 formats for just $5.

Convenient and fully searchable, the PDF version enables you to easily find and copy code—or perform examples by quickly toggling between instructions and applications. The MOBI format is ideal for your Kindle, while the ePUB can be utilized on a variety of mobile devices.

To learn more, go to www.apress.com/companion or contact support@apress.com.

Apress®
THE EXPERT'S VOICE™